# fine lines

Edited by
## David Martin

Volume 22          Issue 2          Summer 2013

**Published in cooperation with:**

WriteLife, LLC
2323 S. 171 St.
Omaha, NE 68130

Fine Lines, Inc.
PO Box 241713
Omaha, NE 68124

www.writelife.com

www.finelines.org

Printed in the United States of America

**Cover Photo Credits**

Front Cover: "Colorful Kayaks"
© Brad Martin

Back Cover: "Rainflowered"
© Kim Justus

Times 10 pt. is used throughout this publication.

ISBN 978 1 60808 083 0

ISSN 1523-5211

First Edition

## About *Fine Lines*

*Fines Lines* is published by Fine Lines, Inc., a 501(c) 3 non-profit corporation. Publishing services are provided by WriteLife, LLC, a non-traditional book publisher. David Martin is the managing editor. In this quarterly publication, we share poetry and prose by writers of all ages in an attempt to add clarity and passion to our lives. Support is provided through donations, all of which are tax deductible. Join us in creating the lives we desire through the written word.

Composition is hard work. We celebrate its rewards in each issue. Share this publication with others who love creativity. We encourage authors and artists of all ages. Our national mailing list reaches every state. Increased literacy and effective, creative communication is critical for all.

*Fines Lines* editors believe writing of life's experiences brings order to chaos, beauty to existence, and celebrations to the mysterious. We encourage readers to respond to the ideas expressed by our authors. Letters to the editor may be printed in future issues after editing for length and clarity. Reader feedback is important to us. We support writers and artists with hope and direction. Write on.

## Donations

Contributions are tax deductible. When you support *Fines Lines*, four journals in book form will be delivered to your front door. Frequently, we send an e-letter with *Fines Lines* news, upcoming events, and the inside scoop on special issues.

In addition, we provide hundreds of copies to students who have no means to buy this publication. You will add to their literacy, too.

We offer two methods of payment for your *Fines Lines* donations:

- U.S. residents should make checks payable to *Fines Lines* for $50. Those living outside the U.S. must send their checks for U.S. $60. Please include your name, address, and email with your payment and send to:

  *Fines Lines* Journal
  PO Box 241713
  Omaha, NE 68124

- We also accept credit card payments via PayPal on the *Fines Lines* Web Site: www.finelines.org.

## Submissions

- We accept email, file attachments, CDs formatted in MS Word for

PCs, and laser-printed hard copies.

- Editors reply when writing is accepted for publication, if a stamped, self-addressed envelope or email address is provided.

- Submissions must not include overt abuse, sexuality, profanity, drugs, alcohol, or violence.

- Do not send "class projects." Teachers may copy *Fines Lines* issues for their classes and submit student work for publication when they act as members and sponsors.

- Address changes and correspondence should be sent to *Fines Lines*.

# Contents

12

# Yearning to Fly
### David Martin

*(These comments were made during the five day, Fine Lines Summer Camp for Creative Writers, June 10-14, 2013, at Beveridge Magnet Middle School in the Omaha (NE) Public School District.)*

Welcome to "Camp Write On." This is *Fine Lines'* 14th consecutive, summer camp for creative writers of all ages and levels of interest, and it is our largest one ever in attendance. Our registered campers are as young as third graders and go all the way up to senior citizens. We started our first camp in the year 2000 with eight elementary students, when we met at the Barnes and Noble Bookstore in the Crossroads Shopping Center at 72nd and Dodge Streets in Omaha, NE. They were excited to play with words and "go to camp" each day, so we decided to try again the next year and the year after that. Each time we held a camp, our enrollment grew. This year, we have a combined total of 174 students, teachers, and presenters. It is wonderful that this dream is collectively supported by so many people.

Many "Angel Investors," who do not want to be publicly recognized, helped in various ways to develop this "magical community without walls or a ceiling." They gave their time, talent, money, and insight, so we can enjoy letting our minds and hearts celebrate the English language and everything that improved literacy means in this world. Some of these *Fine Lines* benefactors are Marty Pierson, Steve Gehring, Rod Markin, Cindy Grady, David Lavender, Michaela Jackson, Ruben Cano, Loren Logsdon, D. N. Simmers, Tracy Schimonitz, Ilka Oberst, and our camp co-director, Yolie Martin.

We are all little birds with broken wings, yearning to fly. Every time we pick up a pen or pencil to write, our wings stretch and get stronger. The more we write, the healthier we become. Our dream is to soar and climb high enough to see over the horizon. Our wings will feel the wind currents under them, and one day we will flap our feathers with enough confidence that we will lift off the ground. Into the air, we will go, our ideas traveling with us. Through years of trial and error, we will learn that the more we write, the more we have to say, and when we become "air-born," we will notice other little birds listening to us. Let's flap our wings, little birds, flap our wings. We write and fly to keep our hopes alive.

***

Isn't writing fun? Every day, I want to write as much as possible. All my life I have been in love with words and books. As a young person, I moved often, and everywhere I travelled, my books were the last items I packed at the old home and the first boxes unloaded in my new place. Without words, paper, pens, and books, I would not be who I am today.

One day in a new town, in a new school, and in a new class, a precocious student asked me, "How do I improve my writing?"

I said, "Well, do you want the long or the short answer?"

"I have time, so I want the long one."

"Every day, read as much as you can about everything you can. Read, at least, one newspaper a day. If you can read three newspapers a day, do that. Read magazines about topics you enjoy. Read magazines about topics you do not understand, so you learn more. Read one book a week for fun. Read all of your text books. Keep a daily journal. Write in it as much as you can, whenever you can, and remember the word "journal" comes from the Latin word "diurnalis" – a daily written record. Write letters to yourself. Write letters to characters in the books you read, and ask them to write you back about what they think is going on in the books where they live. Ask lots of questions. Ask your parents why they believe what they believe and if they ever changed their minds. Then ask them why they changed their minds. They will like to talk about those things. Ask teachers why they became teachers and if they made the right decisions. They will like talking about that, too. Ask questions about what you read. Keep those questions in your journal. Someday, you will write your way into the answers."

The student said, "Maybe, I should have taken the short answer? What would that be?"

"*Fine Lines*. Small book. Big results."

"Do you have another short answer?"

"Write on."

The student said, "Sometimes, doing the writing is hard work, but I always love having done it."

"I always keep paper and a pen in every room of the house, so I can write down new ideas as they appear and before I forget them. Be prepared to capture thoughts before they fly away."

Improved writing brings new opportunity, more change, and needed self-improvement. Good writing is a wonderful adventure, and no one is ever bored when searching for beauty and truth. Rational thought will take you from point "A" to point "Z," but creativity is a magic carpet that carries us anywhere we want to go in the universe. "Until we lose ourselves, there is no hope of finding ourselves" (Henry Miller, American author, 1891-1980).

Answers are the end of searching, but questions are the beginnings of great journeys. Use creative writing to make metaphors and see the world with new eyes. Know your topics well, and sing your songs of discovery with meaning, insight, and pride. Work up to your potential, but only you know what that is. Flap your wings. Let writing unlock your soul and release your fervor, passion, color, and depth. Soar little birds. Go over the horizon.

Metaphors structure our lives. They are most important, and all good writers use them. Emblems and symbols used to apply to topics in unusual and artistic ways enlighten, deepen, and highlight different paths to understanding. One of the quickest ways to improve a writer's effectiveness is to become comfortable comparing two unlike things and paint images into the minds of readers.

Eli, my almost four-year-old grandson, saw a large buffalo crossing the road in Colorado, where his family lives. He said to his mother who was driving the car, "Look at that large buffalo. I am going to call him Metro."

His mother said, "Eli, why are you going to call that buffalo Metro."

Eli said, "He is the size of a bus."

Eli and his mother will always remember Metro. It is not enough to enjoy the stories that we hear. We must unfold our own tales of understanding.

\*\*\*

Ernest Hemingway said, "We are all apprentices in a craft where no one ever becomes a master." Writers dare to string sentences one after the other in hopes of rubbing ideas together, creating sparks of knowledge in the same way campers rub flint and stones together to start fires in the night.

"Where words leave off, music begins" (Heinrich Heine, German poet and critic, 1797-1856). This must be part of the understanding of the

"Mozart Effect." How wonderful it feels to write with music that carries us into the uncharted territory of the blank page. When music can help lift our wings, the writing is effortless, and we cover the most ground. When we hear the music of the message between the lines, we realize how important it is to ask all of our questions. Take the time necessary to ask every one.

"Fear is the cheapest room in the house. I would like to see you living in better conditions" (Hafiz Shirazi). The biggest fear for writers is the fear of the blank page, and every day we go to work in front of the computer screen or in front of the 8 ½ x 11 white page, to show the dragons in the shadows that we are not fearful of them anymore and can still write the truth. The more we write, the more they retreat. The universe is full of nourishment, and all we have to do is inhale, breathe deeply, and write on.

"Life is your art. An open, aware heart is your camera. A oneness with your world is your film" (Ansel Adams). Photographers understand what Adams means. Writers can use this collection of metaphors (art, camera, film) to appreciate their writing craft. Staying as close to the edge without going over allows artists of all kinds to envision things they cannot see from other perspectives. We must create our personal stories and use our lives as textbooks.

"Your heart is the size of an ocean. Go find yourself in its hidden depths" (Rumi). It takes courage to write. Some people want to write for fame, money, egotism, and to leave a record of their existence, but my favorite writers use words to learn about their characters, about the past-present-future, and about beauty-truth-grace. Writers want to know. They do not wait until tomorrow. Writers are not procrastinators. They write today. Let's finish what we start! Dream. Create. Organize. Write.

***

When I stuttered as a youngster, I envied those who could talk easily in front of others. I found writing was a blessing, because I could say what I wanted without mixing up my words in my chaotic speech patterns. The more I wrote in clear, clean sentences, the better my thinking became, and my thoughts were easier to speak. However, talking flies away with the wind, and if I want to keep an idea, I write it down. Anxiety is part of any artistic life, and writing about those concerns brings clarity to the confusion.

There are days when I wish I could call my mother. Even though she is gone, now, I know she will hear me if I play classical music at home and write to her. She always understood me, when no one else did or tried to. I want her to know how grateful I am, for helping me grow up and learn to deal with life's questions. She could open an envelope and step into a quiet place surrounded by her busy world. With her garden, flowers, and smiles, she let peace find me. As I observed her silent ways, her wisdom showed me that we are in life together, but we have to live it by ourselves. Spending our lives in pursuit of worthy passions was her definition of "rich," and it is rare to be called but even more special to answer.

When I was a boy, I often climbed to the top of my favorite tree after dinner and watched the sun go down. This 50 foot maple, right next to our house, was a beauty and displayed its magnificent colors every fall. After supper, Mother would come out of the back door and call for me to come inside and get ready for bed, but I did not answer her and hid quietly on the tree branches like a little bird surrounded by the leaves, while she searched for me. This game between the two of us was a friendly affair. Occasionally, as she stood on the back step with a dishtowel in her hands, after calling me four times, each one a little louder than the last, I could see her smile to herself. She trusted me and went back inside, when I did not answer. Maybe, she knew where I was, but she never let on that she did. She knew I would answer her in my own way. Mother kept opening doors for me, encouraging me to go through them and create myself, while she stayed behind and out of the way. "Mom" was her professional title, and she was good at her work.

After watching the birds fly in the sky, after I cleared my mind of the day's puzzling times, after sorting out what my goals were for the next day, after the sun set, after I found a few moments of peace, I climbed down from the tall tree, went inside, washed up, and got into bed, all by myself. Mom was often surprised to find me asleep under the covers after she finished getting my brothers to sleep. She knew I was a little bird who liked to fly alone.

That special place of mine, high off the ground in my favorite tree, taught me a lot about the power of wings and who I was to become. I have always needed a special place and a lot of quiet time just to be me. Give me solitude, not loneliness. Give me quiet, not isolation. Give me beauty, not shadows and mirrors. Give me hope, not fakery. Give me grace, not buffoonery. Give me art, not lines drawn in the sand. Give me a smile, and help me fly.

***

"Tell me, what is it you plan to do with your one wild and precious life?" (Mary Oliver, *New and Selected Poems*).

# Stress, Darkness and Magic

Russ Alberts

It was a late Thursday afternoon in November, last year in England, and I was bicycling to an engagement group meeting at the Edmund Kell Unitarian Church. Already, the light was fading, and at 5:30, it was dark. Not only was the light of the day fading, but my bicycle headlight was dimming. The route was unfamiliar, since I seldom rode my bicycle to the church from the university. I got lost a couple of times trying to avoid the busy streets, until another cyclist told me to just go down the avenue, and it would be ok. There was a busy pedestrian and bicycle path along the avenue which helped. Still, I got lost, again, approaching the church from a direction I usually did not take.

I arrived late and was urged to store my bicycle inside the church for safekeeping. They said bicycle theft was rampant, and it would not be safe outside, not even on a seldom-used side road. People commented on how dark it was getting so early in the evening at this time of year, and a place one should never go in the dark was the Southampton Commons. My way in had not taken me through the Commons.

At the meeting, we shared our experiences of the past fortnight, since the last meeting, and discussed issues dealing with stress. It was an open and friendly group, and the meeting seemed to go very fast, but soon it was time to go back.

I retrieved my bicycle and said my goodbyes to the group. I checked my map app on my smart phone to find an efficient way home. On the return trip, I would need to go more to the west, since I was not returning to the university. There appeared to be an easy route to follow that went north and connected to my usual bicycle path home. This way went through the Southampton Commons, but it presented fewer opportunities to get lost, and I would be on my bicycle.

After I entered the southeast corner of the Commons, it became obvious why some people were so fearful of this location after dark. Tall trees shrouded the paths, and there were absolutely no street lights. The way was pitch black, and my bicycle light was getting dimmer and dimmer. I followed a street named Cemetery Road in the park, a little beyond where I should have turned north. After backtracking some, I finally got on a path going north and rode for a while but soon realized that the batteries in my light had failed. In the intense darkness, I could just barely see my way ahead. I had to dismount and walk my bike through this area.

I came to a clearing in the Commons, and looking ahead, I saw a grove of trees glowing with a white light. Why were these trees glowing? Looking behind me, I saw the source of their illumination. Rising above the dim meadow was a near-full moon. To the left of the moon, I recognized the planet Jupiter. It was a moment of magic.

Still, I was alone, walking my bicycle in a totally dark park. My situation really had not changed, but my perception of it did. I had a choice. I could interpret my situation as one of darkness, fear, and danger, or I could see it as a moment of magic. I choose to interpret this moment as a wonderful moment of natural beauty.

I continued on the path, and I was not alone, because there were a few other intrepid strollers unheeding the dire warnings about the Commons at night. I continued on my way and arrived home safely, still savoring the magic in Southampton.

# With Your Help
Brad Ashford

Recently, *Fine Lines* readers may have picked up on a newspaper story that millions of dollars are spent on lobbying the Nebraska Unicameral. Those special interests would have better luck putting their dollars on a 50 to 1 horse at Churchill Downs. George Norris, the Father of the Unicameral, envisioned a Legislature free of bias and partisanship. He also noted that the citizens did not expect perfection, but they did expect its Senators to give a darn good Nebraska try. The special interests can spend all the money they want on lobbying, but in the end, we will make the final decisions by listening to voters.

We are finishing up the first session of the 103rd Legislature. This is my 15th year, which makes me next to Ernie Chambers as the longest serving member. I have served with some giants in my years here, and all are good, solid, hard-working Nebraskans. No one is here for personal gain. The only common denominator is fierce independence. We are the only legislative body in the state that does not set its own salary. Voters do. We are the only Legislature in the country that requires a public hearing on every bill introduced by a Senator. We govern from the center. Contrary to Washington, DC, we find solutions to tough issues.

This session was one of the best in my memory. Senator Chambers is back, challenging this legislative body to do its homework. Senator Greg Adams took over from Senator Mike Flood as Speaker, helping to move the body to common sense centrist solutions. Taxes were lowered, and we are ready to do major tax reform next year. The average citizen could use tax relief, and working with the Governor, they are going to get it. Working together, we reformed the juvenile justice system this year and promoted wind energy. We will not shy away from the tough issues. We continue to address the death penalty as the evidence overwhelmingly requires that we do so. Rest assured, we will address health care, until we get it right. The Appropriations Committee, led by a new young legislator, Heath Mello, balanced the budget and increased the rainy-day reserve fund by millions of dollars.

In the Nebraska Unicameral, divisive partisan politics died decades ago. With your help, we aim to keep it that way.

# Vegetarian Diet: Necessary for Change
## Dani Bachmann

Veganism is a diet that amplifies vegetables and fruit as main staples and exempts any animal products including dairy, eggs, and meat. Vegetarianism strays from meat products, too, but does not exclude dairy and eggs. Not choosing these diets over the Standard American Diet (SAD) today, which consists of meat, poultry, eggs, dairy, sugar, and processed food can be directly linked to a disturbance in the health of people, the planet, and animals. The culprit known as "food" has destroyed Americans' health, Earth's ozone, and animals' rights to live a healthy and fulfilling life. Change is needed to reverse the damage done. A vegetarian or vegan diet will heal people's health and the Earth and preserve the animal's right to live a purposeful life.

The times have changed from the "old" days when mothers stayed home to cook well-balanced meals and fathers went off to work, providing money to support the family's health and happiness. In the 21st century, the luxury of a two-parent household is tough to maintain, let alone cooking a well-balanced meal every night. In 1960, 18% of the national income was spent on food while 5% was spent on healthcare (Carr 16). In the 21st century, those numbers are reversed; 9% is spent on food and 17% on healthcare (16). Healthcare challenges today include diabetes, cancer, cardiovascular diseases, autism, and obesity. According to the World Health Organization, "Cancer is a leading cause of death worldwide, and deaths are projected to increase by 45% from 2007 to 2030. Heart disease is the number one killer. More than 180 million people worldwide have Type 2 diabetes, and 40 million (adults) are obese. Every 20 minutes, a child is diagnosed with autism" (9).

The numbers are shockingly high, but they are meant to bring change rather than frighten. The change needed is to keep the cells and the body clean and healthy, preventing diseases like diabetes and obesity from gaining access and damaging an otherwise healthy body. A plant-based diet prevents disease by delivering nourishment to cells instead of depleting them and eliminating fat particles from damaging the body's wellbeing (66).

There must be a change in what is currently not working. The lifestyle habits of most Americans will have to be altered, and most will have to come face to face with the reality that it is not just because of "bad genes." Genetics can result in an ailment that can be traced back through family history, but current research has proven that genes do not dictate our destiny. Family history of disease is a warning of what could pose a threat and should be looked at as a way to prepare the body's defense mechanisms for prevention of disease. There still is the possibility that genes can be the reason behind an ailment, but the possibility is small. "(O)nly 5 to 10% of all cancers are caused by inherited genetic mutations" (10). Researchers at the Dana-Farber Cancer Institute believe that "70-80 percent of cancers are linked to diet and other behavioral factors like tobacco and alcohol - and not genetics" (10). In compliance with current research, the need for diet change is now, while these numbers are projections and the future is capable of being influenced.

Choosing a vegetarian/vegan diet can be as easy as going to the same grocery store but choosing a different aisle in which to shop. Vegetables, fruits, and whole foods are basics in the vegetarian/vegan diet, and all play roles in keeping the body's pH balance alkaline. The body's pH balance kept at an alkaline level will aid the body in oxygenizing cells and repairing damage sustained from eating the Standard American Diet (SAD). Once the damage is repaired by detoxing the acidic waste left by the SAD diet, the body can be in a constant state of balance and prepared to heal itself.

"According to a recent German study, a meat-centric diet is responsible for the emission of more than seven times as much greenhouse gas as a plant-based diet" (Campbell, Esselstyn 37). The plant-based diet that has the power to change the Earth's ecosystem for the better is that of a vegetarian/vegan diet. Greenhouse gases affect normal climate patterns, influencing the heating of our planet and causing global warming. A diet high in meat consumption needs lots of livestock to supply the meat. "The livestock sector accounts for nearly 10 percent of human-induced $CO_2$ emissions, 37% of methane emissions, 65% of nitrous oxide emissions, and 64% of ammonia emissions, a significant contributor to acid rain" (37). Cutting out the need for animal-products will lower the number of livestock farms, which will lower the greenhouse gases.

The Amazon River basin, which was once full of trees, is now treeless and emitting $CO_2$, "unlike standing trees which capture and store $CO_2$, felled trees release the gas" (37). Even just the consumption of meat products, every once in awhile, contributes to deforestation in the Amazon. "For each hamburger produced from animals raised on rainforest land, approximately 55 square feet of forest have been destroyed" (37). With most of USA restaurant meat imported from Brazil, consuming a hamburger at a local eating place will result in the destruction of on average " one giant tree, 50 smaller trees, 20-30 different tree species, over 100 species of insects, as well as birds, mammals, and reptiles" ("Your Grocery Bill"). The risks of not having a rainforest have to be greater than that one hamburger, and not eating meat will be beneficial to the eater and protect the whole rainforest, leaving it for generations to enjoy.

Waste, water pollution, fishery depletion, endangered species, and soil erosion are just a few other things a vegetarian/vegan diet can alter. "According to a 1997 report by the Senate Agriculture Committee, animals raised for slaughter produce 130 times as much waste as the entire human population" (Campbell, Esselstyn 37). The waste from animals is used as fertilizer, sprayed onto the land, and most of it runs off the land into flowing bodies of water. Once the waste is in the water, its toxins acquired from the land (pesticides and fertilizers) spoil the water by depleting oxygen and killing the inhabitants, usually fish. "Scientists project that the population of all commercial fish and seafood species may collapse by 2048" (39). Fish are not the only species that may become endangered and extinct. According to *Forks Over Knives*, "Worldwide we are now losing animal species at a rate that will put us in a state of mass extinction - an event that has occurred five times in the last 540 million years" (39). Not only are animal and fish extinctions occurring, but the soil of the land is rapidly declining. Because of soil erosion caused by livestock farms, the western half of the United States has lost more than half its topsoil. This is a bitter cycle that has a colossal effect on the environment and planet Earth. To end this cycle and eat a plant-based diet would save the world.

Choosing to eat meat, dairy, and eggs, is as much a personal choice as choosing what to watch on television. Making the personal choice to not change to a vegetarian or vegan diet because of individual preference in convenience and taste, will likely be an easy way to justifying not knowing what is occurring in another part of the world, like the Amazon. Failure to see how that hamburger affects the rainforest makes it easy to act as if it does not happen.

Farm cows may stimulate the mind to imagine a big doe - eyed animal, timid and sweet, grown on a luscious green grass farm where it can graze all day, only bothered every morning to be milked and fed, but the cow's story is bleak. On a factory farm, this is the reality of a dairy cow's life. Once born, the baby calf is taken from her mother within 48 hours, so her mother can still produce milk. The baby will either become veal or raised for beef. The mother will then be artificially inseminated to keep up milk production, a cycle that will last until the cow is made into hamburger meat or dies from health complications usually caused by stress on the body (*Vegucated*). "The dairy cow is the hardest worked of all farm animals" ("Factory Farming in America"), but the other animals, like the pigs and birds, live through their own horrific experiences as well.

The female pigs are kept in confinement until ready to give birth. The piglet, after just ten days of being born, is taken away from its mother, and without anesthesia its tail is cut off. After the mother witnesses their piglets taken from them, they are then impregnated again and confined until they give birth. The piglets are either kept in confinement until old enough to be impregnated, or they do not make it to adulthood. The death of a pig is usually from infection, faulty construction, or neglect (*Vegucated*). Birds are victimized by the dismal life of a factory farm resident. Once hatched, the beak and some of their toes are cut off to prevent fighting and pecking the other birds. The birds are kept in cages where they cannot stand up or have room to move around, so they become agitated and aggressive with other birds. Genetically altered birds cannot walk because of other reasons though; their hearts give out, or their breasts are too big, so they cannot walk around and die where they fall (*Vegucated*).

Humans are not mass produced like food has become. They need a diet that will sustain one's own life, the Earth's life, and the life of the creatures who balance the environment. Vegetarian and vegan diets become not only a way of eating but also a lifestyle that influences the world. At each sitting for a meal, a choice is made whether to save humankind, the Earth, and innocent beings or let the destruction of life continue. Healing the connection from humans, the Earth, and all other beings begins with the choice to adapt a vegetarian or vegan diet, and it ends with a lifetime of achievement executed by fork, knife, and spoon.

## Works Cited

Campbell, PhD, T. Collin, and Caldwell B. Esselstyn, Jr, MD. *Forks Over Knives*. New York: The Experiment, 2011. Print.

Carr, Kris. *Crazy Sexy Diet*. Guilford, Connecticut: Skirt! 2011. Print

"Factory Farming in America, Part 5: The Life of a Dairy Cow." *Isfoundation*. Traci Hobson. Web. February 16, 2013.

"Your Grocery Bill and the Amazon Rainforest: What's the Big Deal?" *texasvox*. Ali Walker, April 11, 2011. Web. February 16, 2013.

*Vegucated*. Dir. Marisa Miller Wolfson. Perf: T. Colin Campbell, Brian Flegel, Joel Fuhrman, Stephen Kaufman, Tesla Lobo, Ellen Orchid Mausner. 2010. Film.

# What Does Wisdom Mean?

Matthew Ball

Sometimes, it is hard for me just to let go and accept my place on this planet with billions of sentient beings, and most of them are perfectly content going about their daily lives with a routine, a schedule, and a plan, all the while constantly busy doing nothing important. I am overwhelmed with the activities going on; sometimes, I long for a day, week, month, or year to sit by a river and take in Earth's natural beauty. While I am grateful for technology like cell phones, computers, televisions, and having power nearly everywhere, I feel smothered by the omnipresence of society. It permeates everything. I cannot dodge the addiction to stay in touch with people I hardly know or remember, and for what? For social bragging rights? To comfort myself with a number online to prove that I am not alone? I just do not understand how this happened, and it occurred overnight.

This is not me filing a baseless complaint that technology has ruined our society, as I am not naïve enough to disregard all the wonderful advances in medicine, communication, and the flow of information. This is my meek attempt at rationalizing the incoherent madness of today's daily life. The way our society exists now, time is against us: be to class by eight, to work at five, and the homework done before the next class. Time, time, time, time, time. It is always counting down, slowly ticking off valuable seconds that I can never replace. What if that is not the way the universe works? What if time, instead of being linear, and only flowing one direction, was circular and could be moved or manipulated as the perceiver sees fit?

Mathematically speaking, movement, or the rate of travel is directly linked to time. This is proven by the way we measure the speed of light. We measure light's speed by the distance it can travel in a year. We measure speed in miles per hour. Therefore, the faster, and more often one moves, the further he or she progresses through "time." While a still object may arrive in the same spot through "time," it will have aged more in the same overall time period. Make sense? I did not think so. It is hard to break down walls and barriers we built for ourselves to simplify our existence.

I once watched a film titled *Waking Life*. Warning! Unless the reader

27

feels like having the substructure for all thought smashed with an 85-ton wrecking ball, do not watch this film. It blurs the definitions of life and death. The brain still functions for minutes after death, which could mean the perceiver died and has a few minutes to dream. Well, how does time work in dreams? A few minutes of the brain functioning could mean infinite time for dreams. Far out, right? Well just imagine the possibilities that this could mean, common consciousness, a single consciousness with many different facets, or this could just be plain insanity. How would one be able to tell if he or she was dreaming or awake?

In all reality, I have had dreams where I "woke up," only to see a giant green butterfly pick me up and fly me to my space castle. Would it matter if life were only a waking dream? Would anything change about our lives? If we, as individual people, can achieve anything we want, why are more of us not doing what we love? Life is about perception. I do not have an answer. It may be because I need to hear this. Wisdom is knowledge in action. Maybe, this is my knowledge of life, coming to fruition. I am not wise. Many times, I choose to disregard my knowledge and either take another path or remain stagnant. When water remains still for an amount of time, it starts collecting particles of dust here and there, until the water is so filthy it becomes opaque and leaves a residue on anything that comes in contact with it. I do not want to be a puddle. I would rather be a single $H_2O$ molecule in a rushing river, smashing into rocks, cascading over high cliffs, evaporating, raining, and repeating the same steps over and over again to purify me, to help other living beings grow, and never remain stagnant. I believe there is a difference between living in this world and understanding living in this world.

When I was in grade school, I used to think of my brain as a filing cabinet, and when I had information I wanted to remember at a later time, I visualized opening a file drawer somewhere in my brain, placing the information in the drawer, and closing it. This process worked wonders for my memory. All I had to do was remember where I stored the information in my brain. I could recall whole "documents" from memory. I do not know when I stopped thinking like this. Somewhere in my recent past, I quit organizing my thoughts and let them roam around at will in a frenzied mess. I imagine if one could take a picture of the information in my head, it would look something like an explosion of colored paints in a contained, gravity free environment. This chaotic form of storing information has made me less organized, yes, but it also does something wonderful. Instead of having absolutes or information that cannot change, all the collisions of information have caused me to create new thoughts and outlooks on life and created new "colors" and "murals." New hybrids of thoughts and processes appear at any time, rooted in many different things to form my opinions on life and the way things are. The human brain is an amazing machine. All that is needed is the imagination and desire to try.

While reading *The Element* by Ken Robinson, I was shocked to see some of the queries I posed earlier were not only asked by him as well, but he also gave answers. I need to find my "Element," which Robinson defines as, "Where the things we love to do and the things we are good at come together." I understand that I have a very inquisitive nature. I look for similarities in people and experiences, all the while appreciating those same things for how they are different. Everyone has a past, a story, a beautiful painting of light and dark, which is unique. I was almost slapped in the face when I read, "Growth comes through analogy, through seeing how things connect, rather than only seeing how they might be different." Robinson was speaking to me, in the "time" I exist.

"As the pattern gets more intricate and subtle, being swept along is no longer enough" (*Waking Life*) is a call to put knowledge into action. I have proven I have knowledge, but I was supposed to show wisdom in my writing. Someone once told me "Always, write honestly," and "Tell the truth as you know it." I accomplished these two things by pouring my heart into writing. Being open, honest, and raw is a terrifying rush of emotions.

Sometimes, I want to erase everything I have written, just to save myself from having to let readers into my head. It is a scary thought to let readers into my thoughts and have them interpret this through their own filters. "What if I come across as crazy?" or "an idiot?" I guess the question I really should be asking is, "Did I write anything I do not one hundred percent agree with?" The answer is a resounding, "No."

"Wait a second," thinks the inquisitive reader. "You never provided closure on your technology complaint!"

Thank you for reminding me. As of this moment, sitting in my office, writing this sentence for the prying eyes of the reader, I am using a laptop, listening to Mozart, and I have the lights on. I have to get over my loathing of social norms. It is not logical to complain about something that is not only a necessity, but something I love. Would "escaping" society change anything? If change comes from within, which I believe it does, changing locations will not help me grow. One of my classmates pointed out something I missed in a chapter of David Martin's book, *Little Birds with Broken Wings*. He referenced a poem "Desiderata." It might be safe to say "Desiderata" written by Max Ehrmann, is analogous to what I have written here, only more fluid and direct. Please, read it.

I need to control my "pointless" activities and not be concerned with others' habits. I must use my words carefully, because I am one pronoun away from ruining someone's day. The best way to change the world is to be it; all I can do is show the path I'm on and hope others join, because I believe the future is already here. We, as human beings, have the responsibility to make life what we want, not sit back and watch, like the stone through time and the dirty puddle. Be an active part of society; be the stream that comes down from the mountains, over cliffs, through crevasses, to the bottling plant, to my lips. Affect those around us positively. "Remain in a state of constant departure, while always arriving. Save on introductions and goodbyes" *(Waking Life)*.

*Old Tractor :: Cindy Goeller*

# Bingo with Grandma

Haley Banks

I knew the day was coming after driving down 13th street. A yellow house on the left side always had a mustard colored sign that read "Bingo on Saturday - 6:30" on its chain-linked fence. Bingo was held in a small church on the southwest side of town. Grandma would always call me to see if I wanted to go, and with no doubt in my mind, I always said, "Yes." There wasn't any other way I'd rather spend my Saturday nights than playing bingo with Grandma.

She would pick me up ten minutes before 6:30 and drive to the church. Grandma and I would walk in and be greeted by at least two of her friends near the entrance. The crowd consisted of nearly all elderly folk and a few children here and there. Most of the older people in the crowd knew my grandmother, for they all lived in the same town for years when they were younger. She had the biggest smile on her face when we were in the hall, surrounded by her friends. We would take our usual seat near the back, for most of the seats were taken by the regulars who showed up early. As we took our seats and began setting up the dobbers, more and more people would come over to give a warm welcome to my grandmother and me. The bingo caller would soon announce the call for the Early bird, and that's when the fun began.

The Early Bird was always a special, usually consisting of a frame, where we had to fill in all of the outside numbers to call out "Bingo," and it takes much longer than a normal bingo. Other times the Early Bird special is a shape correlating to the holiday that is around that time of month. Grandma and I would go about filling in our free spaces on the 2 by 3 card and wait for the caller to announce the first number. Maneuvering over our cards searching for the numbers being called out, "B-23," "O-64," "I-29." The dobbers met the number, releasing ink in a perfect circle to remind us that the number had been called. We would constantly discuss how many more numbers we needed and explore all the possibilities of winning the game.

"Look, Haley, one more for four corners!" she would tell me, excitedly. Crossing our fingers together, we would wait for the caller to say the winning number. Numbers upon numbers would be called, and the little old lady across the room would call out, "Bingo." Always staying optimistic, we ripped off the losing sheets and filled in the next round of free spaces. No matter how many times my grandma and I lost, the game continued to be fun.

During intermission, Grandma would give me money to get snacks from the kitchen. I would get her a diet soda, myself a Pepsi, and a supreme nacho for us to share. Eating nachos at bingo was our favorite part. They slopped on so much cheese, not leaving a dry chip in sight. While we ate our perfect combination of meat, cheese, and chips, the ladies who ran bingo at church would walk around selling raffle tickets. People would generously bring items to give away during the raffle. Depending on how good the selection was, Grandma would buy just the right amount to give us a good chance of not walking out empty-handed. We could almost be considered amateurs to the bingo hall. While the professionals were playing twelve cards at a time, we only played six, giving them a greater advantage to win bingo. That didn't matter much; we had the same luck as everyone in the hall when it came to raffles, but it seemed like the odds were in our favor.

The next round of bingo would start when the ladies were done selling raffles, and the cycle continued. The caller would announce the numbers. We bingo players would dob the numbers, and we would hope for a win. Sharing back and forth after every number, we would make a hypothesis about which card was going to be a winner. Now, when either of us came down to one number, we would get antsy.

I can remember the rush when I was impatiently waiting for the caller to yell out my number. I had one number left that was constantly repeated in my head over and over. Suddenly, the mighty number was called. After the constant repeats of the number, it slipped my mind until I saw the straight line on the card. The feeling was unbelievable, and blood rushed to my head like a sugar high. With a slight bit of hesitation, I yelled, "Bingo." Attention was on me, all me. My face turned cherry red, while one of the ladies came to check my card. It was a good bingo, they would say, and then handed me two $5 dollar bills. I felt on top of the world, and Grandma was just as happy for me, while I sat there like a little champion. As the rest of the night went by, we would hope for our tickets to be drawn out of the box for the mighty win of the "jackpot blackout."

On January 12, 2013, Grandma couldn't go to bingo with me because of a traditional spaghetti dinner my brother's baseball team put on. I decided I would still go to bingo with one of my close friends. Until that day, I was ecstatic about going to bingo on Saturday, just like I always was. I searched for my dobbers and didn't make any other plans. Miraculously, like the Grinch, I started to feel guilty. The one time Grandma couldn't go, and I realized that it wasn't the game, the nachos, or the money that made bingo fun, it was being with my grandma.

*Candlesticks :: Kris T. James*

# The Card

Jeanie Boll

"I just wanted to thank you for the Mother's Day Card."

Whenever the phone rings and before I push the talk button, I always check to see who is calling. So, standing in the bright warmth of the spring sun pouring through the living room window, I knew it was my mother. Resignedly, I picked up the phone. We hadn't talked for a while. Dad must have asked her if she talked to me recently and prompted her to call. That was the only time she would call, when my deaf father wanted to know what was going on in his youngest daughter's life.

Usually, she'd even start the phone calls telling me exactly that. "Dad asked if we had talked lately. He wants to know if you and the kids are okay."

If it were not for the phone calls, they wouldn't know how things were with my family. Both my parents are retired, but they seldom came to see us. My children could never live up to the perfection of my older sister's kids, and my Democratic blue-collar parents did not like my husband and his Republican white-collar background. They were devastated when I changed my political affiliation from Democrat to Republican. My parents blamed my husband. I believe that if I had been a serial child molester/ murderer and still a Democrat, my parents would have approved of me more.

But this phone call started differently.

"I just wanted to thank you for the Mother's Day Card."

My insides clenched with dread. My parents always hated greeting cards. Birthday cards, Valentine's cards, Christmas cards, and yes, Mother's Day cards. My working class parents felt event cards were a waste of time and were designed just to make Hallmark rich. Usually, my mother wrapped my children's birthday presents in white tissue paper and drew colorful pictures of clowns, balloons, and flowers on it with magic markers and wrote the message "Happy Birthday." It was important for her to be original.

It was my mother-in-law who introduced me to cards. She loved them and spent a great deal of time and money on them at the Hallmark store. My mother-in-law spent hours picking out the right one for whomever she was sending the card to for whatever occasion, even a Mother's Day card for me.

Like my mother-in-law, I also spent time picking out this card for my mother. Maybe not as much as time as my mother-in-law would have, but still, I did not just run into the store, look at the cards, and say, "I think this will do."

The card had a mixer and egg beaters on the front and said, "Good moms let their kids lick the beaters." On the inside was another picture of the egg beaters lying on a counter with the caption, "Great moms turn the mixer off first." Then I wrote, "Thanks for being a great mom. Love, Jeanie and Doug." I hate mushy cards with flowers and kittens and puppies and sentimental pictures of moms and children with their mushy sentimental poems and sayings inside. This card, I thought, would be perfect. Licking the egg beaters after my mom made a batch of chocolate chip cookies or a cake from scratch was a happy memory from my childhood.

We had our choice, my brothers and I, one of the beaters or scrape the bowl. We had so much fun talking and laughing that Mom usually left the kitchen, while we loudly tussled over our choices. First, we'd size up which had more dough, the beaters or the bowl. Then, we'd vie over which one we wanted. Cookie dough batches left more thick creamy dough and chocolate chips on the beaters. Cake batter was much thinner and left more residue to be scraped with Mom's favorite red and white spatula from the bowl. Each had its merit, and each had to be weighed according to our own preferences and the size of the gourmet treat. Sometimes, just to try to be fair, Mom would leave a little extra cookie dough and chocolate chips on the bowl, but extra cake batter could not be left on the beaters. It just dripped off.

Laughing and joking, we'd choose. Then, in the U-shaped kitchen with its dark brown cupboards of the seventies, we would lean against the brown and orange mosaic tiled countertops merrily enjoying our treat, exclaiming when we'd get an extra large clump of chocolate chips or crying with feigned dismay if we felt one got more than the other. A few minutes later, we would be done, laughing and joking and jostling again, this time at the stainless-steel kitchen sink as we rinsed off our egg beaters and the white Corelle mixing bowl that we licked clean, so clean they did not look as if they needed to be washed. The fun and joy from those little short moments in our lives seemed to draw us warmly together, connecting us with fond memories long after they were done and we were adults. It was because of this childhood memory, this *happy* childhood memory of togetherness, that I picked this card.

My mom had not just called to say thank you. "I was surprised. You know, we never had a good relationship."

Sighing, I unceremoniously plopped myself down on my old brown plaid living room sofa and gazed out of my front picture window at the greening lawn slopping gently down to the rock driveway. The green expanse resumed for a short bit on the other side of the driveway and stopped again at the budding forest. Since it was still early spring, the poison ivy and nettle underbrush had not grown up, and the sun shone through the meager spring leaves leaving the forest exposed for better viewing. I closed my eyes and shook my head. Things were becoming clearer now, as I began to see the reasoning behind this odd phone call: drag up the old relationship hindering the new relationship from growing.

My mother was right; we hadn't had a good relationship. But this was a *good* memory. Why couldn't some of the past be just that, the past? When could she just accept something about me or from me without criticism? I thought this was one thing I had gotten right.

When I was little, I wrote poems, but I did not always have end rhymes, so they were not good enough. When I wrote stories, I misspelled words and had improper grammar. My mother corrected the errors and schooled me about the proper way, believing I just was not good enough, could never be good enough, until I quit.

When I painted pictures, sometimes the grass was purple and the sun green. I just wanted to see how colors worked together. Sitting in our small bungalow kitchen in North Omaha on top of dictionaries put on top of the vinyl kitchen chair so I would be tall enough to reach our green linoleum and chrome, newspaper-covered table, I believed, in my little four-year-old heart, that the colors I did not use as much as others might feel left out and have their feelings hurt if I did not include them in my always the same, never changing picture of a house, a tree, a sun, a child, and grass. I just drove my mother up the wall. In my mother's mind, the sun should always be yellow or orange and the grass green. Before I was five, I got bored, and gave up.

Later, in third grade, we moved to a small town with small classes. I made a turtle out of old boxes and painted it with purple and green tempera paints. Unbeknownst to me, my teacher had sent my purple and green turtle to the county fair. I received a purple ribbon. It was the first of four art works sent to the County Fair and of two chalk drawings, one of a Red-winged Blackbird and one of a brown majestic horse, sent to the Nebraska State Fair that earned me purple and blue ribbons.

When my cousin saw my sixth grade entry, she called to congratulate me. Linda babbled on so excitedly for me that I could barely understand what she was saying. I never knew if my mother approved of them. This time, she did not have anything, good or bad, to say about my attempts at art.

"One day," my mother went on, "I never know why, you just decided you didn't like me." Finally, I saw through the last entanglements and could see where this conversation was heading. Here it was, yet again, but voiced with more clarity than the usual barbs hidden in pleasant conversation.

I was taken aback and speechless, yet, I could have also told my mother a million and one things, but only a shadowy room filled with shadowy images appeared in my mind. The first memory. I knew it was there, yet it surprised and saddened me to remember.

Only my younger brother, my mother, and I were home. My dad must have been at work and my older sister and brother at school. In that little bungalow of a house in North Omaha, way back in the early sixties, mom was busy stripping and rewaxing the dark brown wooden floors. The two front rooms, the living room, and kitchen/dining room were dark as if there were a storm outside or the sun had forgotten to shine. My brother and I were perched on those vinyl kitchen chairs in the linoleum floored kitchen as instructed. We were told to not get down, and we dared not. Truthfully, I was the only one sitting. My younger brother was small enough to stand on the chairs and to peek over the top as he observed our mom at work. When she was done waxing, she got up from her hands and knees and stood in the small kitchen between the white refrigerator and us to survey her work and wait for the wax to dry, wait until she could buff the floor, until it shined and was slippery, when we walked in our stocking feet on it.

It was then, during the lull of work. The conversation started, while she was stripping the wooden floor. It was not the first time my mom had this conversation with me. It was one of those stories of my life moments, like when my parents tell me about when I were born, or things they did when they were my age. It was a conversation we had before, always initiated by her. This time, however, was the first time I initiated the conversation, the first time I knew what it meant.

"Do you wish you hadn't married Daddy?" I asked.

"I should not have married your dad. I was too young. I should have enjoyed life a little more." My mom with her curly black hair and cat-eye glasses frowned her typical frown. She rarely smiled. "If I did it over again, I would not have married him. But it is done. We are married," she told me. "Can't change that."

"And what about us kids?" I asked, knowing what the answer would be before she even answered it. After all, she had told me this story many times before.

"I wish I only had two children. It would have been better to have only two." There wasn't a follow up of, "But I have four children. It is done." Not a, "I wish I had only two, but I had four, and I love you all," just "I wish I had only two children."

This was the beginning of the "whys." When I first understood these words. When I knew what they meant. She wished I was not born. I was not a wanted child. My only consolation was that it meant my youngest brother, the one she loved the most, would not have been born either. Did my mother even know that? There was some kind of evil satisfaction in that.

I closed my eyes a little and slyly, through the slit of my eyes, looked over at my brother sitting innocently and unaware, as he played with a car. He did not know what it meant, but I, the older one, did. "Ha, ha," I thought to myself, "he wouldn't have been born either." I felt evilly gleeful and guilty at the same time. It was a good thing he did not understand. He would be hurt, too.

"Mom," I said into the phone, "I thought you would like the card. It brought back such good memories of when we were children. I thought you would get a kick out of it and laugh."

This conversation was the "why" I did not visit my parents much anymore, why we are limited to the sometimes conversations on the phone. Every time, I go to their home or they visit my children and me, I have to wrestle with something new: something to new to forget, something new to forgive. Sometimes, it is an old memory, like this shadowy memory of a shadowy house, a memory I thought was long gone, buried, forgiven and forgotten, yet carelessly resurrected with rash words and barbed comments. I would never tell my mother, now, why I did not like her as a child. I know it would hurt her if she remembered, and though looking through the eyes of a child, I did not know why my mother frowned a lot, but as an adult, I understand. Her dark memories blocked the sun from filtering into her life. I just wish my parents could forgive me for when I was a child, and how I acted as a child when they were adults.

"I didn't think you had any good memories," my mother said in her monotone emotionless voice.

"Oh, yes mom, I have some really good memories."

# National Anthem: *September 11, 2001*
## Jessica Franke Carr

*Another day killing yeast*, I think with a sigh, as I tumble wearily down the rickety concrete stairs to my car, a 1997 red Pontiac Grand Am that had made the journey from my parents' Kansas house to my first Atlanta apartment just a few weeks ago. After two years confined to dorm life at Emory University, I am enjoying the freedom of living off-campus and commuting on my own set of wheels. Never mind that my apartment is a hovel or that I am so directionally challenged that I only know how to drive to two places: school and the grocery store. To get from school to the grocery store, I have to drive back to my apartment first, because I only know the route one way. Obscuring trees and curvy roads (all named Peachtree) do not create a safe driving experience for a girl who thinks "North" is whichever way she's currently facing.

Today, I know my route. To my second home, the yeast genetics lab where I am doing research for my Honors thesis. Mere days ago, I shocked myself by winning the Poster Contest at the summer research session. I'd been at the awards banquet, sculpting cubes out of the cream cheese frosting from my carrot cake and stacking them into a pyramid, when the announcer started reading off a poster title that sounded similar to my own. It is a testament to my low self-esteem that the first thing I thought was, *I didn't know someone else was doing research on yeast. Of course* they *would win.* But no, it was my name that followed the title, and I might as well have won an Oscar, since I was beaming so much. It was a sign that would point me down the right path in my career. *Yes*, that $200 reward said, *science is the way*.

My steps aren't entirely heavy as I trudge across the cracked parking lot, the morning sun already warm as it wiggles through the trees to my shoulders. I fire up my crimson two-door coupe, which makes me feel like a racecar driver even though it's just a Grand Am, and begin wading my way through the sea of traffic that this city forces through narrow two-lane tributaries, all weaving through neighborhoods so heavily forested that the houses are invisible from the street. I sometimes wonder if the city planners do this on purpose, so that one never really knows how bad traffic is up ahead. With only two or three cars visible at any given time, Atlanta driving is like being trapped in a slow-moving void of uncertainty. You must constantly be on guard, lest the car in front of you stop suddenly. It is a miracle that every day, every route is not littered with accidents, and the sheer volume of traffic streaming through these curly streets doesn't burst through the banks and flood the peaceful, hidden homes with honking reality.

My only company on these drives is the radio. Not vintage enough to be truly cool, my dinosaur of a Grand Am is only outfitted with a cassette tape deck, and 2001 is solidly a CD-playing era. I am severely anti-talk-show because listening to other people's conversations is too distracting, so I generally have to navigate these twisty trails with one hand on the wheel and the other always steadfastly flipping channels in the vain search for a song I like that isn't almost over already.

This morning, however, all I can find is talk. My calloused scanning finger pushes buttons, but every station is yapping. Talk talk talk. After I get all the way through the station numbers without hearing a single bar of music, I start to wonder what everyone is talking about. I go to my favorite station, the one most likely to play some Three Doors Down or Staind, and try to listen to the unfolding story.

At first, I think my radio station must be interviewing an author and is letting the writer read a snippet of his latest work on air. I don't know why my alternative rock station would suddenly be feeling artsy, but that can be the only explanation for what I'm hearing. A plane crashing into the World Trade Center? People leaping from the upper floors to their deaths, because they found that method preferable to burning alive? What a downer. Why in the world are they reading this? Where's Nickelback when I need them?

When the announcer reports a second plane hitting the second tower (at 9:03 a.m.), I know this is not Tom Clancy's latest novel: this is a rapidly unfolding fact, which makes it much more terrifying. I hear a second female announcer softly crying as she tries to cover her mike, leaving the first male announcer to stammer as he is forced, for the edification of his blind listeners, to transcribe the awful scene unfolding on his television into words.

I want to get to a television of my own as quickly as possible, but traffic is barely moving, and I can't see anything but the red tail lights on the gold car in front of me and a veil of trees. Damn trees. At least at home on the prairie, I could high-tail it through the grass in a true emergency. Here I am trapped in a coffin of wood, concrete, and metal.

After what seems like hours but is obviously only minutes because no other action has occurred on the radio, I arrive at the parking garage, pull in to an empty stall at a crazy angle, and half-run, half-stumble on wobbly legs to the lab.

No one is there, but I can hear a radio announcer talking.

I drop my bag in the entryway and holler, "Where are you guys?"

"Over here!"

My lab mates are all simply one aisle over, hidden behind stacks of petri dishes and shelves of sparkly chemical bottles. They huddle around the radio, gathered in a tight group, even though the radio is loud enough to hear from the hall. Some of them are sitting on chairs, some standing behind. All of them have their hands touching their faces. Brenda's hand is over her mouth; both of Reagan's hands are nestled in her spiky blonde hair; sitting Amy has her chin propped on her hand; Caroline's hands are comically one on each cheek, her mouth an O of disbelief. Even Sue is there, hiding her eyes behind her fingers, daring herself to peek.

The lab radio, which, like my car radio, usually blasted chipper tunes, is all talk. I can't tell if it is the same channel I'd been listening to in the car, but it doesn't matter. At this moment, musical preferences are irrelevant. Americans are united in shared horror, and whether we love rap, country, classical, rock, alternative, or pop, we all want to listen to the same track this time.

After about 20 minutes of relative inactivity, I send my boyfriend Jeremy an email. He is meeting with his swim coach, so I don't know if he even knows what's happening. My email informs him to get over to the lab ASAP. I shakily head back to my desk, but I have a difficult time remembering just what it is I am supposed to do with my yeast today. PCR? Freeze cultures? Pour plates?

The radio is still on in the background, still loud, with announcers still yammering. Suddenly, they are screaming again, as another plane crashes into the Pentagon at 9:37 am.

*Ok, I'm done, I'm not doing anything with yeast today*, I think.

"I'm finding a TV," I proclaim, and the rest of the lab follows me into the hall like I am the Pied Piper.

My advisor, Gregg, is half-jogging down the hall. "They set up a TV in the conference room."

The room is packed with scientists. My friends, my lab mates, my professors, the janitor are all crammed in to watch a crummy feed on a network channel because there is no cable in this room. We all watch the feed for a few moments, soaking in the camaraderie, before some diehard researchers decide their yeast or fruit flies or cell cultures cannot wait and leave. I stay. My yeast can be replaced.

Gregg stays, too, along with a couple of other people I know by sight but not by name. While we are watching the footage of smoke and fire streaming out of the plane-sized holes in the towers, my boyfriend arrives. My lab mates pointed him in my direction, and he gives me a big, silent hug, as I continue to stare at the fuzzy screen. Jeremy takes it upon himself to improve the quality of the video, and his tinkering has just brought the scene into clear focus as the South Tower collapses at 9:58 am.

I join in the nation's collective gasp, as we watch the tower go down and the debris go up, exploding into the sky like a mini mushroom cloud.

Shortly thereafter, Brenda pokes her head in the door and informs us that they are evacuating the CDC.

This is extremely bad news. Unlike its typical movie portrayal, the Center for Disease Control is located in a squat, non-descript red brick building on the fringe of Emory's campus. Most of the building is underground, for security reasons. The research building in which I am currently standing is a dozen stories high, made of gleaming metal and shiny glass, a testament to Emory's generous endowment and dedication to showmanship, ostentation, and modern innovation. The tenants of this building have always been proud to call the CDC our immediate neighbor, as if the physical proximity of legend will transfer via laudatory osmosis. Now, the fact that I can look out the window and watch terrified CDC workers flooding out of the building makes me feel nervous, queasy, and panicked. If an uninformed terrorist bomber is planning to run a plane into the CDC, he'll likely mistake our glorious monolith for the real deal and head right for us. I could be moments away from being rammed by a 747 going 500 mph.

The conference room is no longer a silent funeral service. We buzz and flap our arms and flutter around in the tiny room like a vial of fruit flies who realize they are about to be FlyNapped. The danger has leapt from the TV and invaded our lives. *How likely is it that the CDC would be a target?* Well, it is one of only two places in the world where a vial of live smallpox virus is kept, making it pretty tantalizing if the terrorists are interested in bio-warfare. We decide that it is more likely the terrorists will try to infiltrate the CDC, nab the vial, and spread smallpox through the largely unvaccinated population than it is that they would run a plane into us. Somehow, the thought of being 100 ft. from Ground Zero of the upcoming smallpox epidemic doesn't make me feel much better.

Jeremy and I flee back to my apartment, where my roommate is glued to the television. We sit in the dark with the blinds drawn but don't know why that makes us feel safer. No one is peeping in at us. We are peeping out. We spend the rest of the day flitting back and forth from the TV to the window, where we pull the blinds apart to watch for approaching plane silhouettes and mushroom clouds on the horizon.

Gripped by paranoia, I call my parents to make sure they are safe. While Kansas is not likely to be a prime target, possessing neither huge cities nor stockpiles of tantalizing deadly illnesses, it is well-known that the prairie is dotted with this country's arsenal of nuclear weapons, all ready to pop out of corn fields like horrible Jack-in-the-Boxes bent on sparking World War III. The rest of my family is living in Omaha, Nebraska, home of the STRATCOM bunker, from which President Bush convenes the National Security Council teleconference immediately after the attacks. My niece watches Air Force One fly overhead, a grand plane, now the only man-made object marring the unbroken prairie sky.

Like most Americans who are not directly in the line of fire, I feel besieged and unsafe anyway. We have no idea what will happen next, no clue as to how organized this terrorist group is. Are suicide bombers currently hiding in every city, strapped to nukes timed to explode any moment? Will we contract smallpox and join millions of other people in the epidemic that will bring about Armageddon? Are smallpox vaccines even made anymore? If all flights are grounded, how soon will I be able to see my family again? I keep picking up the phone, just to reassure myself that the dial tone is still humming. We fill all available glasses and pitchers with water, just in case.

Gradually we are forced to accept the fact that danger is not imminent and venture out into the blinding light of a new world to sift through the rubble of our former lives. I attend classes. I return to the lab and kill more doomed yeast, and I go on dates and remember how to smile. For some time after the attacks, Americans continue to be united even though our radio stations have returned to their regularly scheduled programming. Our American pride is palpable, a communal swelling of goodwill that affects all of us, Republican or Democrat, conservative or liberal, religious or atheist. When Jeremy and I attend a Lifehouse concert that Halloween, the person dressed as "Dead bin Laden" wins the Costume Contest, hands-down. However, this intense patriotism eventually deepens the political divide as we disagree about how to best safeguard the nation's standing in the world. Sometimes, I wish we could all tune into that same frequency again, when we all sang the same song of fear, hope, and determination.

Faster than I imagine, life returns to normal, mostly. The subsequent anthrax attacks keep the CDC, and therefore Emory, on very high alert for years afterward. The CDC surrounds itself with giant cement barricades and tightens security clearance. Before, I'd often walked by the CDC without noticing it; now, I have to tiptoe along the remaining sliver of sidewalk to get to the lab, and I avert my eyes from the building lest the security guards think I'm showing *too much* interest and shoot me. Instead, I keep my eyes on the road, worrying that any minute an armed terrorist unit will barrel through the cement barricades with me sandwiched in the middle. I hold my breath and walk quickly, like a child superstitiously crossing a graveyard, until I pass safely back into the world of the living.

---

*Words to Ponder*

*"What an astonishing thing a book is. It's a flat object made from a tree with flexible parts on which are imprinted lots of funny dark squiggles. But one glance at it and you're inside the mind of another person, maybe somebody dead for thousands of years. Across the millennia, an author is speaking clearly and silently inside your head, directly to you. Writing is perhaps the greatest of human inventions, binding together people who never knew each other, citizens of distant epochs. Books break the shackles of time. A book is proof that humans are capable of working magic."*

-Carl Sagan

# As the Leaves Change

Sophie Morrissey Clark

"Come on, hurry up," they yell, running into the forest.

I follow at their heels and enter a world of magic. The trees become giants with long beards of green leaves and strong arms of branches. The thorn bushes become evil snakes biting at our ankles. My brothers transform into expert explorers with names like Ziptow and Spirit Iron-Knife. I become a prisoner they have set free from their enemies and have joined them on their journey through the treacherous forest. We run through the trees, swinging our stick swords and fighting off any branch or bush in our way. We don't notice the hours that pass and the sun quickly setting. The sound of my mother's worried voice suddenly awakens us from our world as she calls us for dinner.

\*\*\*

At two o' clock in the afternoon, there's finally a sign of life from my brothers' rooms. Cooper emerges, heading straight for the kitchen to eat whatever he can find. I haven't seen him all day, and this will probably be one of our few encounters.

"Hey, Coop, what have you been doing?" I ask.

"Oh, I've just been on the computer."

I nod and turn to leave, but he quickly catches my attention.

"Hey, do you want to watch a movie or something?" he asks.

I don't give it much thought and say, "Not today, I have homework to do."

\*\*\*

Today, we are pirates. Simon is the captain. Cooper is the first mate, and I am part of the crew. Our basement is underwater, and the couch becomes our floating ship, rocking with the waves that crash against it.

45

Simon calls us to brace for a storm as a huge wave knocks me off board.

Simon yells, "Man over board!" and orders Cooper to help save me. They both pull me out of the water and back onto the cushioned deck of the ship.

"It's a good thing we were here to save you, lassy," my captain says.

\*\*\*

"Hey, Simon do you have a hat I can use?" I ask.

"Yeah, there should be one in my closet."

As I rifle through Simon's possessions for a hat, I come across a plastic sword at the bottom of a pile. I laugh and poke my head out of the door.

"I challenge you to a sword fight," I say, pointing it at him.

He chuckles and says, "Hurry up and get out of my room."

\*\*\*

I lay in my brothers' room on the spare mattress that was placed in between their beds. I have my own room, but I decided it's too scary to be alone in.

"What do you guys want to play tomorrow?" Simon asks, as we drift off to sleep. Cooper suggests we pretend to be the kids from the last movie we watched.

"No," Simon says, "kids can't do anything. Let's be grownups."

We decide on revolutionary war soldiers and fall asleep to the gunshots outside our tent.

\*\*\*

I'm sitting alone in my room staring at the blank notebook in front of me.

"Come on inspiration, kick in," I think.

Where has all my creativity gone? My eyes trace over the framed picture of the buck-toothed, stringy-haired, 8-year-old girl smiling back at me, her arms tightly wound around two adventurers disguised as my 8-year-old brothers. I smile back at them, as I wrap my fingers around my pen.

\*\*\*

"I'm going to travel the world when I grow up," Simon says, through a mouthful of animal crackers. "Me, and my three dogs, and five cats."

As he goes on to list their names, I quickly interrupt, "But Simon, what about me and Cooper? You aren't going to live with us?"

Cooper nods in agreement. "We always have to live together," he tells him.

Simon thinks it over, "Well, it wouldn't be fun exploring without you guys," he says. "Let's explore the world together, and then, we can all live in the shed."

We agree on this with an emphasized slurp of our juice boxes.

*** 

From upstairs, my mom shouts at me to go make sure the boys are awake. I walk into their room to find them both staring at their computer screens, not bothering to look up at me.

"We should do something today," I suggest, hoping to get their attention.

Simon finally becomes aware of my presence and pushes his computer lid shut, "Like what?" he asks.

"I don't know, we used to do a lot of fun stuff together," I reply.

My mom appears behind me, arms loaded with laundry.

"Yes, do something together. You guys only have a few years left with each other, and then, you'll all go your separate ways."

Suddenly, I have the perfect idea. "Get your coats and shoes on," I tell them.

We spend the afternoon walking through the autumn colored forest.

> *"Character gives us qualities, but it is in actions - what we do - that we are happy or the reverse. All human happiness and misery take the form of action."*
>
> - Aristotle

# Zero-Sum

Spencer Cox

I can't put features to the face in front of me - it's a peach-colored glob, floating above the collar of what appears to be aqua-colored nurse's scrubs. I want to rub my eyes and focus on this blurry abomination, but I can't feel my hands. They are either tied down or non-existent; it's hard to say.

I close my eyes. I feel like I'm floating. There is no me, no anything. I want to stay in this dark place, sleep forever, and drift away. The nurse-thing is just a picture hovering in my mind, and it's doing nothing but interfering with my euphoria.

Now, it's talking to me, or at least *at* me, and my eyes pry open again. Its voice is a warbling dissonance, not unlike a trombone missing a few valves. At first, I want nothing more than for it to stop, but then the sound begins to soothe me. I guess part of me is happy to know that I still have ears, in case my hands – and the rest of me - really are gone. Its dialect is slush to me. Two of its words find a way to cut through and shatter my blissful state:

"The baby."

Oh, God, I had forgotten about the baby. *My* baby. The sweet, innocent life that's been growing inside of me for months. My peanut. Is something wrong with him? What's happening?

I focus my psyche and try to cut through the grogginess enveloping me. I can see that it's working almost instantly – the nurse-thing's features twist and morph into an actual face - a college-aged girl with long, brown hair and brown eyes filled with pity and worry. The nametag hanging at the end of her white lanyard reads "Jenny." "What's happening?"

The sound of my voice is rocks and sandpaper, and my tear ducts flare with its use. My throat is a chasm of pain. Jenny puts her hand on my forehead; her touch is like ice, but the sensation helps me to focus.

"Please," I say. I want to say more, but my throat won't allow it.

Jenny takes her hand from my forehead and brings a cup to my lips. "Drink, sweetheart."

The water rushes down my aching throat; its tendrils expand in my chest, igniting my insides with an icy, unconsuming fire. I do my best to not throw up on Jenny's face as my stomach clenches. I wonder how long it's been since I've had anything to eat or drink.

Jenny takes the cup away and returns her hand to my forehead. "She's burning up," she says toward someone to my left. I don't have the strength to move my head in that direction, but by concentrating, I am able to blink and move my eyes, a little. Unfortunately, the other person is out of my view. I can see the hint of someone in my peripheral vision, but that's about it.

"We may need to increase the drip," a man's voice says from the other corner of my perception – the doctor, I guess. I assume that he's talking about drugs, and my psyche flares and cuts at my dazed state again.

"No," I croak, barely audible even to myself. I want to scream, to cry out, *Where am I? What are you doing to me? What is wrong with my baby?* but the only thing I can do is lie here, confused, and drift away.

The lower half of Jenny's face stretches into a grin that reaches nowhere near her eyes. "Honey, it's the best for you right now," she says, standing up. She looks toward my left – toward the *other* person. "Doctor Murphy won't let anything happen to you."

The desire to scream is even stronger than before. "Not me," I manage, and with difficulty add, "baby."

Jenny's fake smile drops from her face. She doesn't need to say anything. I know. It must be the baby. I cast my mental razor away and give in to the void. I close my eyes and drift, content now to go wherever I was before. There's no reason to fight anymore – not if my peanut is gone.

"Please, Mrs. Johnson."

The doctor's voice – it comes from my right.

I am falling back into myself. With what seems to be the last of my strength, I pull open my eyes to see Jenny's face, as it contorts back to the nurse-thing, and my thoughts become nonsensical.

*Where is my bicycle?*

"The baby is fine."

This time, the voice comes from the one on my left – the *other*. It's familiar but sounds strange, choked. I can feel the sensation of someone squeezing my left hand.

At least I still have hands.

Jenny the nurse-thing is hovering above me again, her blurred features like something from Dali's nightmares. "It's true, sweetie. He was born healthy as can be, 7 pounds, 11 ounces." She strokes my hair from my forehead. "Your husband's mother is at home with him, right now."

"Husband," I say in little more than a whisper.

*Warren?*

I had forgotten all about him. My best friend - my love. Somehow, the thought of Warren pulls me back to the surface. I reach again for that sharp edge of my psyche, struggling to cut the webs from my eyes and soul.

This time, nothing is there; I'm slipping back into myself again, and I'm afraid.

"Doctor, we're losing her," I hear Jenny say from within what seems like an infinite concert hall. Her words echo across my psyche, like ripples across a glass lake.

To my right, I hear the maniacal beep of a machine pulsing and thrumming. My vision continues to deteriorate, until Jenny the nurse-thing is nothing more than a smudge. I see another moving shape, probably the doctor, maybe Warren - or whoever is at my left - but I don't care anymore.

I just want to see my baby.

The beeps of the machine slow from a whine to a low pulse, and finally a song - a song that I know.

Shame on us

Doomed from the start

May God have mercy

On our dirty little hearts

My body is gone again. *I* am gone again. The room, Jenny, everything. *Peanut.*

It's all gone. I'm floating, falling. Now, I'm . . . .

*Gliding?*

I open my eyes.

Ahead, I see Warren riding his bike. He looks over his shoulder and smiles at me, his reddish cheeks alight in the sun. I think I'm riding my bike, too, but I can't be sure. Above me, vast blue sky stretches across everything. Luscious, green trees line the rocky path we're on, and the air smells of springtime rain. I want so badly to be here right now, to stay with Warren and be happy forever, but I can't – not while I know my baby is somewhere else, somewhere I can't be.

The trees lining the path begin to grow; they lean forward with audible cracks and reach across the path above us, blotting out the sun and turning the path to a dark tunnel.

No! Warren, please, we can't go this way. We have to go back! Our baby.

Darkness encompasses Warren as he rides ahead, and soon I can't see anything at all. I want to scream, to cry. I want to do anything but be in this place.

*I just wanted to see my baby. Just once.*

Another lick of the song sweeps into my awareness:

Shame on us

*For all we have done*

*And all we ever were*

*Just zeroes and ones*

I open my eyes. The first thing I see is 11:11, glowing bright red from my alarm clock. The tiny speaker belts out the ending of the song.

*And all we ever were*

Just zeroes and ones

I close my eyes and let the relief wash over me. My pillow is wet, and I can feel the tear-tracks on my cheeks.

"Baby, are you ok?"

*Warren.*

I feel his hand reach over and caress my stomach. "I think you were having the dream again, love."

"Yeah," I say. It's all I can get out. I realize I've never been more terrified, elated, relieved – *awake*. It was worse this time; it gets worse every time. I put my hand over Warren's eyes and close mine, letting the dream wash away.

Warren pulls his hand out from under mine and sits up, looking at me. His eyes are wide, and a goofy smile is stretched across his face. "Did you feel that?"

"I did," I say. Tears sting the backs of my eyes - for a different reason, this time. I put my hand back on my stomach and wait to feel my baby kick again.

# The Myth of Insecurity

## Shelley David

Insecurity is the lack of confidence and assurance; self-doubt sums up what insecurity I dealt with in my life. I googled the word "insecurity," and 22,550,000 results came up. For a person who has seen the dragon of insecurity, that number confirms I am not the only one who ever encountered self-doubt. Why should I care or worry, about what friends, even strangers, think about me? I wasted valuable time concerning myself over this dragon. Now that I am older, I can look back and see the ugly dragon of insecurity is an absolute myth.

Going to a small grade school, I was part of a close class. As all young girls do, I quickly realized who was "in" and who was "out." I was never one who belonged to the "in" crowd; it just did not make any sense to me. Who determines who is "worthy" of being a part of the clique? What are the credentials? Whatever they were, I surely did not possess them! I never seemed to be good enough for the basketball team, the volleyball team, or any athletic challenge that came my way. I struggled with getting "A's". No matter what I did, I felt like I was not good enough. One passion I had was a love for the piano, so it was there that I poured out my frustrations.

When I attended high school and college in the 1980s, the super model era ballooned, and I was bombarded with images of beautiful women with perfect bodies. Cindy, Elle, Christie--they were everywhere. Walking through a mall, looking at a magazine, seeing a billboard, they were screaming, "Look at me. Come into this store, and if you buy what I am wearing, your body will look like this, too! If you buy this makeup, you can have this face!" This was perfection at its finest. What they had, I wanted, so I thought. How amazing it would be to look like that! I was the little hungry fish wanting more, and they were fishing for me. I took the bait, hook, line, and sinker. The slimy and hideous dragon reared its unsightly face, glaring at me. What I did not realize was I needed much more than new makeup and "cool" clothes to change my ongoing battle with insecurity. It helped temporarily, but soon I needed more. Clothes and makeup helped my outside appearance, but they did very little with the deep feelings I was carrying in my soul. What did I need? What was I lacking that other students seemed to have in their lives?

Getting rid of insecurity and self-doubt never happens overnight. I needed a daily dose of confidence, an inner conversation affirming who I was, and I was not the only one who ever had these ugly feelings of unworthiness. I spent time in prayer, as I still do. I sat at my piano with the door closed and played my heart out. I stopped listening to sad, depressing music and listened to uplifting harmonies.

Surrounding myself with people who completely accepted me was crucial in making sure that dragon did not show up again. I needed that support and unchained love that only they can fill. Dealing with the media throwing their ideas of what is worthy and beautiful toward me is a constant battle. Why are so many women drawn to plastic surgery and tummy tucks or anything else they can do to alter their bodies? Obviously, they are insecure in how they look. They are dealing with the despicable dragon in their lives, too. Being a parent of a teenage daughter, it is my responsibility to teach her that she is loved and treasured just the way she is.

The mythical dragon that took so much of my life from me is now in its dungeon, where it belongs. At my age, I can look back and see how God abundantly blessed me. It does not matter to Him if I fit into a size 4 or a 22, if I have a high paying career, if I am a stay-at-home mom, if I have wrinkles, or a flawless face. I have nothing to prove to anyone, ever. God created me the way I am and the way I was meant to be: pure, loved, blessed, and whole. When I see the fiery eyes of the dragon of insecurity, I find a way to throw it back in its dungeon, where it belongs. Sometimes, it takes a pail of water to put out its projecting flame, and other times, it takes a fire truck. This I know for sure, the dragon will not have any control over my life ever again! It was a heavy burden to carry, but now I am free.

# Hope on a Wing
Deborah Duffy

My husband died of pancreatic cancer three years ago. Each day since then, I wait for some sign that he's still with me. Even three years later, I'm looking for him to reach out to me. I have been holding onto this hope, while I was also telling myself to move on and accept that he was simply gone.

I looked for comfort by doing things we enjoyed doing together. Lanny taught me to fly-fish, and we spent many hours on creeks and rivers together. When feeling especially sad, I put on the Orvis waders and boots he gave me for our first anniversary, and I grab the Winston rod he taught me on and head to the Bitterroot River that runs through my valley.

One September day, I went camping at Wade Lake in southwestern Montana, with my adventure seeking friend, Diane. On the second afternoon, we decided to try our fishing luck in the Madison River, one Lanny and I never had time to fish together. We parked at the Three Dollar Bridge, and with one look around, I knew this water would test my skill level. Even after over ten years of fly-fishing, I'd have to count myself as a beginner, having intermittent moments of brilliance and finesse, enough to keep me heading back out with rod in hand and brimming with optimism.

I walked toward the river, glancing up-and-down stream trying to decide which way to go. Out of the corner of my eye, just upstream from where I stood, a rush of movement caught my attention. As I worked my way through the heavy brush lining the bank, I saw what took me a few seconds to sort out, bald eagle bobbing up-and-down on the water in a fast and wide riffle. Its wings splayed out on the water, flapping and splashing, as the rushing current carried the eagle downstream.

I watched anxiously, sure it was drowning, as it was pulled under and fought its way back to the surface. Then, it suddenly emerged from the water, just as it reached the end of the riffle. I first took in the wide wingspan and how hard it struggled to free itself from the fast current. When it took flight and I saw the huge trout dangling from the eagle's talons, I couldn't stop myself from letting out a whoop, much as I did when I had a big trout on my own line. What a great catch! I knew exactly where I was going to make my first cast of the day and started readying my line.

Diane came running up to me. "That was Lanny you know?"

I tilted my head looking questioningly at Diane.

"Deb, Lanny is showing you the perfect place to fish. He's also taking the first catch of the day."

A huge smile spread across my face, as I understood what she was saying. It was true Lanny always caught the first trout when we went out. Later that day, a huge trout burst into the air trying to catch my fly. The trout played with me that afternoon, and I never did catch one. Despite my lack of success, it was still the best fishing day I have had since Lanny died. I felt like he was fishing right beside me.

Over the course of the next several weeks, I frequently glanced up into the sky and was surprised to see eagles circling over my head. Each sighting would leave me with a comforting sense of being watched over. I had been looking for a way to feel a connection with Lanny, and now, I had it. I realized my spirit was freed at the same moment the eagle broke free from the water. I'd been stuck under the currents myself for the past few years.

Living in Montana where there is a strong Native American culture, I learned the bald eagle represents protection, wisdom, and strength. Native Americans believe birds bring messages to those who will listen. I'm so glad Diane was at my side to help me learn to listen on that sunny September day on the bank of the Madison River. Diane continued, like many of my friends were doing, supporting me while I gained the strength to let go. Lanny will be forever a part of me, but I've given myself permission to start healing now.

I continue to head out to a river with fly rod in hand whenever I need time alone with my memories. As I stand at the water's edge readying my lines and deciding which fly the fish will be hungry for, I tell Lanny he's welcome to the first catch, but it's my turn to bring in the biggest trout. I'm discovering that the heavy weight of sorrow began to lift, and hope was delivered on the wings of that eagle, as it took flight over the Madison.

# My 1%

## Trinity Eden

I never put much thought into how much of a difference one person can make in this world. Historically, a small group of people have made big changes in this country: the American Revolution, many religions around the world, and in my life. Too many people feel their lives do not matter, and I can relate to giving up and not trying, because I felt like my life was not going to matter to anyone, and my efforts were not worth anything. I tried different activities in school, but nothing I did made a difference, until I was older.

In my high school years, I was just a statistic that involved various forms of breaking the law. There was grand theft auto, running away five times, possession by ingestion, petty theft-three times, and minor probation violations. On my journey of self-destruction, I did not think about the impact my actions would cause at home. I was just a statistic, a young American Indian girl from the Pine Ridge Indian Reservation in South Dakota, who was abused by her alcoholic birth mother, relatives, and a middle-aged Caucasian married couple. My case was one that projected alcoholism, Battered Woman Syndrome, my children taken away by authorities, and many confused adolescent years followed by adulthood filled with resentment.

During my late pregnancy, after my legal troubles subsided, I became interested in changing where my 1% was going to be placed. I wanted my case not to read, "Young American Indian mother of two from the Pine Ridge Indian Reservation suffers through life." Instead, I now want it to read, "Young American Indian mother from Pine Ridge defies the statistics, graduates from college, has a healthy lifestyle, and is making her 1% matter in this world."

# The Relation between Art and Anatomy: Artistic Instruction as a Remedy for Medical Dispassion

Hayley Faber

Students of art and medicine share many similarities. From the time of the Renaissance, when the pursuit of knowledge and the study of the human body were rescued from the Galenic and Hippocratic theories, to the present day, both artist and physician have worked together to study this fascinating window into the human condition. Both learn their crafts from an illustrated text that is dually science and art in classification. "The doctor studies the body to improve its fate, the artist to improve its spirit" (Rifkin 8).

The world owes a great debt to the famous artist and anatomist, Leonardo da Vinci. His illustrations are early examples of objective, scientific exactness in rendering the human figure, a value that would become the undercurrent for anatomical drawing and study up to the present day. The connections between anatomical illustrations and dissections run deeply throughout history, and medical students undoubtedly benefit from developing an appreciation for them. The study of art history and life-drawing during pre-clinical training has the potential to counteract the dispassion that students often adopt from a biomedical ideology, re-sensitizing students to the humanity and wholeness of the patient, and ultimately resulting in greater compassion and better patient care.

The study of anatomy can be traced as far back as 300 B.C. in Alexandria, but the earliest surviving anatomical illustrations date to the 12th century C.E. (*Dictionary of Art* 840). In the Renaissance, dissections were performed for medical students only once or twice a year. Artists were often present at these events, keenly interested in this rare glimpse of the human form. Often, they who would use this knowledge and not their medical student peers, for in these days, the anatomy was only useful to verify the text of the second-century Greek physician, Galen of Pergamon (Nuland 32, 68). Since the physician could study Galen, he had little use for performing his own dissection. Additionally, religious teaching prior to the Renaissance, namely the Christian Church's high value of the soul over the body, lent little importance to anatomical study (66). Thus the contradictory legacy of Galen was allowed to persist. His work was grounded in dissection, experiment, and clinical observation and it proposed that an understanding of structure and function is necessary to comprehend pathology, although it was peppered with errors and inconsistencies. One of the main problems with Galen's research was that he only performed dissections on animals and based his human anatomy on the animal components (46). So complete and detailed was his writing that it became the standard mode of instruction and was scarcely challenged for the next fifteen hundred years.

The first illustrated anatomy book was published in 1522, but it was not until Andreas Vesalius published his *De Humani Corporis Fabrica* (*The Fabric of the Human Body*) in 1543 that scientific observation would prove a real challenge to the founding tenets of Galen's anatomy (Rifkin 14). The woodcuts in *de Fabrica* were "the most accurately detailed and solidly rendered images of the human body ever produced, then and for some time after" (16). At the time, printing of books with images was still a novel technique. This new modality allowed for the widespread dissemination of the same information, "a founding tenet of modern scientific method" (16) and set a standard for the modern textbook. *De Fabrica* showed the human body in motion and displayed more than the mere forms; it showed their functions (63)

Vesalius enjoyed privilege in his lifetime as the personal physician to Charles V, the ruler of the Holy Roman Empire, and a professor of anatomy at the famed University of Padua. The real significance of *de Fabrica* was not in his explanations, but in the illustrations he oversaw. Vesalius performed numerous dissections in an age when anatomical teaching consisted of animal dissection and study of Galen's famous text. Performing human dissections and comparing them to Galen's illustrations allowed Vesalius to discover numerous errors that previously were considered dogmatic and truthful (Rifkin 69). *De Fabrica* exposed these fallacies and ushered in a new era of scientific understanding based on observation and experimentation.

During the Baroque period, artists and anatomists continued to refine and reinterpret the figures of the body. In contrast to the old view of religion as a hindrance to scientific progress, many men of anatomy saw themselves as pioneers on the forefront of discovery of God's creation, a pursuit that glorified the creator (Kemp 201). One famous text from this period called the *Anatomia Humani Corporis* is more famous for the controversy surrounding the so-called plagiarism of its images than for the images themselves. Two editions were published by Govaert Bidloo in 1685 and 1690. He was born in Amsterdam and became a professor of anatomy in addition to serving as the personal physician to King William III of England (Rifkin 132). The meticulous drawings were done by Gerard de Lairesse, but the volume was rejected for being "too technical for artists, too inaccurate for surgeons, and too expensive for everyone else" (43). In that time, "publishers retained the right to sell the printed sheets of a work to any who applied," and so in 1697, the British anatomist and surgeon, William Cowper, bought and published many of the same images set among his own text and some new illustrations (Roberts and Tomlinson 412). Though criticized and attacked by many for its appropriation of illustrations without proper credit to Bildoo or de Lairesse, this volume became a success, and in its second edition, they are acknowledged for the figures.

Following in the footsteps of his predecessors, Bernard Siegfried Albinus set out to produce an anatomical book. Albinus was a student of Bidloo's in Leiden and went on to become a professor of anatomy and surgery, but unlike those before him, Albinus aimed to show the "ideal" human figure (Rifkin 177). For his 1747 text, *Tabulae Sceleti et Musculorum Corporis Humani* (*Tables of the Skeleton and Muscles of the Human Body*), Albinus chose a "slender male cadaver" to "replace the weighty forms of the Baroque" (51). He also compelled his artist Jan Wandelaar to utilize a squared grid system set in front of the skeleton to avoid any free-hand errors or distortions. For all of its careful precision and attention to scientific accuracy, the backgrounds of Albinus's images can be criticized for subverting that same ideal with their aesthetic detail and design (54). The anatomist was clear, however, that the backgrounds were made to compliment the figures, render them more aesthetically pleasing, and heighten their sense of depth and relief. To the anatomist, "stylishness and accuracy were not seen as conflicting aspirations" (Kemp 198).

The illustrated anatomy was the physician's atlas to the complexities of the human body before the advent of photography and continues to be an important didactic modality in our current age. Human anatomy texts today utilize photos, alongside illustrations which serve to highlight specific parts, demonstrate kinetics of joints and limbs, denote regions of bone, muscle or organ that would not be clear to the naked eye, mark boundaries, insertion points of muscles, or show contrast between structures. It is clear that art and anatomy are connected. However, the value of scientific objectivity is a difficult one to obtain with any graphic illustration. Three potential threats to objectivity, namely period style, personal instinct, and technique, are also elements that add to the artistic quality and training of any draftsman (Rifkin 10).

The idea of "style" is familiar to any artist and at its best represents an important connection or process of communication between the artist and the viewer (Kemp 192). It is a manner of representation that conveys aspects of production, patronage, and meaning (Kemp 192). For these reasons, style is a highly valued part of artistic study. In science and medicine, style has been regarded as "irrelevant adornment to the business of communicating information" (Kemp 192). Since 1850 when the famed Henry Gray's *Anatomy* was published, a conscious effort has been made to promote a "style-less" representation of the human figure (192).

One can trace the loss of "style" from its use in the early baroque anatomical texts to the present day. Vesalius shows his figures in classical poses or acting out dramas. Figures of Christian martyrs and Christ himself by artists like Titian are prototypes for the poses in some of Vesalius' images in *Fabrica,* such as the "7th plate of muscles" (197). The figures were meant to portray a certain philosophy of the "whole organism" and at the same time show a grand, romantic view of man's place in creation (196). One image of a skeleton contemplating a skull is drawn in the *memento mori* fashion and includes the quote "genius lives on, all the rest will perish" (Kemp 200). The image was obviously intended to draw the viewer into a certain mode of contemplation of life, mortality, and the human condition.

Another artistic style can be seen in the figures of Albinus in which everything is perfected and smoothed. Albinus deliberately chose a subject for its proportions, and according to his own words, he took care to "render the likeness more beautiful [by removing blemishes]; so those things which were less perfect, [in the skeleton] were mended in the figures" (Roberts and Tomlinson 324). His ideal images are "far removed from the flesh-and-blood reality of dissection" (Kemp 198).

One early example of the shift toward "style-less" representation is Bidloo's anatomy with de Lairesse, whose records of dissections take on a "still life" quality, comparable to depictions of flowers and fruit that were popular during the Dutch Golden age (Rifkin 131). Included in these images are the dissection instruments, the pins that mount the specimens, and even flies perched atop the decaying flesh (Kemp 195). Such elements follow in the tradition of *trompe l'oeil* in order to emphasize the reality of the depiction (Kemp 200). The skeleton drawings, however, still utilize lush backgrounds and somber *memento mori* qualities (Roberts and Tomlinson 312).

This realistic trend culminated in the publication of Henry Gray's *Anatomy: Descriptive and Surgical* in 1858. Gray's goal was to avoid any "taint of philosophic anatomy" in the illustrations (Kemp 205). Artistic elements are kept to a minimum, and there are no stylized backgrounds, little use of light or shade, and no heroic poses to be found. Deliberately absent in Gray's *Anatomy* are any depictions of full skeletons or whole bodies. The accompanying text presents the anatomy by system and is equally unembellished and "business-like, "but this "non-style" with all its limitations and conventions becomes a style all its own which set a precedence for medical study that continues to the present day (205).

The value of remaining unemotionally involved in medicine can arguably be traced back to its foundations. It was the Hippocratic physicians who "established dispassionate observation as the first rule of clinical medicine" and Galen who "applied it to research" (Nuland 45). "Hippocrates had introduced the healers to the concept that medicine is an art. Galen now taught them it can be an art that is based upon the truths of science" (45).

In the 16th and 17th centuries, the anatomy theater was the preferred didactic mode for medical students. The theaters were dark, crowded, and tainted with the smell of the decaying cadaver, as effective preservation methods had not yet been discovered. The very nature of this systematic dismemberment of the human body created a mental framework for understanding the human body, and in the 17th century the philosophical concept of the human body as a machine, exposed by Rene Descartes, furthered this line of thought (*Encyclopedia Britannica*). Surviving manuscripts from the time emphasize the deliberate presentation of the body, "sanitized . . . [and] devoid of its former humanity to the students in the audience" (Payne 46). This presentation comes in sharp contrast to the view of the patient in the hospital bed or on the operating table, which presents a greater challenge to the physician's emotional disconnect. "Nausea, loathing, and foeter" are emotions English Physician William Harvey (1578-1657) recounts feeling during his medical practice (47). In the 17th century, the sensual and emotional reaction to human body cavities filled with fat, fluid, slimy organs, undigested food, and fecal matter was seen as a feminine and cowardly trait. "Masculine bravery" was a prized characteristic of a good anatomist and physician (48). Writers of the time criticized this style of anatomy as an "inhuman art" (49) and argued that "those who frequently cut on the dead lost, or perhaps never learned, a humane bedside manner toward the living" (50). It seems apparent that there are instances when a certain level of emotional disconnection is necessary for objective treatment and clear thinking by the medical practitioner. In order to learn the human structures and perform surgical operations, a medical student must overcome visceral reactions to unpleasant bodily functions and components and avoid attachments to individual patients.

In response to the valid criticisms that too great a dispassion leads to a poor bedside manner, one might suggest a remedy in the study of art alongside anatomy in medical school. An appreciation for the intersection of art and anatomy will allow students to recognize the humanity and wholeness of patients and counteract a reductionist and dispassionate tendency, ultimately resulting in greater compassion and better patient care. Awareness of how images and anatomical teaching can desensitize a person to the realities of the human beneath her knife and cause a mental block to emotional investment in patients is an important realization for the medical student. For this, the study of Art History and the tradition of anatomical drawing would be a valuable lesson.

Studying the living anatomy would be an asset to the 21st century medical curriculum. As one British professor of anatomy, William Anderson, expressed in his 1895 address to the British Medical Association, without the study of surface anatomy, the student is "forever ignorant of the knowledge that the surgeon and physician should possess, for he knows only the fully dissected anatomy of the corpse and little or nothing of the living normal anatomy of the people whose diseases it is his function in life to treat" (357). This instruction could take the form of drawing from the living model, a common practice for students of art. Artistic instruction would serve to focus the physician's awareness to minute features, "every eminence and depression, ridge and sulcus…every wrinkle in the skin itself…and the relation of these points of observation to physiology and pathology" (357). This attention to detail and artistic mind-set could both cultivate a greater appreciation for the uniqueness of every patient and provide a new mental framework in which these particularities aid the physician in his search for pathology. In today's advanced society where disease is investigated at the molecular level with proteins and cellular components, recognizing the aesthetic quality in all of these created things can add joy and fulfillment to scientific study and provide a vibrant source of creative inspiration for clinical and artistic endeavors. An artistic view of medicine and the study of historical medical texts like those of Vesalius, Bidloo, Cowper, and Albinus, when viewed not for their anatomical correctness but for an understanding of where medicine has come from and how previous generations understood their bodies and themselves, can inspire a return to a more "holistic" view of the person and an appreciation for the debt medical students owe to artists who dared to enter their dissection rooms.

## Works Cited

"Anatomical Studies." *The Dictionary of Art*. New York: Grove's Dictionaries, 1996. 840-44. Print.

Anderson, William. "A Discussion on Art in Its Relation to Anatomy." *The British Medical Journal, 2*.1806 (1895): 349-358. Print.

"History of Medicine." *Encyclopedia Britannica. Encyclopedia Britannica Online*. Encyclopedia Britannica, 2011. Web. 01 May. 2011. <http://www.britannica.com/EBchecked/topic/372460/history-of-medicine>.

Kemp, Martin. "Style and Non-Style in Anatomical Illustration: From Renaissance Humanism to Henry Gray." *Journal of Anatomy, 21*.2 (2010): 192-208. Print.

Nuland, Sherwin B. *Doctors: The Biography of Medicine*. New York: Alfred A. Knopf, 1988. 1-489. Print.

Payne, Lynda. "'With Much Nausea, Loathing, and Foetor": William Harvey, Dissection, and Dispassion in Early Modern Medicine.' *Vesalius, 8*.2 (2002): 45-52.

Rifkin, Benjamin A., and Michael J. Ackerman. *Human Anatomy: From the Renaissance to the Digital Age*. New York: Harry N. Abrams, Inc., 2006. 1-340. Print.

Roberts, K. B., and J. D. Tomlinson. *The Fabric of the Body: European Traditions of Anatomical Illustration*. Oxford: Clarendon Press, 1992. Print.

# Letters from the Front

Marcia Calhoun Forecki

"It's the police, sir. Open the door, please."

Marcus Lightner stood to the side of his front door. He reached across the jamb, unlocked the dead bolt, turned the door knob, and jumped back. The officer stood outside, running his hand over the surface of the door.

"Is this the door you say was shot?" the officer asked.

"He shot the laser aiming thing right through the door."

"Aiming thing?"

"The red laser dot they use to aim high powered weapons. I saw it right here."

Marcus indicated the closet door, directly opposite the front door. "If the sniper had rung the bell, and I had answered, I would have took one right through the cranium."

"Are you alone here?"

"I am."

"Is there anyone you can call. A son or daughter, maybe?"

"Are you ordering me to evacuate?"

"If you give me the number, I can call for you."

"There was someone in front of my house."

"Where?"

"On the sidewalk. Blue pants, white shirt, white shoes, baseball hat, clean shaven."

"Was he running?"

"Could have been. Did you see him?"

"Let's step inside, sir. Can you get me that phone number, please."

"That door's solid oak, but it won't stop an automatic weapon. I know weapons. I'm a veteran, you see."

"Yes, Mr. Lightner. I remember you told me that the other times I was here. Do you remember meeting me before? I am Officer Presser."

"No. I might know your grandfather, but you don't look familiar."

Officer Presser waited as Marcus went into the kitchen. While Marcus brewed a fresh pot, the officer made a call on his cell.

As they finished their coffee in the living room, a car pulled into the driveway. Marcus opened the front door for his son, Neil, and returned to the living room. Officer Presser rose from the high-backed, brocade side chair. This had been Marcus's wife's chair when she was alive. The touch of her arms on its arms had worn the flowers to where they looked out of focus. Anyone except a police officer would have been asked to choose another seat.

"Are you all right, Dad?" Neil asked entering the living room.

"Your father is concerned that he is in danger here. Maybe you could talk about that with him."

"Sure. What's up?"

"I'll let your dad explain. Mr. Lightner, I'll drive around the block before I go."

"All right," Marcus whispered. He slumped into a corner of the sofa. His eyes filled with tears.

Neil spoke cheerily, "Hey Dad, any more coffee? Let me get a cup, and we'll talk."

After they talked a few minutes, Neil walked his father to the front door. Showing his father the peephole, Neil explained, again, how the morning sun came through the lens and reflected on the coat closet door. The house was a split level. One entered onto a landing and walked up steps to the left, into the living room, or down steps to the right, to the garage and basement. There was a coat closet directly opposite the front door.

"Your mother used to hang a wreath on the door. If she wanted to look through the peephole, she pushed it aside," Marcus said.

"I remember," Neil said. "Now, without the wreath, the light comes through the lens of the peephole and reflects on the closet door. That's what you've been seeing in the mornings. See, it is gone now, because the sun has risen high enough, so it does not shine through the hole," Neil explained.

Marcus hung his head and walked into the kitchen. He poured coffee into his empty cup and stared at the dark liquid. He felt foolish and ancient. He stared into his coffee. A tear fell into the cup, and he heard it "plop." Marcus flushed with embarrassment, when he realized his son was right behind him and saw the falling tear.

"I'm just useless since your mother died," he said softly.

"Not at all. Just a little confused, at times."

"When will I see Ruth again?" Marcus implored. He looked into the eyes of his son and saw her eyes. Neil had his mother's cheekbones and her green eyes ringed in gold. Sometimes, it was torture to look at his son's face. Marcus hated that his son got to carry a part of his mother inside him forever, and he could see her whenever he looked in the mirror. More often, Marcus craved seeing his son, which humiliated and confused him, so Marcus remained alone, determined to stay strong for her, until she returned.

"I have an idea" said Neil. "Let's look in the basement. Mom had a bunch of wreaths for the door. Remember, she changed them with the seasons. You can pick one out, and we'll hang it on the door."

"No," Marcus said.

"Come on. I'd like to see the door decorated again."

"I'll do it myself, later."

Marcus did not want Neil to know that he spent hours in the basement among his wife's things. They were scattered around the laundry room, even on his work bench: her clothes, her cookbooks, her crafts; all the things Neil and his wife had worked so hard to pack and label in plastic totes and shelve like drawers in a morgue.

"Okay. I'll see you tomorrow."

"What for?"

"I'm picking you up after work, remember? Tomorrow is Friday, and you're coming to dinner at my house, with my family. Your grandkids."

"Sure. I remember," said Marcus. Now, he wanted Neil gone.

"What is your plan for the day?" Neil asked. A psychiatrist suggested that early stage dementia patients should have a plan for each day. Neil read it in an article. He asked his father every morning, when he called or stopped by on the way to work, what his plan was.

"Cut the grass. Mulch Ruth's roses, I guess."

"Do you have something for lunch?"

"I'll make a sandwich. I've got some roast beef left that your wife sent over."

Neil felt relieved. He had brought Marcus home with leftovers from Sunday dinner at his house. This was Thursday, and he still remembered. He would be all right for another day, Neil hoped.

"I'm leaving now, Dad. I'll call you tonight."

"Why?" Marcus really could not understand why a call was necessary so soon after a visit.

"To make sure everything is okay and because you're my dad."

66

"Oh."

After Neil left, Marcus spent more time than necessary cleaning the coffee maker and wiping down the kitchen countertops. He mowed the backyard and then went back over it to mulch the clippings. He raked up the clippings and put them in a metal garbage can near the garage. He cut out the bottom of the garbage can and found an extra lid. He put the grass and leaves he raked up into the garbage can. Then, he flipped it over, took off the bottom lid, and extracted a few hands full of the compost. He mixed the decayed grass with some plant food and laid the mixture around the rose bushes.

After taking care of the roses, Marcus cleaned and oiled the lawn mower blades. He swept the flagstones between the rose bushes and pulled off the dead petals. He cut two blossoms and carried them into the house. He put them into a silver Revere bowl filled with water. It had been Ruth's favorite way to display her roses. Marcus set the bowl on the dining room table and made a sandwich for his lunch.

Marcus stared at the rose in the silver bowl in front of him. He thought of his wife, and tears fell onto the paper napkin in his lap. The drops grew into perfect circles on the napkin. Marcus watched the circles grow, fascinated, for who knows how long.

Marcus took a small tablet of paper from the top dresser drawer in the bedroom. He found a pen in a mug on the night stand. "World's Greatest Grandpa," the mug declared. Marcus carried his writing equipment to the table on the patio in the back yard. He inhaled the fragrance of the cut grass. It reminded him of a girl's hair, freshly rinsed with rain water. Marcus opened the writing tablet and started a letter to a girl who lifted scarlet cheeks from her rose bushes and blew sweet breath on strawberry curls stuck to her sweaty forehead.

*Dearest Ruth,*

*I don't want you to be upset, but I feel I have to put down some lines about what happened here. We have to face the possibility that I might not make it home, and I want the truth to be told, at least about what I did on the beach that day.*

*They teamed me up with Slattery, a skinny kid from Arkansas or Alabama. He had this crew-cut of carrot-orange hair, thick as moss. The guys razzed him about being so skinny that his hair looked like an eraser on top of a pencil. Good man, though. We were both carrying the big 30 cals. We were supposed to fire rounds at the top of the chalk cliffs where the Germans set up machine guns, while the other guys ran off the landing craft*

*up to the beach.So, there we were, standing in the ocean before the gate
of the landing craft was even down so the men could run up on the beach.
Half of them were still puking over the sides, when me and Slattery jumped
over the side and took our position. We were to fire on the pillboxes up on
the cliffs over Omaha beach. Inside the pill boxes were German machine
gunners. A regular rifle was no use against those concrete boxes, so we
had to take them out with the 30 cals, and that's what me and Slattery were
trying to do while standing in freezing waves that came near to pushing us
over. Slattery pointed to a flash on top of the cliff. I had seen it, too. I got
off quite a few rounds. The men in the boat ran through the water under my
fire and onto the beach. Then, I saw a flash on the barrel right in front of
my face. It was the spark of metal on metal. That weapon jumped out of my
hands and into the ocean. I wasn't hit and neither was Slattery, not then.
Well, that ended our mission, so we crouched down and ran toward the
beach. We joined the mob running from the other boats.*

*Imagine, dear Ruth, an inch to the left or the right, and a Nazi bullet
would have gone right through my heart. When a man is surrounded by
death, he can't think too long about who is spared or why. The next battle is
a new roll of the dice. Someone safe today can roll craps tomorrow. If I am
allowed to return to you, I ask only that you let me lock this war away and
continue our life together, so cruelly interrupted by unforeseeable chance.*

*Your loving husband,*
*Marcus*


*P.S. I saw the most lovely and sad sight yesterday. We were marching
through a bombed out Belgian village. This one house had been flattened,
but some of the flowers in the garden were still there. They were those little
white rose moss plants, like you planted up close to the house. Well, there
were drops of blood on those tiny white flowers. I pray whoever lived there
made it out alive.*


Marcus laid down the pen and stretched the fingers of his right hand
against the palm of his left. Of all the pains that invaded his body, the
ache in his hands troubled him the most. Holding a pen was excruciating,
sometimes.

Neil kept pushing him to get a computer and use e-mail, but what a
waste of money. A big machine just to write a few letters? Marcus picked up
free pens at doctors' offices, the V.A., and from mechanics who serviced his
car. The house was full of them. Ruth squirreled away enough note pads to
write out an encyclopedia. Letters to loved ones should be written by hand,

Marcus believed. The ache was part of the effort, for someone he truly loved.

The afternoon sun was peeking under the patio cover. Soon, it would be in his eyes. Marcus moved around the table to a seat facing away from the roses. He considered the rock wall he built in the southeast corner of the yard. He brought in fill dirt and built a terraced perennial garden of Hollyhocks and Fox Gloves, backing up Purple Dragons, yellow Alyssum, and Snow-in-Summers. In the long shadows of the afternoon, the little walled garden reminded him of Belgium and the flowers that nestled up to the old stone cottages.

Marcus picked up his pen and wrote again, to the girl who wove sweet clover into her braids, wore a white apron, and made him laugh when he thought his happiness had been suffocated by fear.

*My lovely Marie,*

*I think so much about our last time together that I believe I may have distorted it out of all proportion in my mind. Was the sun exceptionally bright, the air fragrant with morning glories, and time held at a complete stop? That's how I remember it. Marching every day, toward the finish of this war, I saw so much misery on either side of the roads we traveled through Belgium and on into France. People walking with determination, but no destination. They carried every possession they had left in a pack or on a cart. They either looked down at the ground or straight ahead. It was impossible for me to tell if they were leaving or returning to their homes. Their expressions were the same, either way. Was it wrong for me to feel happy in the presence of such sorrow?*

*Marie, when a man is at war, all he thinks about is going home. He longs for the familiar, the quiet, the unconditional love of his family. I was no different. I dreamed about my wife, our home, and the life we had planned for ourselves before that war took me away from what now seems an easy love and brought me to you.*

*I still carry the picture I took of you, with your dark curls blown around your face, your hands shoved into your apron pockets. You hid your hands you thought were ruined by farm work, but they felt like silk against mine when you let me hold them.*

*All I wanted in those June days was to be home. Now, alone in the house, I dream about you every time I close my eyes. Did you find another man to love you? Did you raise children in the country or move back to the city? Are you sitting in a garden now, looking at a stone walled flower garden? Do you ever think, in the sleepless hours, of an American who*

*loved you when love was so urgent and so fragile?*
    *Yours forever,*
    *PFC Marcus Lightner, 299th Combat Engineer Battalion*

Marcus folded his letters. He covered them with his arms and laid his head upon his hands. He dozed without dreaming. When dusk covered him, Marcus lifted his head and wondered whose roses they were on which the sun's last rays fell so softly.

*Forgotten Baseball :: Magie McCombs*

# Five Grandparents

Adriana Gradea

When I think of my childhood, I think mainly of my grandparents. I spent most of my early life around my paternal grandparents who lived in Cluj, Romania, in a small brick apartment.

The apartment was on an elevated first floor of an apartment building in a military complex built in the 1950s. The building had two more stories, as well as a semi-basement and an attic. Each floor had eight units, and for each four, there was one communal bathroom and two toilets rooms. With time, most people converted their pantries into very small bathrooms. The staircase and corridors were made of a sort of cement called Venetian mosaic, gray with some white and blue pebble-like shapes in it.

Sensuous smells were always in the air in Grandma Anica's kitchen. I especially enjoyed Easter and Christmas, when the gas cast-iron oven baked traditional sweet breads with walnuts or poppy seeds. In the other two rooms, the heating systems were also on gas: tall hearths covered all around by ochre terra-cotta square tiles. As children, we had to learn not to touch them because they could get very hot. I burned my fingertips a few times. In the cold winter nights, one had to wake up in the early hours to turn them on, with matches, because they took a while to warm up a room. I remember those hearths in my parents' basement apartment also, which was in the same military complex. There, however, the tiles were dark brown and their pattern, to my unutterable amazement, miraculously made them look precisely like the chocolate cookies I used to have with my milk.

My earliest memory was of Grandma Anica and me in front of her tall mirror, having my long hair combed. My small, frail grandma had hazel eyes, looking at me from underneath beautifully arched, dark eyebrows. I dreaded the comb and gave her a hard time, but to see two little me's was fascinating. Who was the little girl in the mirror? Was she a princess? Then,

Grandma would braid her hair and twist it in a little bun. Magic.

I belong to Romania's baby-boomer generation because of a decree-law issued by dictator Ceausescu in 1966 which interdicted abortions and contraceptive measures, but that is a different story. However, as we were a large generation of children not expected or particularly wanted, I consequently had always lots of children of my age around. The complex was surrounded on one side by a sloped dead-end street, which had been unpaved, and where we would ride our sleighs in the winter. On the other side of that street, there was a military base separated from our complex by a cement fence. Next to it there was a bakery which supplied bread to the neighborhood's food stores. The smell of freshly-baked bread and pastry filled my long summer days. Occasionally, we would get a hot, steaming pastry bun, if we asked nicely. Other times, we got a bucket of water poured onto our heads.

On the fence that surrounded the entire military complex, we walked fearlessly every summer. Especially after Nadia Comaneci became the 1976 Montreal Olympic champion in gymnastics, we made up competitions around the yard, so the fence became the beam apparatus. It was five feet high, but who cared? Nadia *was* the quintessential Romanian girl, and every little girl identified with her for years after that. I modeled my pony tail and bangs after hers.

During school days, every afternoon, hungry and tired, my first stop was at my grandparents' place. Something was always cooking in Grandma Anica's kitchen. The smell was of tasty food, whether it was stuffed, green, bell peppers, baking in the oven, polenta bubbling in a pot, my favorite chicken soup with homemade angel-hair pasta, or crepes sautéing in sunflower oil on the old stove. I could smell the aroma from afar, as it was floating through the corridor like sheer ribbons fluttering in the wind.

Grandma Anica would be at the stove. I would greet her and kiss her sticky cheeks. "I kiss your hand, Grandma," I would say the traditional way women are greeted in Romania by children and men.

I would go into one of the rooms where Grandpa Constantin was painting in oil colors. For an accountant, and for someone with no formal art training, he painted with courage and joy. Art took him out of depression. The raw colors he used for his landscapes and flowers filled the room with a smell familiar to me from the art studios at school.

"Adriana, glad you're here. Grandma made your favorite soup and crepes," he would say in his Moldavian accent, raising his bluish-green eyes to greet me. He was of Greek and Sicilian descent, but was born in the south of the eastern Romanian province of Moldavia, a place with vineyards, where the speech is mild, fairy-tale-like, with diphthongized vowels influenced by Russian. Even after many years of living in Transylvania, he never lost his regional Moldavian accent.

They happily spent their afternoon with me and shared their food. The tasty rolled crepes were soon on my plate, hot and soft to the touch, oozing crimson homemade sour-cherry jam. Grandpa was watching me happy and smiling. Even after I got married, he would call and tempt me with grandma's cooking, inviting me to visit.

Grandpa Constantin was a quiet man, but a little depressed, I suspected. I think he didn't want to die. Having all the family around, however, would uplift his spirit and make him happy. I remember him telling all sorts of stories after Sunday dinners. Once, when my cousin Cosmin and I were little, he tried to make us fall asleep in the afternoon, so he told us stories. Cosmin was a year and a half younger and, at the time, my only cousin and the closest to a sibling. We all fitted very well on the large divan at my grandparents' place, which seems quite unbelievable today. One quiet afternoon, he had us both around him, comfortably seated, and he started making up a story.

"Once upon a time, there was a princess, Adriana-the-Fairy-ana. And a little shepherd, Cosminel-the-Shepherdel," he said, adding a rhyme to my name and suffixes to Cosmin's names to make them diminutives. By then, our mouths were open, and our eyes didn't blink. The way he worked out those names, molding them onto well-known fairy-tale names, had both of us stopped in our tracks. It took us a good few moments to grasp the meaning of our new names, during which we could not follow the plot, usually involving a dragon and a rescue. Shortly after, Grandpa himself fell asleep, and we emerged from the room announcing victory: "We did it! We made Grandpa fall asleep!!"

Grandpa had other stories, too: war stories, stories with Germans and Russians, with bombs and shelters, and about running for cover every time the alarm blared. I still have clear memories of stenciled messages in black on the city's walls directing people to shelters. They were there well into the late 1970s. Grandpa once fell into a ditch full of tar in the panic of running to the shelter. After Romania turned against Germany in 1944, when the Russians were in the country, a zealous young Russian soldier almost shot him. Grandpa was on a train, wearing his Army uniform.

At one point, while trying to buy a cigarette from another man, he suddenly heard from behind: "Don't move, or I'll shoot you!"

Grandpa thought he was going to die. It turned out that, since the Russians didn't know Romanian military ranks, they couldn't tell that

Grandpa was a noncombatant. Only when the Russian soldier's superior arrived was the gun taken away from Grandpa's head, and he was allowed to leave.

I regret now not paying more attention to Grandpa's stories. I truly believed he was going to live forever, as was everyone in the family. Today, when I remember my grandparents, I also remember that for a while, I was the only grandchild to five grandparents. In fact, once when I was about four years old, a work colleague of my father's, Mr. G., kept asking me, trying to be funny, "Adriana, explain it to me again: How come you have three grandpas and two grandmas?" I'm sure he was winking at my father, smiling an old-funny-man's smile, behind my back.

I didn't know what to say, thinking that counting and naming them was enough clarification. Upon returning home, I told my mother that something was wrong with Mr. G., since he couldn't understand the simple fact I had three grandpas and two grandmas.

All I knew at the time was that apart from Grandma Anica, I had the grandma on my mother's side, Valeria, whom I called my "Other Grandma." Her story, when I learned it years later, seemed unbelievable. Honestly, I did not *want* to believe it. I didn't know what to think about being the granddaughter of a political prisoner. It was already enough that my mother and her sister were the daughters of one. These things were not talked about, but rather whispered, so we did not talk about it.

I learned later that my Other Grandma used to be a notary public for the city hall in Satu Mare, a northern Transylvanian town close to the Hungarian border. Grandfather Ioan was one of the chiefs of the local police at the time the communists came to power. His position made him an "enemy" of the newly instated communist regime in those years of Soviet occupation. It was the Stalinist period, also known for the witch hunts that put away "enemies," and an "enemy of the working class" could be anybody who had been an important part in the previous regime or even people who had not been actively fighting for communism in illegality.

The night of December 15, 1952, they descended into the house and took my grandpa away with no explanations. They made Grandma divorce him, as they did in all such cases, probably in an attempt to have her redeemed in the eyes of society. Besides, the local communist leaders wanted his house, so they took it. The procedure was, "You get up from the table 'cause I wanna take your place;" or: "You get out of your house 'cause now it's mine." I found out later that what happened to them was all too common in those times, and many people went through exactly the same scenario.

They put Grandma and her two daughters in an apartment consisting of one room at the top level of a building, which did not have a bathroom or a kitchen. She was 30 years old, and her daughters were 3 and 1. Consequently, she was also terminated from her job. Later, she did find work as a typist and moved to a village near Cluj, and then to the city of Cluj, in the same apartment complex where my other grandparents lived. That's where my parents met in the 1960s.

Grandpa Ioan was put in prison with no trial, and he was released with no apology after seven years. By then, everything was too late for him. He was never the same man as before. He died in the 1970s. I have only one memory of him.

I remember my grandfather Ioan as a very slow man. The communist prison life, with hours of standing in cold water up to the knee level, among other terrible things, as I learned later, left him an ill and disturbed person. In my memory, he was a warm and kind presence, with loving, bright blue eyes. He had been a handsome man. Smiling at me, he walked very slowly, in obvious pain. They told me he had water in his knees and also in his lungs. I did not know what that meant, as I had never heard a thing like that before, but for the five year old that I was, this explained the way he walked.

One day, Grandpa Ioan came to see me. I was playing in my other grandparents' yard, at the military complex. There were lots of kids in the inner courtyard, between the gray-stucco buildings, playing in the grass-covered yard. Summers were long and sunny, so I used to play outside all day long. Nothing could beat the fact that the sun stayed up in the sky until 9 or 10 at night. I observed Grandpa Ioan's walk as he came closer and talked to me, calling my name, smilingly, wanting to capture my attention. I saw him going away again, only to return a few moments later with a piece of cake he bought at a small pastry store across the street.

We both went inside to my grandma Anica's, where he sat down and calmly watched me devour the dessert. It was a brown, square piece of cake with a hard, chocolate frosting with some white curly lines as decorations on it. Grandma and my mother always made all the food from scratch and were not fond of store-made pastry, so I almost never had such cakes. I always wondered how they tasted, though, and this was probably the first time I had ever touched one. Being the busy child that I was, as soon as I finished the cake, I ran outside to play with my buddies. I still remember that visit and the cake to this day. However, my next memory related to him is attending his funeral, my first one ever.

My Other Grandma remarried in 1968 with my grandpa Josef Unk.

To me, he was Buni-Tata, a corruption of "grandpa-daddy," widely used in Transylvania by the Hungarian minority. Being partly German-Romanian, partly Hungarian-Romanian, his Romanian was bad, and he spoke Hungarian with my Other Grandma. I believe she was happy. He was a good man. Rather tall, with a red face, he had thick, blonde hair full of gray and big, wrinkled hands. He loved riding his bicycle even in his seventies.

I remember how once, when putting sugar in his tea in a beautiful gold-rimmed porcelain cup, he turned to me and said, "Adriana, do you know how the Germans dance? Like this," and he stirred the liquid with his spoon, clockwise. Then he continued, "And do you know how the Russians dance? Like this," and he hit the bottom of the cup with the spoon, making short, up and down movements. "And the Romanians, do you know?"

I shook my head no, smiling.

"Like this," he said again, stirring counterclockwise. "But do you know why?"

I didn't know why.

"Just so that the sugar melts," he said happily. He was my fifth grandparent. None of the kids I ever knew had divorced grandparents, let alone remarried ones. No one could understand.

My Other Grandma loved having me over. She made me "furred" bread, as the translation from Hungarian goes, a kind of French toast but savory, without the sugar. It was good. Or she would toast sliced bread in a pan, and then put oil on it and rub a garlic clove against it. She cooked in a more Hungarian-Transylvanian way, with sweet fruit soups made from cherries, sour cherries, gooseberries, plums, and apples; plum-filled potato dumplings rolled in sugar and breadcrumbs; pasta with cabbage, pasta with poppy seeds, and pasta with ground walnuts and sugar. That was quite different from my Grandma Anica's food.

Thinking of my Other Grandma now, I realize she was also the one who talked to me about God. I am grateful she taught me how to pray because God was not talked about anywhere in the communist years. One evening when I was about four or five, before we went to bed, she was talking about something, perhaps heaven, when I suddenly said, more in the form of a question, "And there is a big golden book in heaven, and an angel is writing in it." She looked at me amazed, probably thinking I had some kind of inkling of the heavens and hugged me tight. That scene often pops up in my mind when I least expect it, and when people talk about angels. It came to mind when she died in 1994. I wish I could still believe in either the book or the angel.

My grandparents were there through my childhood and young adult life, to fill my soul with memories. Remembering them through the years gives me the dimension of their love for me—a love I mindlessly took for granted in the first part of my life. In 1996, I won the Green Card Lottery, which gave me the possibility to get a visa for the United States. When I was about to leave for America, Grandpa Constantin tried to make me stay. He didn't understand what else I wanted when I was already lucky enough. My career was taking off as an English teacher at a famous high school, and to have the kind of parents and a loving family like mine was all he thought I could ever want. Excited about the adventure of my life that was about to happen, my mind's eyes wanted to see only roses in my future.

I will never forget the last time I saw Grandpa Constantin. I was in a hurry, and even though I had seen them every day before that time, I did go one more time to my grandparents' little place that was so familiar to me. I went to say goodbye. That Grandma Anica was crying was actually expected, but to see Grandpa's clear eyes tearing up and looking away, in that small kitchen, chipped on my euphoria. It moved me that my serious grandpa was hurting. Couldn't they see they would always be with me, in my heart? And that their place had always been my home that I would never really leave? But that was the last time I ever saw Grandpa. He probably knew it then, or just feared it. He died of a stroke the following year.

I visited that complex again, almost ten years to the day I last saw it. The place I remember from my childhood was considerably larger. The place I found shrunk to a miniature of what my memory retained. A small part of me is still hiding around there and will never leave.

# The Old Barn

Susan Graham-Ulsher

Across the pasture where the horses grazed, there was an old barn that sat in the middle of a field. It was built in the late 1880s and had seen better days. It was old and faded looking. The paint that once covered the oak planks had worn off with time, leaving the wood to dry and splinter from exposure to the hot sun in summer and the cold winds and rain in winter.

The wood was dark reddish-brown and rough to the touch. Around the paddocks and stalls the railings had been chewed down by its previous four-legged tenants. Cobwebs hung in every corner of the barn. They were covered in dust, and when the breeze blew through the open doors, they swayed and vibrated in the wind. Surrounding the pastures, huge eucalyptus trees stood tall and proud. Their wide branches hung heavy with silver leaves.

I spent my adolescent years riding the horses that lived on the ranch. After school my sisters and I would hang out in the barn with friends, grooming the horses and ponies, talking, laughing and telling stories. One summer in 1976, we watched as bulldozers tore the barn to the ground to make way for twenty new houses. We stood and watched as machines tore at the wood planks. We could hear the cracking of the hundred-year-old wood as it split into pieces. The trees were the last to go. Tough, resilient, prolific, and tenacious, their roots clung to the life sustaining soil. Grinding their gears, the bulldozers bore down one last time, and the last tree fell. The field was dead and barren.

A hate grew inside me. I could not accept the fact that the city was growing and needed room for growing families like mine. Like other families, we were forced to sell our horse because there was no affordable boarding in the area. The property had been condemned and deemed unsafe. I hated the developers who stole my pasture. I hated the construction workers and all of their equipment, but most of all I hated the new homeowners.

Time passed by, and many friendships ceased. What had been a common meeting ground for riders around the neighborhood was turned into a noisy corner. A part of our lives was erased that day and a way of life.

Living in cities that grow every year, I guess I just have to accept the fact that growth will continue, and land will change hands, and buildings will sprout. It is not a thought I enjoy. I think often of that field and the old barn. I remember the friendships and all the fun I had. I can still see, in my mind's eye, all of the beautiful horses that grazed among the trees. I can only hope that somewhere in this country, someone will leave an old barn standing in a field, for many generations to come.

# The Seasons in My Life
Maria Gutierrez

The red and orange leaves are dancing to the rhythm of the wind. Their gracious movements are a delight, cracking with every turn before they go out of scene. Soon, the stage will fill with snow, Christmas carols, and the smell of hot chocolate. Children will be cheerfully sledding, excited about the colorful bows and wrapping hiding their presents. The birds, in expectation for the new spring to come, wait for the flowers to begin blooming again, so they can suckle their nectar and sing to it. Later, when the warmth of the long days of summer embraces lovers, the trees will again be full of new leaves to prepare for their next dance.

My childhood, as spring, had its own young beauty and happy-go-lucky moments. Cuernavaca is called *La Ciudad de la Eterna Primavera* (Forever Spring City). There, my older brother, my younger sister, and I enjoyed going weekends and holidays to my grandparents' country home. Trees were always green, and flowers of all colors filled the garden. The thick and wet grass served us as a bed as we rolled down the hill shouting, "Green! Blue! Green! Blue!" to each turn, before landing in an unexpected place and begin running again to the top of the hill to roll once more. Chutes and Ladders, Bingo, Checkers, and all sorts of games were covered with the scarlet beans that we collected from the ground of a nearby garden full of *colorines* (erythrina) trees, but our favorite game was playing with the ants. We spent hours watching them and providing sticks and leaves to help them build their cities. Their teamwork amazed us. When they marched, we sang songs for them to march along.

Summer came, and I found love. Joy was everywhere. I could see myself reflected in the eyes of my soon-to-be husband. Weekends were full of parties with friends and picnics with both his family and mine. One of the best trips we made was to *Las Grutas de Cacahuamilpa* (grottos). Going down the caves, the cool air relieved us from the heat. The large salons with stalactite and stalagmite formations in one of the largest cave systems in the world filled us with awe. Just thinking about the water droplets falling over millions of years to become The Fountains, The Throne, The Bell Tower, The Goat, The Cherubim's, and hundreds of other formations, made me feel a very tiny part of a vast universe. These large natural rock walls witnessed lives of Olmec people, the Chontal tribe, the Spaniards after the Conquest, Maximiliano the Emperor of Habsburg, and now, our family and the awakening of love.

Many years later, when the leaves fell down from the tree of my life and my husband passed away, a friend gave me a book called *El Otoño de Freddy la Hoja* (Freddy the Leaf's Fall). Reading this story to my children helped me explain to them the meaning of death. It gave us the opportunity to open our eyes and, in the midst of our pain, admire the beauty of different trees. A big oak tree stood in majesty in front of an office building where we had to go once a week during several months. This tree became our friend and gave us solace, and now, when I look at the trees in Nebraska, their rainbow of colors makes me vibrate. I love walking under the cool shade of trees in the summer at Lauritzen Gardens, and I watch how they turn red, orange and yellow before they take away their clothes in the fall. I love the sound of the thick and fluffy bed of leaves of all colors under my steps. The graciousness with which they dance to the wind is music for me and reminds me that the true meaning of loss is only transformation.

After my children grew up and married, winter finally presented me with "The Most Beautiful Thing I Ever Saw": the picture of my son holding for the first time his own son. At this time, my daughter-in-law's mother and I lived in Mexico. We came several weeks before the baby was due, because the doctor had told them the baby would arrive earlier. After many hours of labor, Mariana, my daughter-in-law, was having a hard time, and my son Rafael was very worried. Mariana's mother was also worried and mad at the doctor, who, for several hours, was reluctant to perform a c-section.

When the baby was finally born, they took him out of the surgery room, and Jose, my other son, and I received him, while Rafael and Mariana's mother stood by her bed. We were watching him and taking pictures while the nurse weighed and measured him, and the doctor checked that he was healthy. When Rafael came into the room, the doctor handed him the baby. His eyes filled with amazement and tenderness. All the tension of the past hours having his wife deal with the pains of delivery was now over.

The baby had been crying since the moment they took him out of the delivery room, and when he felt his father's arms around him, he suddenly stopped crying and went to sleep. Jose could not take his eyes away from his brother and his nephew. When their eyes met, they connected like when they were children, and did not need to say anything to read each other's mind. This time, they were perplexed. They were captured with the prize they had won, the prize of being father and uncle. This little baby took them to a new dimension.

My thoughts took me to the day Rafael was born. I was full of joy. My husband was very excited. As soon as he had a chance, he ran to the store to buy a boat toy larger than the baby. My mother and my mother-in-law looked at each other with pride. A few days later, my son was very ill and could not leave the hospital when I was released. We felt an immense pain.

As I looked to the sequence of my life passing before my eyes, I felt a great love for life. There was ugliness, and there was beauty. There was pain, and there was happiness. There was sorrow, and there was joy, and this day, I knew that I was ready to begin my spring again.

*Sainted :: Kris T. James*

# After the Storm

Shawna Hanson

It's usually towards evening after a hot, humid, windy day that the wind suddenly becomes still. I would be sitting on the swing set in a cutoff shirt and gym shorts covered in dirt and sweat when I would look around and notice the roar was silenced by an unseen hand. Instead of being consoled by the calmness, the air radiated an eeriness. The humidity seemed to intensify and grow in strength, yet there was no breeze to blow it away this time. Puffy white clouds could be seen on the horizon. The animals on the farm, including the insects which had been so merciless earlier that day, had hidden away from sight. It would then dawn on me that a storm was forming.

Everyday after school, I rode home on the bus. As soon as everyone was seated, we were off through the grid-like gravel roads jostling around in the seats. The bus driver wove through farm after farm dropping off my classmates, one by one. When I was ten years old, I followed this familiar routine and got home around 3:50 in the afternoon. I knew that my parents and all of my siblings were not going to be there. Yet, within three minutes of being home, my sister Alisha and her friend Mason walked into the door. Alisha had forgotten to bring a pitcher for water to use for Parent's Night, after the high school volleyball game.

As she headed out the door, she said, "Shawna, please don't tell Mom and Dad that I was here. I only have a school permit, and I'm not supposed to have Mason with me, pretty please?"

I said I wouldn't tell, and they left. Less than ten minutes later as I was unpacking my lunch, I heard the telephone ring.

"Is Mark or Judy there?"

"No, but I'm their daughter."

"Did anyone just leave your house recently? Your sister maybe?"

"My sisters are still at school, I think."

"Are you sure someone didn't just leave?"

"Well, my sister Alisha just left."

"Okay, thanks. Bye."

The calmness never lasts long. The wind takes a quick breath and fashions its way into a storm. Then, the rain comes, and the wind clinks against the windows, beating them down. The wind swirls around the house in a continuous roar. The lightning creates a strobe-like effect, and when it takes a snapshot of the outside, the trees are bending and swaying trying to keep afloat. Suddenly, the hail makes a heart dropping sound and pounds on the side of the house, and I'm praying, please God, save the crops, and don't let them get damaged. There's that moment when my Mom shouts, "Let's get in the basement!" and we rush down and huddle together, hoping it passes.

It took a call from my Grandma to realize what was happening. I rushed outside to spot the ambulances and flashing lights a mile away. I just stood there not knowing what to do. From the corner of my eye, I saw the cop car drive up to my house. A tall, middle-aged, policeman stepped out. He asked if my parents were home, and when the answer was, no, he asked if he could call them. This was in the days before everyone had a cell phone. Luckily, however, my sister Natasha had one, and she was shopping with my Mom in Lincoln.

"Ma'am, this is Deputy---, and I'm sorry to inform you that your daughter Alisha has been in a rollover car accident on the gravel road near your home. She is being life-flighted to Lincoln right now."

As soon as a storm has passed, the earth seems relieved. The unspoken tradition around where I grew up is to load up in the pick-up, and drive around to survey the damage. This doesn't come from an idea of morbid curiosity. Instead, the intention is to help those who need it. One night, a thunderstorm rolled in, and the wind blew furiously throughout the night. As the tornado warning flashed on the TV screen indicating our county, we dashed to the basement for safety. The tornado missed our house, but it did not spare our neighbor's three miles away. Within a couple hours after the storm, ten or more pick-up trucks were parked on the road, and people were picking up debris. Despite the hard times and bad luck, the neighbors were looking out for each other and slowly putting their house and lives back together.

Mason broke his collar bone and was out of the hospital within a couple of days. My sister was in the hospital for over a month. Her left arm had been broken and the gravel and glass had become embedded in her skin. She had twenty surgeries on her arm to repair the damage, trying to prevent infection, and hoping to restore the skin on her arm. There were countless hours of physical therapy to allow her to stretch out her arm completely straight. Every time we went to visit her in Lincoln, we passed the spot on the gravel road. The skid marks and ruffled grass were still glaringly visible.

I also remember when she tried playing the piano again for the first time. She couldn't stretch her hand to an octave, and she could barely move her fingers. It was heartbreaking to watch, but she had a look of determination. She was going to play the piano again.

The neat thing about a storm is that a couple of days later new growth appears. The earth has taken a drink, and it has restored the land. There is hope for the rest of the year. The corn and soybeans become greener and produce more fruit. The rain washes away the marks on the road and cleanses the earth of the pain from the night before.

One morning while I was in college, I woke up early and turned on my computer. I typed in the website and was watching a graduation ceremony over the Internet, Alisha's. She was graduating from a Physician Assistant program at a school in Winchester, Virginia, after two years of arduous studying. Her husband was visible on the screen and was proud of his wife. Alisha crossed the stage and was awarded her white coat. She wanted to become a Physician Assistant to help people going through tough circumstances. Her story was her inspiration. Out of pain came renewed purpose.

# Trichotillomania: The Dream of Writing On
## Abby Hills

A few pages here, a couple of chapters there, when I was only six, I wrote my first story. It was about a girl who wanted to enter a neighborhood talent show, but she didn't think she had any skills. Eventually, the girl finds out she can dance and wins the show, pretty deep writing for a six-year-old. In school, I loved writing class the most. The number one comment on all my report cards from my teachers was that I had amazing voice, the one aspect of the six traits of writing that is the hardest for students to learn.

"I am a writer." That is what I say when people ask me who I am. "I am a writer." Though my journey through life has had a lot of downs, it has also had some high points, and today, I am on my way to becoming a published author.

At age eleven, I had a life changing experience. It seemed like an unfortunate event in a young girl's life, but it ended up changing who I was. My grandparents were babysitting me one day, because my parents went to see a college baseball game and would not get back until late. My older sister was staying at a friend's house that night. There was a barbeque going on at my aunt's house, and my grandparents were going to take me, but my grandpa began to feel badly. He was a little under the weather and didn't feel like going, he said, so we went without him. After a wonderful time at my aunt's house with my relatives, Grandma drove us back to her house. We walked in, and all the lights were off except the one in the bathroom. My grandma 'tisked and said that grandpa must have gone to bed, and then she asked me if I would turn out the bathroom light for her, and she would go dish us up some ice cream. Happily thinking about vanilla ice cream with chocolate sauce, I walked over to the bathroom and let out a scream.

My grandpa was lying on the floor. I can remember his exact pose. He was lying between the toilet and the wall, one arm reaching out toward the door where I stood and his head lying on his arm, as if he tried to call out to us, but we weren't there. He wasn't blinking or moving. I stumbled back and hit the closet door behind me, my mouth hanging as far down as it would go.

"Grandma!" I screamed more than once until she came running, clutching a kitchen towel in her hands.

"What, what?" she asked frantically, pausing in the doorway. I couldn't say it; the words wouldn't come out of my paralyzed throat. Eventually, I went behind her and pushed her body toward the bathroom door, and she let me lead her there. "Go call 911!" she told me quickly, and I sprinted to the kitchen and grabbed the phone. Before I even had a chance to dial, she was there snatching it out of my hands to talk to the dispatch woman.

I numbly walked into the living room and stared at the only light in the entire house, realizing the reason the lights were off was because he collapsed before nightfall. I slowly bent to my knees, not feeling my body at all, and sat perfectly straight and erect, staring at the light coming through the door. When my grandma hung up the phone, she came into the room and stood at the top of the steps ahead of me, turning on the living room light, and her body blocked my view of the bathroom door.

"I just feel so badly," she said, her voice quivering as we could hear the faint sound of a siren in the distance. Her chin began to wobble, and she put a hand over her mouth to keep from crying in front of me. The EMTs knocked, and my grandma answered, then they rushed up the stairs and closed the door to the bathroom, the three of them alone in there with my grandpa.

The rest of the night was a blur of activity. My grandma called her priest, and he came and spoke to us both, and he made me feel a little better. My parents came home, and I explained what happened to them, while grandma talked to the police. My dad took me to get my sister from her friend's house; he forced me to go with him, because he thought I needed a break from the scene. My mom couldn't leave her mother alone at a time like this. When we got back, my aunts and uncles who had been laughing and joking all evening were all there, somber and sad, and they did not allow my cousins to come with them.

The EMTs rolled my grandpa out on a stretcher, while we were all waiting in the basement living room, and they asked if any of us wanted to see him one more time. For whatever reason, even though my dad was against it, I said I wanted to see. I walked up the steps with only one aunt and uncle, and we stood stiffly and stared down at him. I remember thinking that this was strange. Why did I want to see him when even my mother didn't? Why did I want to look at the body of a man I loved, after he was gone? I had never seen a dead person before. I looked at his hands folded peacefully, his immaculately creased pants, and his collared shirt. I couldn't look at his face, I just couldn't. My uncle put a hand on my shoulder, and it made me feel really good, because he didn't show outward signs of love very often. Just then, I felt as if he thought I was brave, and that was important to me. As the EMTs were zipping up the bag, I glanced at his face quickly, and then let my uncle take me back down the steps.

A few days later, after the funeral, after I had slept off all the tears I sobbed, I went to the family computer and started writing. I wrote down everything I could remember about the night. I was insanely worried I would forget the details. For some reason, I was desperate to remember that night exactly how it happened. I printed the three sheets of paper and stashed them in my room.

A few weeks later, my best friend was with me, and my mom had driven us to the video store to rent a movie. As we were driving back home, I blinked a few times, rubbed my eyes, and an eyelash came off on my finger.

"Make a wish!" My friend said. I looked at her, confused, and she explained, "It's good luck for an eyelash to fall out. Make a wish and blow it away." I did as she said, and I wished that I would start to feel better. It had been four weeks, and I still felt the same way I had the night grandpa died. Frozen, stiff, stuck, it was hard to breathe. The next day, I looked at myself in the mirror, paler than ever, and my blue eyes had large purple circles under them. I couldn't force myself to smile, no matter how hard I tried. I lifted my fingers and pulled out an eyelash from my eyelid, expecting it to hurt. Instead, it felt really good. I made a wish, and pulled another. Pulled, wished. Pull, wish, pull, wish. I did this for about an hour, almost in a trance, until I had no eyelashes left. I got scared, not understanding what I was doing to myself. I brushed the eyelashes off the bathroom counter and went to busy myself with something else. "That did not happen," I kept telling myself.

Two weeks later, another friend was staying over for the night; it was summer break, so my parents let me have friends over more often. My friend was already asleep, but I couldn't stop thinking about my eyelashes and wishing I had more to pull out. I just couldn't stop thinking about them, and it almost hurt because I wanted to pull them out so badly. I fingered the line of my eyelid, searching for more to pluck, and then my knuckle grazed my eyebrow. My fingers frantically reached for the tiny hairs there and began to pull; it felt so wonderful! I briefly thought that my wishes wouldn't come true, if I was using eyebrow hairs instead of eyelash hairs. It didn't matter. I wanted to pull them, no, *needed* to pull them. I wished on them anyway. I wished that I wouldn't feel so sad anymore. I wished that I could feel like me again. After half an hour, I glanced down at my pajama top in the dim blue light of the TV that was still on and saw a spread of tiny hairs all over the material. I panicked. I went to the bathroom and looked in the mirror; my entire right eyebrow was gone. I knew I couldn't hide this from my mother. I was too upset to go back and lie down; I had to tell her now. It was three in the morning, and I crept into my parent's room and up to my mom's side of the bed and shook her awake. I explained what I'd done, and she sat up quickly and turned on the lamp.

"What have you done to yourself?" she asked, obviously upset. She got out of bed and pulled me into the bathroom and closed the door, so as not to bother my dad and turned on the light. She took my chin and stared at my face for a long minute, and then let it go. "Don't you ever do that again, do you understand?" she asked. Her tone was harsh, but I expected her to be more disturbed.

"Yes," I answered, ashamed of myself, and unable to explain what I had done. I went back downstairs to sleep, but for months, I tried to leave my eyelashes and eyebrows alone, but I couldn't. Eventually, all my eyelashes and brows on both eyes were gone, and my mother couldn't ignore this behavior anymore.

Mom took me to the doctor, and she suggested a therapist for me. I was frightened; did this mean I was crazy? Would they lock me away? I cried all the way home, and my mother tried to explain to me that this didn't mean I was "nuts," it meant that I was having a hard time and needed a little extra help. Her words didn't make me feel any better, and a week later, when we saw the therapist, I was skittish and upset, but I knew I had to talk to her about what I did to myself. I was diagnosed with trichotillomania, a psychological condition that involves strong urges to pull out one's own hair. After a little while in therapy, I was also diagnosed with both depression and anxiety. The doctor believed I had anxiety my entire life, but the depression and trichotillomania were just now making themselves known, because of the traumatic occurrence I experienced at my grandparent's house.

Over the next few years, all three conditions worsened. When I was fourteen I had to wear a wig every day to school. I had too much hair missing on my head to cover it with a bandana. I created eyebrows for myself with an eyebrow pencil. I felt like I looked like a clown, despite my mother telling me I looked normal. I had so much anxiety that I missed school often and got violently ill every day before school, before road trips, and before sleepovers with friends. I was put on increasing dosages of medication for my depression, but none ever made me feel like "me" again. I was never the same.

I had a lot of problems with my conditions. Kids are cruel at all ages, but when people have something blatantly wrong with them, they are always targets. A vicious rumor went around in seventh grade that I ate my hair. Some people with trichotillomania do eat their hair, but I didn't. I was frequently asked if I had cancer. Once, a boy ran up to me and snatched the bandana off my head and then froze, and every student in the hall, which was every student in the seventh grade because we were lining up after lunch, stopped and looked at me. If there had been any doubt that I was a freak, there wasn't any more. I grabbed my bandana from his hand and put it back on quickly, pretending nothing happened, even though my entire body was hot, and I was fighting tears. The next day, my small group of friends would no longer speak to me. I was now such an outcast that if they associated with me, they would be outcasts, too.

In ninth grade, people always asked if the hair on my head was a wig, and I had to lie and say it wasn't. In high school, I couldn't go through what I did in middle school. In tenth grade, people pestered my new friends for information about my hair, and not realizing how big of a secret it was, my friends would tell them, which made everyone make fun of me even more. In eleventh grade, if I walked too closely to other students in the hallway, they would move away from me, as if I had an infection they could catch by being within ten feet. "Ha ha." I would say blandly and keep walking. No one ever knew how much those things hurt me, but I would come home and cry on one of my parent's shoulders for hours every single day.

Through all of this, I wrote everything I was feeling and everything kids did to me. I wrote down everything my therapist said so that I wouldn't forget. Over the years, I tried everything to quit pulling. I got hypnotized. I bought relaxation CDs. I covered the bathroom mirror with wrapping paper, so I couldn't see what I was pulling. I kept a rubber band on my wrist and stung myself every time I pulled. I kept a pen I could click in my pocket to replace pulling with that habit instead. I went on and on, and nothing ever helped. It only got worse. I wrote everything down, and I kept meticulous notes. The only thing that ever got me through the pain of both the depression and the extra sadness I felt at being the school's biggest freak was writing. I made up stories replete with characters going through much worse things than I was: characters who were dying, who lost an arm or a leg, whose mom or dad died, and kids who couldn't talk or see. I channeled all my feelings into writing stories as escapes. Reading was also a getaway, but writing was my true passion. I took many writing and English classes in school and honed my skills. I was actively using my fingers to put down words, instead of pulling my hair. Every time I got the urge to pull, I grabbed a pen and wrote on the nearest piece of paper I could find. Once, I accidently did this on the edge of an important document of my mother's. Oops.

By the time college came, I had gotten past most of the hardships with the kids around me. Yeah, I still got the occasional, "Nice wig Abbie. What's it made of?" thrown at me, which is a line from the movie *Mean Girls*, to which I would reply, "Your mom's chest hair!" just like the girl in the movie did. I simply decided that those people were immature. They had made fun of me since sixth grade. Honestly, weren't they sick of it by now? I decided to major in literature, because I wanted to be a writer. Over the past few years, it became a dream of mine to become a published author. I wanted to write books about my experiences. I wanted kids who were going through hard things to know that they weren't alone in their suffering. Others went through the same things and made it out on the other side.

By my junior year in college, I still wore a wig every day, but my eyelashes had all grown back and about half my eyebrows. I was still working hard toward stopping the pulling, but I made a lot of progress. I was taking an English class that fall semester, which was about writing argumentative research papers. I briefly thought of arguing something about one of my conditions, but I knew my professor would have to read about me, and I knew that the other students around me would have to peer edit my paper, and I wasn't ready to proclaim my circumstances to the world. I was worried it would become the same way it was in high school: ostracism, no one speaking to me, whispers of "freak" and "hair eater" behind their hands. Instead, for my first paper, I decided to write about a famous writer I loved, Homer.

My professor was very hard on us, and the second day of the class I had so much anxiety I even accidently cried in front of him, something I had never done before. My professor told me that if I did not give up on the class, that he wouldn't give up on me. That meant so much. I felt like he was on my side, and he would teach me what I needed to know.

For the second paper, I already began some research when the professor called me into the hallway during class. I was worried I was in trouble. Was he kicking me out? Had I done something terribly wrong? When I got out into the hallway, my professor told me I was a good writer, and he wanted to know if I would be interested in writing a piece that would go into a collection of student writing he was developing. He was a publisher and editor as well as a university professor. I couldn't believe it. Me?

I wanted to glance around and see if anyone else witnessed this or if it was just in my head. He said he wanted someone to write about a specific topic, and he thought of me. I was going to be a published writer, my dream. After all I had been through, so much humiliation and heartbreak, I was getting my first steps toward my dream.

Two weeks later, I received an e-mail from my professor that said, "Abbie, I am trying to convince the editors to also publish your Homer paper as well." I started to cry. I was so happy I didn't know what to do with myself. I hadn't been this happy since I was a kid, and for the first time since I was eleven, I felt like myself. I was doing the thing I was meant to do. I could feel it. I was still struggling with my conditions, but I was happy that I had them. If I hadn't gone through such hardship, I would never have gotten the strength to become who I needed to be to achieve my dreams.

> *"Most of the basic material a writer works with is acquired before the age of fifteen."*
> - Willa Cather

# The Blue Story

R. C. Hoover

*"Only those know truth who either Suffer or Dream."*
*Sheolian folk saying*

"I am in pain," she said, "so much pain. Dreamer, please take away the pain."

"I cannot take away the pain," the Dreamer said.

"Then give me courage," the woman said.

"I cannot give courage," the Dreamer said, "but let me find what I can give."

And that night he dreamed. He was a boy again, listening to his father and uncles and cousins as they told of finding courage to face battle, to face loss, to face loneliness. And the Dreamer, as a young boy, said to his father, "Father, give me courage that I may give it to another." His father smiled and said, "I cannot give you courage, but I can give you this." From the air, his father gathered a stub of candle. "Light this," his father said, "when all seems dark."

In the dream of the woman who had asked for courage, a boy offered a stub of candle.

The next day, those beside the bed said, "Her pain is less."

Her eyes opened, and she said, "A little less, but now I am afraid." She looked at the Dreamer and said, "I am so afraid. Please take away my fear."

The Dreamer said, "I cannot take away your fear."

"Then give me peace."

"I cannot give peace," the Dreamer said, "but let me find what I can give."

And that night the Dreamer dreamed. He dreamed of the forest, and the lake, and the mountain where he had found peace long ago, amid his greatest sorrow. And he asked the mountain, "Mountain, give me peace, that I may give it to another." The mountain whispered, "I cannot give you peace, but I can give you this." And in his strong hands rested a stone, etched with the likeness of forest, lake, and mountain. He reached out.

And in her dream, she received it.

In the morning, those who stood by the bed said, "She seems less afraid, but Dreamer, you seem weary."

The Dreamer smiled at the woman on the bed and replied, "Yes, I am weary, but I am content."

Days passed. Now, neither courage nor peace could long sustain the woman. She whispered to the Dreamer. "I thank you for the gifts that allowed me to find courage and peace. I am content."

The Dreamer nodded, and said, "Yet you would ask again."

"Yes," said the woman. Her voice was weak, but her eyes were shining. "That I might sit with you before your father and uncles and cousins, and walk with you in the forest and see the lake and the mountain."

The Dreamer took the woman's hand. And they dreamed:

A boy and a girl sat and listened to stories of courage by the light of a thousand candles. And as strong youths, they ran and swam and climbed. And in their dream, they sat atop the mountain and held each other as the sun set.

> *"Find the key emotion; this may be all you need know to find your short story."*
>
> - F. Scott Fitzgerald

# Pale Faces

Shelby Jones

The moment the door opened I knew something was different. I was just getting off work, and it was about 10 p.m. A very long day, no matter how you look at it. I went in at the normal time, 6 a.m., but I had to stay late to finish some paperwork. These 16-hour workdays were killing me.

I took a look around my apartment. The lights were off, as I had left them, but I knew there were people there. The door had a slight creak, an annoying reminder to oil the hinges, which I hadn't gotten to.

There were people everywhere. They were hanging around with no expression on their shadowed faces. I didn't know if I knew them, but then again I couldn't have recognized the characters in such a dark scene.

"Hello?" I questioned. I was standing in the doorway for at least 30 seconds, and no one moved or said a word. It was a frightening moment, seeing a whole bunch of weird people scattered throughout my apartment.

I quickly flicked the light on to reveal the horde of people, frozen in time. Their faces were pale, their eyes dark, sunken against their hollow faces. They all looked straight ahead at me. They were tall, resembling long, thin trees in a forest.

I didn't know what to do. Call the police? Run? I put down my bag slowly, without turning my eyes away from them. I didn't know what to call them, either. I knew they weren't exactly people, but I didn't know what else they could be.

I stood there as still as I could, thinking back to my Boy Scout days, when I learned how to avoid a bear attack. This was like that, right? I tried not to make eye contact and hoped to appear the least threatening as possible, not that I was at all threatening in the first place, because I was awkward and lanky looking. They all continued looking at me. I guess that didn't work.

The next tactic I used was trying to get to the phone to call the police. I'm sure I would sound like a total lunatic if I told them about the pale faced strangers with no eyes taking over my apartment, but I couldn't think of anything else. I looked up at the beings, and they were all as still as could be.

I forgot my cell phone at the office. I never forgot my cell phone. Of course, this was the only day that I really needed it. I relaxed my tense posture and turned my head to the phone, about 10 feet away sitting on the coffee table. I wasn't a big fan of caffeine, because it always seemed to make me sick. When I was a teenager, my friends and I attempted to have an all-nighter, with dozens of bottles of Mountain Dew and energy drinks. It didn't take much to get me sick. I ended up being the lame one and going home at 11 p.m.

I sized up the number of steps needed to reach my destination. I thought I could make it with one long jump. After all, I *was* a track star in college, one of my many achievements.

I took a small step towards the phone and took a look at the pale faces. They all had their heads turned slightly to get a better look at me. I knew it was now or never, so I quickly lunged toward the phone, but I ended up doing half-splits on the floor, hitting my shinbone against the coffee table and stretching places in my legs that had never been stretched before.

I'm sure the whole scene was a humorous one, and I probably would have laughed ,if I saw it myself. I felt like the character in the online game of QWOP, with my limbs flailing around and hitting things.

I heard a giggle come from the pale faces, and I began to laugh myself. This was quickly turning into a freaky horror movie spoof. They had smiles as bright as the sun. Oddly, they had full sets of teeth! They looked as if they could be veneers, or possibly the highest quality dentures. It was an odd sight, for sure. Then they started chuckling, but no noise came out. I could definitely tell they thought it was funny, because smiles came across all their faces and their bellies kept moving.

I slowly got up, careful not to make sudden movements. They laughed and laughed and laughed, but I didn't think it was that funny.

I was beginning to question whether or not these beings were dangerous. They had chances to lunge their bony bodies at me and devour me, but they didn't. I then decided to try and talk to them.

"Hello? What are you?" I asked them, speaking to no one in particular. I didn't get a response, just a slight head nod from them all.

"Okay. Well, why are you here?" I asked again, trying not to sound annoyed. They did not answer.

"Well, guys, I thank you all for stopping by, but it's getting late, and I have to be getting to bed. See you later." I said with a wave and walked to the bathroom, shutting the door behind me.

I put my ear to the door, and I heard shuffling, then nothing but silence. I opened the door slightly, and I peered through the crack. They were gone!

I tightly closed my eyes and looked again. Nope, nobody was there.

I opened the door all the way and examined my apartment, finding no one. *Finally*, I thought. It was just before midnight now, and I was beyond exhausted. I didn't bother to change into comfy clothes to sleep in, so I just plopped down on the springy mattress in my bedroom. I closed my eyes, and all I could see were the pale faces. I realized it was going to be a long night of tossing and turning.

I pulled the covers over me, stopping just below my neck. I turned onto my side, and closed my eyes, trying to not think of them, but I guess that's a form of thinking about them.

I opened my eyes again, and it was bright outside the windows. I looked at the clock. 7 a.m. I shot up, looking around for any evidence of what happened last night. I pulled back the covers and examined my leg, the spot where I banged it on the coffee table and saw a big, purple, bruise mark on my skin.

*So it was real.* I thought. Then, I remembered I was late for work, but oddly, I didn't really care. I had just gone through a traumatic experience last night, and I wouldn't be bothered to show up to work!

I didn't go to work that day. I didn't go the next day, either. I stayed in my apartment for the majority of my days. It's not like I could actually try to explain to someone what happened to me. They would put me in a mental institution!

So, this is the first time I've told anyone about my experience. Who knows if someone will read this at all. Have the pale faces visited me again, you ask? Indeed they have! They're here most of the time, just quietly sitting here, like always. Now, they're my friends, my pals, and my buddies, although they don't do anything. I like to just sit with them.

I never went back to work. People visit me, but whenever the doorbell rings, the pale faces shake their heads at me. They're my friends, so I wouldn't want to disappoint them. That is what I'm going to continue to do. It's been about a month, now, and I have been doing just fine. Who needs human interaction, anyway?

# The Back Alleys of Ecuador

Parth Kapadia

With bodies moving and hearts racing, with the beat of the bass and the most gorgeous women in the world, they were all over me, touching my body. Maybe, this was because I was the tallest man on the dance floor, and, quite possibly, the entire country. The nightlife at the world's 0 latitude was never ending. We partied until the sun came up every night on our quest at the equator of the world. Global Petals, my Internet startup, my baby, and my job, steered us to the green lands of Ecuador.

Michael, my business partner, and I were not only there as tourists, we were there on a mission. It was our duty to unite Ecuadorian Flower farms, while connecting them to the United States through our innovative Internet marketplace: GlobalPetals.com. The girls, the women, the *mujeres* could have possibly been the biggest tourist attraction next to the Galapagos Islands, but we were seeking fields of green with our eyes set on the Flower Industry in South America. Our main contact and friend, Jose Rosales, the owner of R&G flowers, picked us up at the Quito International airport on a hot December night.

"What's up Parth!" he said to me while grasping my hand like an American. He then talked to Mike about our trip in Spanish the rest of the way to the hotel.

"Hotel Cumbaya," read the blue-amplified letters. The light projected onto my face and reminded me of a Chicago diner. The streets were pitch black at 3 a.m. in Quito, but I could still see that the hotel was nicer than the other structures nearby, and I thanked IIT for funding our trip. When we checked in at the hotel, I noticed there weren't any computers, only pen and paper. I guess they were fine with that, for now at least. We were there to change that by bringing technology to a technology-limited part of the world.

The sun surfaced, and our voyage began on a bright Sunday morning. The streets of Quito were flooded with vendors, cantinas, and dogs. Locals swarmed Mike as if he was a tourist, trying to sell him relics of all sorts. I wasn't hassled because of my Ecuadorian roots, although I was darker than most. It was ironic because Mike was fluent in Spanish and learned a bit about the culture during his study abroad there. I only knew the curse words that I learned from my Mexican roommates. We brought plenty of change with us. Ecuador was dollarized in the early 2000s during their slumping economy. It only cost 10 cents for a bus ride that would take us all around town. The autobus only stopped for women and slowed down for men, so we needed a running start to catch it. Ecuador's terrain is mountainous, and bus rides always felt like roller coasters, but I didn't mind.

Before we set out to meet farmers during the business week, we spent our Sunday discovering the city without any sense of direction. I felt safe everywhere I went. The Ecuadorians were friendly. Despite the language barrier, it was easy for me to communicate with the locals by waving my hands. I glanced at an old woman who was selling ironed shawls at the corner of an old tavern market. She looked at me, welcoming, and smiled. She could tell that I had no interest in her items, but I felt her warmth through her deep brown eyes. It seemed like they were worry-free and easygoing. They seemed as if they weren't achievement driven like us but were driven by the people around them. They were humble and appreciative of the little they had.

Our expedition started early Monday morning. We backpacked to various flower farms throughout every corner of the country. One farm's greenhouses were colossal with flower stems tripling my height. Over 170 hectors (10k sq meters) of multi-colored flowers filled my peripherals, and my body was immobilized.

"Thank you," I whispered to the Dean of Engineering of IIT. "This is what Americans want to learn about, what they need to know about. How such a stunning living being is grown, treated for, and imported to us. That's what sells nowadays, knowledge."

Flashing forward and Powerpoint projected, we trained over 80 farm owners on how they could benefit from technology in such an ambiguous industry. Their faces appeared convinced as Mike wrapped up our pitches, reassuring them in their native tongue. My cheeks grazed farm owners' cheeks, as we kissed, one side after another. This was success, I presumed. One after another, farm owners inked the dotted line as we logged them to our online community.

Every evening we celebrated our accomplishments at a cantina with greasy empanadas and bitter homegrown beer over Skype with team members back home on our smartphones. Ah, technology.

"You do good for us" applauded the aged restaurant owner.

The flaky crusts melted in my mouth every time, as we managed to persuade over 300 farms to fall in love with our services. The feeling couldn't have been better. We were cashing out and learning so much in this beautiful oasis. Ecuador began to love Global Petals, because the people knew that we were there to empower them. We loved it back.

One day, after a fattening dinner, we decided to hike up the steepest avenue in town back to our hotel to get ready for another party. We heard yells coming from around the corner. It was a construction site, and the workers were a group of young boys, no older than 10. They were gnawing away at hashed limestone, sledgehammers in hand. Why weren't those kids doing homework or something on a weeknight? The beauty of the country dissipated, as my shoulders began to slouch into my chest. My shins were "gassed" from the walk, but my heart charred for the children. They probably never experienced Saturday morning cartoons or field trips. I couldn't swallow.

Ecuador, the country of a million magnificent blossoms, concealed the country's depths of hell, but that's everywhere right? I guess. For us, it paved the road for our fragile startup company in which we created dozens of jobs, increased international commerce, and developed a marketplace that houses hundreds of relationships. I'm not sure when I'd get the opportunity to travel back to the equator of the world. If or when I do, I'll be sure to bring elementary math books.

# Glorious Wave

Jody Keisner

I. Seven days had passed since the tsunami first plowed onto the shores of Asia. On my Internet home page, in a picture box smaller than a business card clipped in two, an Indian toddler clung to her mother. The child's face expressed what might be anger or anguish, her eyes pinched shut. She couldn't have understood what was happening. From my safe distance in Mid-America, I barely understood. The places she knew and people around her had vanished suddenly, in minutes, into a colossal, roaring wave. The headline under the toddler read, "Tsunami Aid."

In a picture box three times the size of the toddler's, Dr. Phil encouraged America's obese to end their weight struggle. Then he disappeared and was replaced with a plaid chair strewn with beer bottles and half-eaten slices of pizza. "Why She Hates Your Apartment" the caption read. I wanted to drag my mouse there, to the purported insider's peek at a bachelor pad (I was newly single and interested in bachelors), but I clicked on the crying mouth of the toddler anyway. Aerial pictures showed the tsunami waves on December 26, 2004, curling in and around each other like shrimp, swamping what used to be coastal towns and tourist resorts. I was afraid of absorbing the tremendousness of what was happening to another part of the earth, to another people. I looked at the pictures for only a moment before turning away.

II. "One-third of the thousands swept into the ocean are thought to be children," a newscaster said into the silence of my living room, startling me. I held a memoir open in my hands, a welcome reprieve from the stress of being a graduate student and adjunct college instructor. I closed my book and reluctantly watched the TV. Ignoring the news didn't make the tsunami any less true, but hearing about the lost children was terrifying.

Nine days had passed since the media began its report on the "Sea of Sorrow." In Sri Lanka a man howled over the dead body of his son which had been laid on a metal table for identification. The father's face crumpled in the kind of pain that was meant for solitude. The mother covered her son's eyes with her hand, stroking his hair off his bronze face even now. In

India, a man bent to search the photographs posted on a bulletin board. Who was he looking for—a neighbor, brother, child—or maybe all three? The room was wallpapered with pictures of the dead.

If it wasn't for the devastation it had caused, the enormous wave was glorious. I tried to understand. I began filling my bathtub with cold water, letting the faucet run while I hunted for something to act as the seafloor. I settled on a plastic draining board for my dishes. With sudden violence I pulled the piece of plastic up, and water rushed over the lip of the tub, rushing across tile and soaking my socks. I imagined the great hissing sound the ocean was said to have made when the sea caved in, giving birth to two giant waves.

III. My mother prophesized that the ocean had sent warning of Armageddon. She delivered this revelation over the phone, 600 miles from the small city in Michigan I had recently moved to in hopes of breaking an unhealthy relationship. I heard my mother sigh and imagined her settling back into her brown couch, a quilt my great-grandmother had made from old dress scraps covering her legs, as she sunk in to watch reruns of her favorite sitcom, *Will and Grace*.

"They've uncovered scriptures that say as much," she continued, when I didn't respond to what I believed was a knee-jerk Christian response to disaster. "In seven years, all of it could be over for everyone."

I knew she didn't truly believe the world would end in seven years, but she liked to warn me that humans had no control over when or how we would die. *It was meant to happen,* she would say after tragedy. I wanted to yell at her, "Who meant for it to happen? *Who* would mean for such a thing?" But instead I said, "Many people won't recover from this."

She sighed again, and then said, "Did you use cranberry or orange peel in that muffin recipe I sent you?"

The ease with which she moved from national disaster to cooking assuaged my own guilt. My family and friends were all okay, untouched. Such enormous tragedy wouldn't happen to us. We were safe in our everyday, ordinary details as long as we didn't linger on the glorious wave for too long.

At Catholic Mass, the Indian Ocean and the millions it had betrayed competed for a prayer with a parishioner's husband who was being eaten by his cancer, the American soldiers in Iraq who were dying, and a newborn with congenital heart failure. Bodies were bobbing in the seawater, waiting to be claimed, the very moment we said in unison, "Lord, hear our prayer."

The young mother's shoulders shook beneath her blue shawl when the priest said her daughter's name, born just two days before with an ineffective heart. I wondered if she had room in her for anyone else's suffering.

IV. Like a nightmare, the day was first calm. Then the ocean swelled into an unbelievable wall of seawater, twenty feet high, washing away fishermen in Galle, resort workers waiting at a bus stop in Beruwala, vehicles full of tourists on their way to Penang, a couple on their honeymoon snorkeling off the coast of Koh Surin, and three teenage girls sunbathing on the shore of Phuket. Thousands more disappeared without surviving family or friends to tell their last story. The majority of those dragged into the ocean were the poorest of the poor. So many died that they were laid into mass graves, shoulder to shoulder, feet to head, one on top of the other.

Survivors of the tsunami were the walking wounded, left to beg for food. Some searched the brown waters for family members and friends. On the Asian shores, bodies scattered the beaches like washed up seaweed, arms and legs splayed like starfish.

After class one night, I asked my friend, Ann, what the disaster meant to her. Red splotches jumped up on her neck and cheeks. "So much pain," she said quietly.

I was scared that my heart, too, could be irreparably pained in an instant, that my family and friends could be taken, every last one of them, all at once. The death count had reached 120,000, and 5 million were left homeless when I stopped watching.

V. At night, I dreamt of the sea.

I am over thirty years younger, a child. I float on my back in the velvety blue water. I am but a few feet from the shore. If I put my legs down, the water would be just at my shoulders. My father and mother are in the ocean, also, but I am not paying attention to them. Instead, I concentrate on my hair, which is tendril-like reaching into the cool water behind my head, on the sun warming my damp swimsuit, on my feet that kick lightly, so I don't drift into a coral reef. The water is filled with algae, gelatinous creatures, and schools of small fish, darting here and there. I feel my body, its buoyancy, the wetness creeping up to my knees, the goose bumps forming where the wet ends and the small patches of dry begin. My fingertips are wrinkly.

When the waves start to swell higher, my father reminds me to stay close. He and my mother are retreating to the shade of an umbrella that my mother has planted firmly in the sand near mangrove bushes. A wave rushes over my head, and I cough the salty water out of my mouth. In my dream, I am unafraid even as the water begins to lift me up and down and away from my parents, rocking me like a lullaby. My father's voice is muffled, as if traveling down a long corridor to reach me.

"Come back," he calls. "I don't want you to get hurt."

I can see a hump of white water rolling in the distance, but I don't care. I squeeze my eyes shut. I want to float in the ocean forever.

*Sara and Water :: Magie McCombs*

# Theory of Relatimeity or Time Is Money

Wendell Kuhlman

*"All that really belongs to us is time;*
*even he who has nothing else has that." –Baltasa Garcian*

*"Time is at once the most valuable and the most perishable*
*of all our possessions." –John Randolph*

*"There is never enough time, unless you're serving it." Malcolm Forbes*

*"This time, like all times, is a very good one, if we but know what to*
*do with it." –Ralph Waldo Emerson*

*(The above quotations, taken in order, pretty well sum up the attitudes*
*my life has taken in regard to the relative importance of time and how we*
*humans choose to spend our allotted portion of it on this planet. While*
*universal agreement on anything is nearly impossible, I think most of us*
*would agree that time is relative; it seems to disappear much faster during*
*some portions of our lives than others. Yet, a clock (or a calendar) measures*
*time with exasperating regularity, and I don't even want to get into the*
*vast complications of the time-space continuum. Suffice it to say, time is*
*important to each of us, mostly for our own individual reasons. This writing*
*contains one man's odyssey through the various aspects of time, particularly*
*as it inter-relates with money. Both are spendable commodities, and both*
*are given inherent value in American culture.)*

I was literally born in a farmhouse in Smith County, Kansas, in
December, 1943. My parents and all four of my grandparents were farmers,
probably little better or worse off financially than most Kansas farmers
in the years of recovery following the Dust Bowl of the 1930s. My father
had two particular talents that soon provided an avenue to modest wealth.
Dad had an affinity for mental math calculations, and he was an excellent
judge of livestock, whether in a sale barn or in a farmer's pasture or feedlot.
Dad became a cattle buyer for Swift and Henry, meatpackers in Kansas

City, and a hog buyer for Cudahy in Omaha. Both of these positions were highly lucrative by Smith County standards. We soon moved off the farm to a nice house in the "city" of Smith Center, approximate population of 2,000 people. Dad made shrewd purchases, and two of his brothers (Uncle Jude/Julius and Uncle Shorty/Allen) reaped the accompanying profits from transporting these animals to market. The three brothers accumulated enough profits that in 1949 they built their own stockyards adjacent to the Smith Center sale barn. The Kuhlman Stockyards boasted its own scale, more space for cattle and hogs than the sale barn itself, and two semis for transportation. I have a rather hazy memory of many of these events, but most of the details came from family members.

The financial disaster happened in 1951. The various sale barns in northern Kansas each held their sales on a given day of the week. Dad established a regular weekly circuit of those sale barns, going as far away as Atwood. I remember going with him on some of these. The speed limit for Kansas at that time was "reasonable and prudent for the existing conditions," and Dad regularly shot the hills along Highway 36 at 120 mph in his new Dodge. After all, time is money, and it's not smart to waste time on the road. The problem is that all the Kuhlman brothers were heavy drinkers, and Dad virtually always consumed more than his fair share of beer by the time he headed home from these sales. It's at least a minor miracle that he didn't kill himself on one of these trips. One day, Dad imbibed enough alcohol to cloud even his impeccable judgment regarding livestock. He bought a huge herd of diseased cattle. When they arrived in Kansas City, Swift and Henry refused them, and Dad was then left with the entire cost of that cattle purchase. It more than wiped out his savings and his one-third equity in the Kuhlman Stockyards; it plunged him so far into debt that he (our family) never got out from under this mistake until my parents sold everything they had after a tornado struck the farmstead in 1972. All this is a long way to establish the fact that ever since I can remember much of anything, we had nothing, except time.

Time is an invaluable commodity. Many people tried to convince Dad to take out bankruptcy in 1951, and we undoubtedly would have been better off financially if he had, but whether it was due to stubborn German pride or an innate sense of fairness to creditors, Dad could not bring himself to take that step. So, we grew up dirt poor; "spending money" was a term that had no place in our lifestyle. This does not mean that we feared for our next meal at any time. We always had large vegetable gardens and livestock (cattle, hogs, chickens) on whatever farmstead we inhabited. Also, the Kuhlman Brothers enterprise and Dad in particular were fairly well known in the Northern Kansas farming community, and Dad's inherent honesty stood us in good stead as he/we struggled to establish a different financial identity. We moved around to a couple of farm homes, paying rent on those houses by the work we did as tenant farmers. We certainly had more modest clothes and cars than our classmates at school, but we always had something to wear (Mom and Grandma Kuhlman made many of our clothes.) and a way to get wherever we needed to be. We had time. My brother and I excelled in the classroom and in athletics and in moral virtues, so the community (especially the local bank) regarded our family as good risks for future success. Time belonged to us, even though we had virtually nothing else in terms of spendable commodities.

***

I earned my way through McPherson College with athletic and academic scholarships, student loans through Pell Grants, and a job at McPherson Concrete Products. I married my high school sweetheart (Wilma Dettmer Kuhlman) in 1964 after my sophomore year of college, and she dropped out of college to work at Kansas Jack, a local company that made equipment used in auto-body shops, where she earned her PHT degree (Putting Hubby Through). Time during these years was certainly "the most valuable and the most perishable of all our possessions." Of course, Wilma and I still had virtually no physical possessions. We were, truly, *spending* our time to buy the future. After I graduated with a degree in English Education, I began to teach in the McPherson Public Schools for $5,200 for the year. That was very little money, even in 1966. We struggled to survive from paycheck to paycheck, but, fortunately, we were both accustomed to that lifestyle.

In 1967, we had our first child, a daughter we named Sheryl. Our first son, Roger, came along 16 months later in 1968. Then Number Two Son, Doug, joined us in 1973. These years with the children were simply crammed with monumental moments celebrating their individual achievements and our joy and pride in each step they took, yet they now exist in my memory almost as an indistinct blur.

During those years I arrived at school somewhere around 7:00 a.m., taught classes until 3:15 p.m., coached either football or wrestling or track until about 5:30, and then often either officiated at a football or basketball game or ran the clock at one of them until whatever time they ended. Summers were spent teaching driver education and painting houses. Wilma was "just a housewife"—and ran a daycare in our home while she sewed, both clothes (for our family and as a paid seamstress) and curtains and drapes and shades. We never had anywhere close to enough time or enough money. Attempts to accumulate either of these elements belonged somewhere in the hazy future. It was all we could do to keep up with current demands for them.

This was an incredibly happy time for me and for Wilma, too. We still had nothing but each other and the promise of the future, but somehow that was usually plenty to sustain us. My McPherson teaching salary did gradually grow, and I believe one incident from our lives hastened that growth. In 1978, after Doug was in school full time, Wilma resurrected her college career. With that additional expense, we reached the point that we simply could not stretch our income to meet demands, so we applied to the school system for reduced-cost lunches for our children. We certainly met the federal income guidelines for reduced prices. That was the only time I ever got called to the school superintendent's office. He appeared mortified that my teaching salary was so low that we qualified for government aid, and I am sure he was concerned that the local newspaper would hear about this situation and create negative publicity for the McPherson school district. He was well aware of the salary scale in the district, of course, and he certainly knew the income guidelines for free/reduced lunches, but I doubt that he truly recognized the overlap of the two. I'm sure our situation was not the only reason, but teaching salaries in McPherson rose considerably faster for the next few years than they did in the surrounding school districts.

In 1981, when Wilma began teaching elementary school in the neighboring town of Inman, the time/money balance shifted almost perceptibly for me (us). Now the demands on Wilma's time were at least equal to my own. She had always been equally busy, of course, but those time demands were sufficiently flexible that she had always filled the role of primary caregiver for our children. *She* had been available for the school to call if one of the kids got sick. *She* had taken them to doctors, dentists, orthodontists, church meetings, etc. *She* had gone to PTA and parent-teacher conferences and served as room mother, choir director, and party planner. Now, all of a sudden, *she* was committed to a classroom in a town 25 minutes away, and *I* very rapidly became aware of the time drain these activities place on a schedule. I cut back some on activities outside my classroom, and all five of us juggled some time priorities. The income from Wilma's job did allow much more flexibility in our attempts to juggle! I became acquainted with the term "disposable income." I had never before been in a situation where all the money coming in was not already spent or at least committed for basic necessities.

While I would hardly say that we had ample amounts of either, for the first time in my life, we probably had more money than time. Time was non-existent. Even our weekends were totally eaten up. Gymnastics tournaments for Sheryl and/or wrestling tournaments for the boys took up Saturdays from 6 a.m. until usually 4 or so in the afternoon. Sundays were often spent at church or at least in church-related activities. At least, we *were* now able to drive a vehicle to these activities, and we were pretty sure to make the trip without breaking down or running out of gas; we could even afford to eat at McDonald's, sometimes, instead of always packing peanut-butter-and-jelly sandwiches. By this time, I finally finished paying off my college loans, so we could start paying for Wilma's. The money side of the "Time is money" concept was definitely improving for us, but time moved past in a blur. Time was, without doubt, "the most valuable and the most perishable of all our possessions."

***

When Doug went away to college, Wilma decided she would rather be a college professor than remain in elementary school. She spent 1992-1995 at the University of Missouri in Columbia and earned her PhD. She chose to join the faculty at University of Nebraska at Omaha. At that point, her career was certainly the priority in our marriage, so I followed her. Since I spent my life in public education, my first thought was to become a teacher for one of the Omaha area school districts. I quickly learned that I priced myself out of consideration for such a position, too much education and too many years of experience to compete with a beginning teacher with only a BA. I had a variety of jobs for a few years in the private sector of our economy. One of the major adjustments was accepting the concept of only a 40-hour work week. In a large sense, I've considered myself semi-retired since we moved to Omaha. The concept of time being a precious commodity to be savored was still present in my life, but I certainly had an abundance of it compared to what I was used to. Then in the year 2000, I again became a teacher, but this time it was in a prison setting. Officially, I was employed by Metro Community College, but I spent virtually all my time in the Omaha Correctional Center for men, working with inmates to help them get a GED. This was a highly educational experience for me in several ways. What a revelation there was in the differing lifestyles and expectations of individuals! All my life, I had been surrounded primarily by fairly industrious, upwardly-mobile, ambitious people. In prison, not *quite* so much!

As I re-assumed the role of teacher, I set about lesson preparations with much of the same diligence I used in public schools, planning the use of the vast majority of the 3 hours each inmate was in class. I always had a curriculum that I intended to cover in a given time period, usually breaking up the semester into several shorter time blocks, each with its own learning emphasis. When I arrived at the prison for the first day of classes, however, I learned that Metro (due primarily to the prison officials refusing to have materials being carried to and from the prison facility on a regular basis) mandated the same 40-hour week I had become used to in private sector jobs. We were *not* to take anything home to grade. Also, the GED program Metro was using had a set of textbooks for each of the GED subjects: Reading, Writing, Math, Science, and Social Studies. We were expected— no, we were *instructed* to use those texts and not to deviate from them because they contained everything the students needed to know to pass the GED test. So I did. I was pleased to learn that the program texts did cover a fairly comprehensive study of each subject. But the pace was much slower than I was accustomed to. I adapted my time expectations to fit this situation as well as I could.

One example that I clearly remember occurred as I was ushering a small group of students from the large general GED classroom to a smaller, quieter room in the prison complex where I was to monitor an actual GED testing session. I had the tests set up prior to the scheduled start time, of course, as I was wont to do. I was bustling through a door leading from the regular classroom when I nearly collided with one of the other students coming into the room—late as usual. "Slow down, Mr. Wendell," he said. "There's no hurry. We ain't goin' nowhere."

At the moment, I brushed off this remark and continued with my planned mission. But as I was sitting, monitoring the students taking the GED tests I had laid out for them, I reflected on the truth of what the tardy student had stated. These men were truly NOT going anywhere, at least, none of them in the near future, and some of them never! "Time is money"? Not so much, not here, not with these men. Time was an infinite commodity, and money was supposedly non-existent within prison walls. It made my brain hurt to try to wrap itself around the disconnect I was truly experiencing for the first time. I knew these inmates were all sentenced to stay within these wire walls for various given amounts of time, but the idea that this caused time to be of *no* importance so violated the inter-relatedness of time to real life as I had known it was still a revelation. Time meant nothing to these people! At first I thought, "What a waste." Then, I began to ruminate on what I could learn from looking at time from their perspective. I'm still trying to digest that concept. Those who are serving time really do have enough of it, plenty of it, even too much of it.

Now I am retired. Time has taken on a whole different aspect again. For one thing, its passage varies so tremendously now. Each given day and/ or week seems to move past at somewhat normal speed, but as a group, they just disappear. When we had the kids around and we were both so enmeshed in our careers, time was very rushed; it passed in a blur, a frenzy of activity. Now, it's not so much that time rushes past, it just seems to disappear. Whole chunks of it, sometimes months together vanish. I've not yet reached the point that I miss appointments or forget the kids' birthdays, but, sometimes, I look back, and whole seasons are gone. Where did autumn go this year?

I understand the concept that time really does appear to go faster as we age, because we experience it as a much smaller fraction of our personal existence. A year is less than 1.5 percent of my life, but to grandson Trevor, it's 20 percent of his life. We always view things in perspective from what we know. And I've known a much longer lifespan than younger people. That's probably one reason why children usually view individual events in their lives as being much more important than do adults. Asking them to "Put things in perspective" doesn't really help; their much shorter perspective is the root cause of their anxiety. The older I get, the more sense that theory makes.

As Emerson mentioned in the quotation cited at the beginning of this piece, this is indeed a very good time, if I know what to do with it. Amazingly, Wilma and I have accumulated enough money in the past few years (Although we're far from rich if one uses the world's standards, I feel rich due to my background.) that I don't feel a great deal of pressure in that regard. I am able to serve as a driver to take kids to and from school. I volunteer half of each Wednesday at the NE Works employment office, helping people create or improve their resumes. I enjoy my role as a "Big" in the Big Brothers/Big Sisters program of Omaha. Periodic visits with children and grandsons provide highlights. A full life? Not in comparison with what I have lived, but it seems enough. It's good to have enough time to invest in working in the ample yard we now enjoy and to spend probably too much time simply playing video games. It's a very comfortable life, and I love it, at least for now. However, if some totally tempting change appears in the future, I could change my mind.

# The Problem Solver or New and Improved

Loren Logsdon

Nestled on the flat but nourishing bosom of the great American Midwest, surrounded by dairy farms and vast fields of corn and beans, far from the din and smog of the great commercial cities, lies the peaceful and picturesque town of Weeder's Clump. Illinois. In almost precisely the center of this idyllic community is situated a prosperous place of business called Provender's Market, owned and operated by the most benevolent grocer in all of downstate Illinois, a kindly, soft-spoken, gentle soul who is loved by everyone in town and whose reputation for honesty is known throughout a three-state area. This grocer's name is August Provender, and on an early Saturday morning in April of last year he was putting a roll of pennies in his cash register and humming "The Sunny Side of the Street" when suddenly the door opened and in rushed the first customer of the day.

The customer was none other than Horace "Oinky" Poindexter, the popular mayor of Weeder's Clump and the recipient of three honorary degrees from San Andreas Fault State University. Grim-faced, Oinky approached the checkout counter, obviously in deep trouble and in need of wise counsel.

"Good morning, Your Honor, I see that you are up and about rather early on this fine morning. I hope that nothing ignominious is amiss in our fair city to put such a troubled look on your visage," August said, revealing that he had been influenced by a lifetime of reading stories by Nathaniel Hawthorne.

Oinky peered about the store to see if any elderly ladies or young school children were within hearing distance. Even though no one else was present, Oinky addressed the kindly storekeeper in a hushed whisper, "I haven't been the most regular of fellows lately, and I was wondering if you might suggest something that would help me."

Even before Oinky had finished his sentence August was bounding over to the pharmacy section of the store. He picked up a dark blue bottle and rushed back to Oinky. "Yes, I have just what the proverbial doctor ordered. Try this, Mr. Mayor. It's called BALM OF ALACRITY, and it is a new and improved miracle fast-acting elixir that helps fight irregularity or your money back."

Convinced that relief was only minutes away, Oinky beamed at August Provender and said, "God bless you. As mayor of this town I am pleased to present you with The Weeder's Clump Distinguished Service Award, suitable for framing for display in your home or place of business." Oinky then left the store singing "Once in Love with Amy."

No sooner was Oinky out the door when in came Bradley Winsome, a senior at Weeder's Clump High School. Bradley had the physical build of a young Greek god, the strong jaw and jutting chin of Val Kilmer, the majestic charm of Brad Pitt, the toothy smile of Tom Cruise, and the voice of Kevin Kostner. In addition, Brad had worked for countless hours cultivating that sullen, underprivileged look that Elvis had perfected to earn fame and fortune. However, Bradley was much more than the typical hunk; he was intelligent, hard working, courteous, fair minded, talented, well adjusted, imaginative, considerate, compassionate, and modest. He had earned varsity letters in every sport at the high school, but, as he explained, when he contracted a stubborn case of athlete's foot while trying out for the debate team, no one, including his parents and his faithful dog Growler, would have anything to do with him. Even worse, all the mothers who had dreamed that their daughter might lure Bradley into a life of connubial bliss now rather openly made snide remarks about him in the post office and the beauty shop. In desperation Bradley said, "Mr. Provender, I feel as doomed as the Frito Bandito. Please help me."

August Provender waved his hand as if this problem were merely a pesky insect; then he told Bradley that he needed a can of Achilles Foot Powder, whose miracle ingredients could cure anything from athlete's foot to existential angst.

As Bradley held the little can of magic in his hand, he had a mystical experience in which he heard either the voice of God or Charlton Heston booming out of the sky to announce that Bradley Winsome was the most perfect male specimen that Weeder's Clump had ever seen or would ever see for that matter.

After thanking August Provender politely, because Bradley was also polite, the handsome young senior opened the door of Provender's Market and stepped out into the street. To his utter surprise, he was greeted by a crowd that had come to cheer him. Moments earlier, when Bradley had entered the store, the street had been completely empty; in fact, the only living creature in sight was a noble dog named Bosco who had run away from his master and was checking out the canine history recorded on a CILCO utility pole. But now both sides of the street were lined with people, and some say that one person in the crowd was holding a sign that read "BRAVES GO HOME AND TAKE JANE WITH YOU." Bradley glowed with well being when the brass band began to play and twenty baton twirlers were swaying enchantingly to and fro. Bradley flashed a broad grin as the photographers took his picture. He knew as he looked at the crowd that the world stretched out before him in infinite possibility.

As the crowd moved away from the store, August picked up his newspaper to see if the Heliotrope University baseball team had won yesterday. As August was perusing the paper and humming "The Cobbler's Song," he heard a commotion and looked up to see Ms Darlene Maxwell enter the store. It was obvious that Ms Maxwell was a mess, and he wondered what could have caused Weeder's Clump's most dignified and cultured lady to be so agitated. Ms Maxwell was sobbing so uncontrollably that August could not understand a word she was saying. Finally, in sheer frustration, Ms Maxwell flung herself upon the checkout counter and beat on it with her fists.

"It's either *fin de siecle hysteria* or the heartbreak of psoriasis," August said to himself, "and my money is on the heartbreak of psoriasis because no one in this town knows what *fin de siecle hysteria* means." August didn't even try to talk to Ms Maxwell; instead he went over to the Beauty Aids section and picked up two miracle products that he knew would transform Ms Maxwell's day from rats and pumpkins into glass slippers and beautiful gowns. After several minutes of August's assurances and explanations, Ms Maxwell left the store with a jar of Aphrodite Skin Cream and a bottle of Bright Eye and Bushy Tail Eye Wash. But even more important, Ms Maxwell was singing "It Ain't No Sin If You Take Off Your Skin and Dance Around in Your Bones," and August could understand every word she was singing.

August had scarcely a moment to catch his breath when in rushed Bryce Nimbus, who looked as lost as a fog-bound child. Although some folks thought that Bryce had his head in the clouds because he had claimed when he was ten years old that he wanted to be a hero, August Provender had always had great respect for the idealistic young man, believing that the world needed real heroes instead of the shallow celebrities and self-absorbed obnoxious clown princes of the prepubescent libido that are foisted off on unsuspecting children these days. So August was concerned to see Bryce in such a state. To August, Bryce's loss of direction was no small matter.

"Mr. Provender, I don't know where to turn. I was helping my friend Sharkey bury some old razor blades in his backyard when I had this haunting mystical experience.

For no apparent reason I looked up at the sky—a Claude Monet sky, to be precise—and saw the word WHY? painted in huge letters, and I found myself thinking, "Yes, why do we humans endure pain, suffering, and heartbreak? What does it all mean? Why do we line up each day to take our poison? Why even attempt the heroic act? Why even ask if there is balm in Gilead? Why sail the seven seas, travel to the four corners of the world, and do battle with formidable adversaries?"

August Provender knew for certain that Bryce was undergoing a severe crisis, and he also knew that he had no miracle product in his store that would help Bryce. But August had a moment of divine inspiration, and he knew exactly how to restore the young idealist's faith. "Bryce, first of all you must stop hanging around Poindexter's Garage and listening to Tug Armstrong and Boone Fowler trying to outdo each other in hanging crepe. Second, you need to read my autographed copy of Ray Bradbury's *Dandelion Wine*, which I am going to loan you. Third, I recommend that you take long walks at night and look at the stars, sit by a river and dream, make a small child laugh, take flowers to your mother, delight an elderly person, befriend a dog, chase after the wind, sing to a bird, create a new philosophy, improve the quality of the day."

"Thank you, Mr. Provender. You are a genius. I'm ok now. I feel fine." Bryce left the store singing "Let's Go Down to the Café and Count Seed Caps."

The next customer was Melody Bombast, the youngest daughter of Woodrow "Bear" Bombast, Heliotrope University's famous football coach. Bear had huge hairy paws and the personality of a sex-starved grizzly, but Melody could have been mistaken for Helen of Troy. Furthermore Melody was Sweetness Itself.

"Mr. Provender, do you remember what a beautiful day it was yesterday?" Melody asked, not waiting for an answer. "Well, Bulgy Hypotenuse and I decided to blow off school and go for a long walk in the country. I mean it was a perfect day. The sun was beaming forth its

115

generous warmth, the sky was so blue it made my heart ache, the flowers were blooming, the arboreal brachiators were singing sweetly, and a gentle breeze was wafting through the tender leaves of the trees. When we reached the top of Weeder's Hill, Bulgy put his arms around me, looked imploringly into my eyes, and asked me if I wanted a Salem. Oh, what's wrong with me, Mr. Provender? Do I have bad breath? Do I have body odor? Am I the Ugly Duckling or what?"

"No, Dear, you just aren't using the right perfume," August replied, trying to calm Melody and keep her from embarking on another monologue. "What you need is an economy bottle of Snake in the Garden Perfume and a copy of the Surgeon General's Report on Smoking. There's really nothing wrong with you that a liberal dose of Snake in the Garden can't fix. And by the way, here's a tube of Adolph's Scalp Tenderizer for your father's problem dandruff. I wish he had asked me about it, but I guess he's too stubborn. I have been afraid to bring up the subject with him, especially after his star quarterback transferred to the Sam Houston Institute of Technology."

"I know what you mean, Mr. Provender. Dad can get downright crispy at times, but I am sure that after the NCAA investigation of his slush fund is over he will thank you for curing his problem dandruff," Melody said. Then she turned abruptly on her heel and skipped out of the store singing "One Way or Another I'm Gonna Getcha, Getcha, Getcha, Getcha, Getcha."

A few minutes after Melody had left, August saw the door open and a thinly disguised young man sneak in stealthily. The disguise was so pathetic that August had no trouble identifying the young man as Cuff Harvest, the only son of Weeder's Clump's wealthiest farmer. Cuff peered suspiciously around before he approached the checkout counter. Known all of his life as "The Prince of Stinkers," Cuff had decided that the time was ripe to do something about his body odor. For years his best friends had tried to tell him, but Cuff could not understand the language of cows, ducks, and chickens. Seriously, Cuff was afraid he would not be admitted to the big state university at Cornsylvania even though he had an ACT score of 99 and ranked third in his class behind Bradley Winsome and Twinkie Bumpass. Using his best John Wayne voice, Cuff said, "Whatdya got for body odor, Pilgrim?"

"I have exactly what you need, Duke," August replied, playing along with Cuff's disguise, and he sold Cuff a can of Beast on the Prowl Deodorant, a bottle of Animal Rage Aftershave Lotion, and a tube of Pearly Glitter Toothpaste. August hummed "Against the Wind" as he saw Cuff sail his John Wayne Cowboy hat high into the air before he got into his car.

The rest of the day passed quickly, with the usual flood of Saturday customers buying their weekly groceries. August was not presented with any more special problems to solve, but he was so busy that he didn't have time to talk baseball with his carryout boy, Gort Rumson, who was trying to put together a complete set of Topps Baseball Cards. Boone Fowler went by, no doubt on his way to fish for manta ray at the lock and dam or to see if he could find any mushrooms in the river bottom. Dr. James Canada dropped off the latest issue of *Oops! The Journal of Medical Malpractice*, with a note suggesting that August read the article on existential angst.

August was tired, but fortunately it was getting toward closing time. As August was preparing to close, in sauntered Menard T. Hawker, a veteran salesperson for Madame Eileen Circe Beauty Aids. Hawker was hoping to convince August to carry a brand new product that his company was trying to market.

"First I have to know if it's improved," August said. "I don't stock products that aren't improved."

Menard thought a moment, rolled his eyes heavenward, stared off into the middle distance, and scratched his head. "But since it's brand new it can't be improved; it will be improved next year."

The new product was called Clear-A-Mind. It could cure the following problems: road rage, elitism, greed, envy, nail fungus, alcoholism and other forms of drug addiction, criminal behavior, urban blight, sexual immorality, and the impulse to engage in wild Dionysian partying.

After Menard explained how wonderful Clear-A-Mind was, August said, "It just won't sell. People will not waste their hard-earned money on a silly product like that. Furthermore, I will not stock a snake-oil product that makes such outlandish claims, promising people the moon and then leaving them stranded in Levittown." August prided himself on his eloquence and his ability to turn a phrase on the spur of the moment. August's communion prayers at the First Malthusian Church of the Recently Enlightened could lift a soul from the very depths of the abyss of despair to the lofty mountaintop of hope.

Menard T. Hawker and August Provender had been good friends for several years; consequently Menard did not take umbrage when the convivial grocer denounced Clear-A-Mind as being nothing more than a gallimaufry of junk. Instead, Menard winked, smiled, and said, "August Provender, you're a live one, you are."

"Well, Menard, old friend, I would really like to help you, but that product just won't sell," August said confidently.

As August was escorting Menard to the door, the two friends were almost trampled by a mob of people rushing into the store. Cuff Harvest, on the outer edge of the mob, yelled, "Hey Mr. Provender, where do you keep that new kind of Clearasil that just came out on the market? The one that is endorsed by Martha Stewart, Oprah Winfrey, Dick Clark, Casey Casem, and Dr. Phil."

*Stone Path :: DiEtte Henderson*

# The Nebraska Junk Jaunt
## Norm Lund

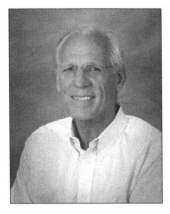

For a city boy such as myself, The Nebraska Junk Jaunt is always a wonderful opportunity to go out and see the real Nebraska. The Junk Jaunt is a 300 mile garage sale through the central part of Nebraska, starting at about Grand Island and forming an oval route that reaches northwest to the edge of the Sandhills. Approximately 35 small towns participate at various levels. In some towns there are yard sales all over town, in really small towns they all have their wares on sale in the community building, or a church, or a school gym.

Why in the world would anyone really want to travel around to a gazillion garage sales? There is a reason that it is called the Junk Jaunt, because there is a lot of junk to see. However, the Junk Jaunt is held during the last weekend in September, almost guaranteed beautiful weather. Although, one year it was chilly enough that I bought an almost new down filled vest for $4 in order to be a little warmer. The terrain that is included in the tour route is varied and absolutely some of the most beautiful in Nebraska. Nebraska is not all flat, as many believe. Nebraska is made up of valleys, rolling hills, plains, dissected plains, sand hills and valley side slopes. As you tour through the route you see every one of those terrain types, and this year the leaves were particularly brilliant in color.

Is it really all junk, or are there treasures to be had? Last year, 2011, there were estimated to be 20,000 participants from 34 different states and 79 of 93 Nebraska counties. Amidst all the junk, of which there is plenty, there are a lot of treasures, some of which can only be found in the mid-west and western states. One of the problems with the success of the Junk Jaunt, which is advertised as running Friday, Saturday, Sunday, but which in fact opens on Thursday, is that the "dealers" are rushing around on Thursday buying up as much as they can before the normal citizens such as myself start touring on Friday, not that anyone is precluded from Thursday. However, they cannot get it all. What are they looking for? For sure antiques, of which there are many. The stuff they really want are things that are western in nature, having to do with cowboys, Indians, cattle, farming and ranching.

The Junk Jaunt ran for the ninth year this year and has become more successful each year. Because of that success you will sometimes see some bizarre pricing. A lot of things can be bought for $.50 or a dollar, and prices go on up. But the funny part is when you see true junk priced sky high; some of the vendors price their items as though you have no idea what things are worth. It's all part of the experience. In fact, you do have the opportunity to buy all kinds of items that are unique to the Western United States. Saddles, branding irons, livestock bills of sale, rodeo posters, tanned hides, lariats, authentic western cowboy chaps, barb wire samples, and the list goes on.

We take a pickup truck, because you just never know what you might find; one year I got a picnic table for my mother-in-law for $15. We go with my brother-in-law and his wife and he is the real deal when it comes to being a "junker." His stuff overflows to my truck when his is full. In actuality, I am not even close to being a junker, I just like the experience of being out in the country for three days. However, I watch for good art, not museum quality art, but good solid art, some done by Nebraska painters, others not. What I look for are rural scenes of Nebraska. I always manage to find one or two great pieces to bring home each year; so far, the price range has been from $7 to $35. Sometimes, I even keep the frame; other times I have the picture re-framed. I am up to six good quality pieces of art that I have found on the tour. Another aspect to the Junk Jaunt are the bake sales. I specialize in finding homemade brownies, some I eat along the way, but I always buy enough to bring a stash of them home with me. There are always good ethnic pastries like kolaches and other specialties.

There are often old cars for sale which are fun to look at; so far I have resisted the urge to buy one. One year we discovered an old junk yard just outside of town that had well over a hundred old cars from the 30s, 40s, 50s and 60s. It was like a treasure trove of old cars. We spent a couple of hours with the owner of the junk yard just walking around and looking at everything.

So, when you add it all up, if you are interested in seeing some of the best aspects of Nebraska in an entertaining way, while un-hooking from the internet for a while, the Junk Jaunt is a great way to get out and enjoy the fresh air. One of the beauties of the Junk Jaunt is the opportunity to talk to lots of outstate people, conversations that you would not normally have; when the Junk Jaunt is going on people are more open to conversations, even if you are from Omaha. With the speed of life ever increasing, we need to find ways to de-compress without resorting to unhealthy habits.

The rural people are very resourceful with regard to the activities and economics of making their small towns survive. Even though the economic odds are against them, the rural folks have absolutely no desire to abandon their small towns. I have talked to ranchers that are struggling financially and they will tell you that they will spend their retirement money if necessary to keep their operations going. Nebraskans are tough, smart, resilient and lucky to live in Nebraska.

> *"It's better to write about things you feel than about things you know."*
>
> - L. P. Hartley

# Estes Park in Eighth Grade
### Garrett May

The summer of my eighth grade year I went on a trip to Estes Park, Colorado, with my Uncle Doug, Aunt Mashelle, my brother Matt, and my two cousins Wesley and Wayde. Colorado was an awesome experience. We have been there twice since my first trip, but whenever we talk about that first time we went, all my Aunt and Uncle have to say is "that camper smelled terrible." For some reason, my brother, my two cousins, and I couldn't stop farting at night when everyone was trying to sleep. The whole camper smelled really bad. My uncle threatened to make us sleep outside because it smelled so bad. Luckily, my Aunt wouldn't let him because of the bears! But I knew she wanted us out.

Our second time going to Colorado, our truck broke down on the way there. We sat at the only mechanic shop open on a Sunday for five hours. My cousin Wayde fell asleep on the sidewalk. They ended up "fixing" the truck and said we should be able to make it to Colorado. But my uncle was smart and got a hotel, and then made a switcharu with my dad's truck. Later that night in the hotel, I was trying to sleep when I noticed that there were bugs crawling through the walls. We all looked at each other, and we all wanted to say, "Lets just go home," but nobody would say it. *Finally*, my uncle said it the next morning. So we packed up and drove home.

Every time we are at a family gathering, somehow those two stories pop up. Back when they happened we were all really mad and couldn't believe what was going on, but now we look back on it and can't help but laugh. These stories were life lessons, teaching us to not dwell on the past but to make good laughs out of the past and move on and learn from our mistakes.

# Mt. Fuji

Sosuke Nakao

Mt. Fuji is the Japanese symbol well known around the world. No one knows what Fuji means, but there are some theories. For example, Fuji means wealthy, abundant, and immortal. Another theory says Fuji means the fire erupting mountain in Ainu, which is old Japanese, and it is the god of fire. I believe that theory because Mt. Fuji is a volcano, and it is beautiful. Many people love Mt. Fuji, and it is my favorite mountain. My first time seeing Mt. Fuji was when I was ten years old, and I climbed it seven years later.

I lived in Kyushu, which is in the very South of Japan, so Mt. Fuji is very far from there. One day, my family and I went to Shizuoka to visit my cousin on vacation. I was very excited about it because it was my first time going to Shizuoka and seeing Mt. Fuji. I remember that I did not sleep the night before we left. We left our house at four in the morning, and we went by car. It took seventeen hours to get there. My parents drove the car alternately. They looked very tired, and I was also tired because I was just sitting and looking outside from the window in the car. I was very sleepy and wanted to sleep, but I tried to not sleep until getting to Shizuoka because I wanted to see all of the views from my city to Shizuoka. We still had five hours left to get Shizuoka, and I was sleeping in the car before I realized it. After a while, I heard my mom call my name, then I woke up. When I looked up outside, I saw the huge mountain with snow on the top, and there was the sun behind the mountain. It was so beautiful, and I was very impressed. At the time, I decided to climb Mt. Fuji someday in my life.

Seven years later, I still wanted to climb Mt. Fuji. When I was looking at the web page about Mt. Fuji on the Internet, I found one tutorial to climb Mt. Fuji, and it only cost 150 dollars. I immediately booked that tutorial myself without asking my parents. I talked to my parents about it the next day. They were worried about me first, but I was playing soccer, so I had enough stamina to climb Mt. Fuji, so they let me to do it. I started to run every day since I booked the tutor. I had one month left, and thought I could climb it without any problems. I was taking it easy, and I did not know how hard it would be to get the top.

Finally, the day of climbing Mt. Fuji came. I stayed at my cousin's house the night before. I woke up at five a.m. and ate breakfast. My aunt kept saying, "Sosuke, please be safe. Do not strain yourself!" But, my uncle cheered me on because he had climbed Mt. Fuji when he was fifteen years old. He told me, "If you climb Mt. Fuji and see the view from on the top, you can consider about your life, and you can feel the power of nature." At six in the morning, my uncle and I left their house. During the ride, I was nervous because I could see Mt. Fuji, and it was like a boss in a video game. When we arrived at the meeting point, there were about twenty people,who were climbing with someone they knew, so I was the only person who was alone. After we listened to the explanation, we headed to the starting point by bus. Before we left, my uncle said, "Hey Sosuke! Remember do not make so much noise when you arrive at the top of Mt. Fuji." I did not understand why he said it to me, but I kept it in my mind. In the bus, I talked to \one of the couples, and they were from Kyushu, too. It was their third time climbing Mt. Fuji, so I asked them some questions.

We were half of the way up, and I was already tired. I could not believe I was already tired because we still had half of the distance, and other people, who were older than me, still looked fine. I was disappointed in myself at that time. I could not think about things like that anymore because I had to finish my goal, so I just stood up and walked without thinking about anything. When we took a rest next time, I took off my shoes because my right foot was in pain. Then I found that I got a corn, and it was already broken. I looked in my bag to find a band-aid, but I forgot to bring it. When I was looking at the sole of my foot, the couple that I talked to in the bus came to me, and they gave me some band-aids. I was very happy about seeing them. During the trip, I saw many people were walking down, and some people were carried by rescue workers. I got scared when I saw them because I could be like them. I tried to focus on walking, but it was hard since the air was thin at that point.

We had one mile left to get to the top. I was only looking at the ground in front of me, and I did not look back because I wanted to see the view from on top of Mt. Fuji. When I saw the top, my walking speed became fast, and I forgot fatigue and pain. I reached the goal with the couple who helped me a lot. I almost shouted at that time, but I remembered what my uncle said, so I said it in a low voice. The reason why my uncle said I should not have made so much noise on the top of Mt. Fuji was because it is a spiritual spot, and there is the god of mountain. If I made so much noise on the top, the god was going to get angry, and I would not be able to go back safely. When I arrived at the top, I felt something weird coming from my feet. It was like an electric shock. I thought it was the power of nature as my uncle said. The view from the top of Mt. Fuji was so beautiful. I never saw a view like that, and I was lost for words. I cannot explain exactly how beautiful it was, but it was incredibly mysterious. It was a very good experience because I got to see the most beautiful thing in Japan. I want to climb Mt. Fuji again, and I have an American friend who wants to do it, too, so we will probably climb Mt. Fuji together, sometime.

*Ballet Camp 2013 :: Ed Vogel*

# Ocean Child

Lauren Narducci

The ocean stared back at Gracie. The bright blue waters lapped onto the surface of the Atlantic shore, the sound of the waves sang through her ears as she closed her eyes, breathing in the salty air. A breeze blew through her hair, causing it to billow softly across her face.

"Gracie," her mother called, interrupting her thoughts. "It's time to go sweetheart."

Gracie looked over her shoulder to see her mother, Jane, waving at her from the driveway of their beach house. Gracie lingered, taking in one last breath of the sea air, then turned around and walked back to her house. As she approached her mother's Suburban, Gracie found Jane engaged in a conversation on her cell phone.

"No Frank! Gracie needs normalcy; she needs her home where everything was normal, where Todd was." There was a short pause. "*Fine.* Uproot your daughter from her home, and then we'll see who the better parent is." Jane covered her face with her hands, mumbling under her breath. "Oh. Hi, Gracie. That was nothing, just a little tiff between your father and me." Jane's eyelids drooped from exhaustion. She continued, "You ready?"

Gracie shrugged. "I think I might stay here. You know, hang out at the beach for a while."

Jane's eyebrow rose. "Gracie. We agreed. The weekends are for your father." Her shoulders slumped. "Besides, it's going to storm soon. You don't need to be by the water, it's not safe." She rifled through her purse, looking for her keys.

Storm clouds were forming, and thunder cracked through the air. Tourists were evacuating the beach, picking up their crying children, and beach gear from the sand. The wind picked up, Gracie shivered, and pulled her sweater closer to her.

Twenty minutes in the car was just enough to make Gracie antsy. Her mother's words echoed in her ears. Gracie watched cars blur by the window and Gracie leaned her head against the cool glass. They passed a bright green sign reading "Welcome to New Smyrna Beach, Florida. Pop. 22,464."

"Don't worry honey; we'll get this figured out." Jane fiddled with the radio, finally settling on a country station.

Every Sunday night was the same, drive the twenty minutes to her father's, then stay with her mother during the week.

"It'll be something new," her father said, after throwing the news at Gracie during their last weekend together. "I just don't think that Daytona is a good place for you right now, not after what happened to Todd."

"Don't I get any say in the matter?" Gracie had shouted, standing up so fast her chair fell back hitting the wall of her dad's kitchen with a thud.

He'd looked up from his newspaper, and sipped his lemonade, "Well of course you do honey. I'm just trying to do what's best for you."

"What's best for me is staying here with Mom. Todd would've wanted us to stay in Florida. Not have our family split across the East Coast," Gracie had taken the newspaper from his hands and had thrown it to the ground. "Move to Boston with your new girlfriend. I don't even care."

***

"We're here," her mother said. Gracie shook her head, trying to brush aside thoughts of her and Frank's last stay together.

Her father waved from the front porch of a blue beach house. Gracie opened the passenger door and stepped out. Heavy clouds dangled above them, and the wind moaned.

"I missed you, Gracie," her father said into her hair, his arms wrapping around in a bear hug.

Gracie cringed, and pushed away. "Dad, it's only been a week." Her gaze shifted to the vast ocean peeking through the fence.

"I know, but it feels like a lifetime. I get lonely down here," he teased, tousling Gracie's blonde curls.

Her mother snorted.

"Is there something you'd like to say, Jane?" Frank glared.

She shook her head, pulled her sunglasses back down to her nose, and said, "I'll pick you up on Monday, Gracie."

Frank turned to Gracie. "Why don't you go put your things in your room," he said. "Tell your mother goodbye."

"Don't tell me what to do," Gracie shot back.

"Gracie, what did we talk about?" Jane asked, her eyes narrowing. "It's only a few days," she tugged on Gracie's shirt sleeve, and whispered in her ear, "We'll get this figured out." She nodded towards the house.

As Gracie walked away, Frank and Jane bickered behind her, keeping their voices low, careful not to let her hear.

Instead of going to put her suitcases in the house, Gracie walked the couple feet to the fence and climbed over, going down the hill to the water. The wind ripped through her hair, and rain sprinkled her skin. She slipped a toe into a wave. The water sent a shiver up her body.

"Gracie girl, come on in, the water's great," her older brother Todd yelled, a smile plastered on his face. His body splashed through the cold Atlantic. Gracie smiled, soaking up the sun, warming her sleepy skin. It was the last week of summer, before her junior year, and the last week before Todd left for Duke.

He waded out into the water, splashing his hands like a little kid.

"Gracie, come on. You know you want to," he teased, swimming further away from shore.

Gracie dipped her big toe into an incoming wave. She jumped back as the water sent a chill through her body. She didn't know how Todd could throw himself into the waves and not be freezing. "Todd, it's too cold!" she whined from the sand.

Todd yelled back at her, "Gracie girl, don't be a baby."

"The water a little cold?" a voice next to her asked.

Gracie jumped and looked over to see a gangly boy looking back at her from a freckled face.

"I'm the same way; it's always cold this time of year."

Gracie didn't respond, just looked at him with a blank expression.

"Oh, sorry. Where are my manners?" he said. "I'm Dylan, and you are?" He held his hand out, but when she didn't take it, he shoved it back into his pocket.

"I'm Gracie."

"Are you new? I haven't seen you around before," he asked.

"Uh, my dad lives here, I've only been staying with him for a couple weekends," she said. Off into the distance a shirtless toddler splashed in the water.

"That's cool. So I should be seeing you around more then?" he asked.

"Well, it depends; my dad wants to move to Boston." Gracie looked down at the sand then back at Dylan.

"Man that bites. My parents are divorced. It's always been one week at my mom's, and then my dad's the next." He kept his eyes on Gracie.

"Gracie," Frank called from the porch, motioning for her to come back to the house.

"Well, that's my cue."

"Hey, if you wanted, I could show you around town sometime. You know, in case you get tired of bumming around your dad's." He rubbed his forehead, his nose crinkling as he waited for an answer.

"Uh, yeah sure. My house is right up there." She pointed towards her dad's. "Come by whenever." She turned, and walked up the sandy path leading to her dad's beach house.

A storm blew in later that night, and rain pelted the house. Gracie lay in her bed, listening to the wind moan. She rolled over, peering at the clock on her nightstand. 4:01 A.M. She closed her eyes, taking in the sound of the rain, and drifted back to sleep.

***

The next morning Gracie faced her father across the coffee table in the beach house's small living room. The sky was still gray and clouds covered every inch of the Florida sky.

"So," Gracie asked, her elbows digging into the arm of the couch. "What am I supposed to do here? I don't know anybody." She examined her nails and looked up to see Frank with his eyes shut. "Okay dad, whatever. It's not like I was talking to you or anything."

"Sorry, I'm just so tired," he rubbed his eyes. "That storm kept me up." He got up from the recliner and put his jacket on.

"Where are you going?"

"I have a meeting with my lawyer. He wants to go over some paperwork." He fumbled with the strap on his briefcase.

Gracie groaned and fell back on the couch. "This is great, I'm going to be bored. All. Day."

"Gracelynn Jane, don't give me an attitude," Frank replied, searching his pockets for his phone. "I'll call you later and let you know whether or not to order out."

She waved her hand at him, shooing him away. He blew a kiss goodbye.

***

A few hours went by, and Gracie scanned through all the available channels the beach house offered, called her best friend Kayla, and even did a load of her dad's laundry. She needed to get out.

A note lay on the kitchen counter. "Don't leave the house while I'm gone. Will be home later, love you."

Gracie snorted. "Good joke." She grabbed her book from her bag and then opened the sliding door to the deck outside her room.

She was already nestled in the deck chair when she heard someone call

129

her name. Gracie looked down over the deck to see Dylan standing in the sand waving.

"Dylan, what are you doing?" she shouted, leaning over the railing.

"I was just wondering if you wanted to go into town with me," he shouted back, putting his hand over his forehead to shield his eyes. Even though clouds covered the sky, it was still pretty bright.

"My dad said I can't leave the house," she said. "But then again, he won't be home for a while." She put up a finger. "I'll be right down," she went inside, threw her book onto the bed, and slipped on her flip flops.

***

A few minutes later, they were down the street walking towards town.

"So, what have you been up to all day?" he asked, running a freckled hand through his hair.

"Oh my God, I was so bored until you came." She released a sigh. "Is it always this boring?"

"Once you get to know more people, it's not that bad. I felt the same way when I moved here." He scuffed his shoe against the pavement. "I've never seen so many old people. It's kind of like 'God's Waiting Room', where people come to die," he said, laughing to himself.

Gracie stopped walking.

Dylan kept on and then stopped when he realized she wasn't next to him anymore.

"What?" Dylan asked, a blank stare covering his face.

Gracie didn't say anything.

"Gracie, what is it?"

She turned her face away from him, tears flooding her eyes.

"Gracie, I'm really sorry if I upset you." He placed his hand on her shoulder.

"My brother drowned last August," she said. "My parents are divorced, so my dad's staying here until he can get the custody agreement settled." Tears streamed down her face. "He wants to move to Boston, where his new girlfriend lives."

"You don't want to move to Boston?"

"I don't even want to live here. My mom lives in our old house, and I feel like if I leave that house, I'm leaving my brother behind." She rubbed her eyes and continued, "I don't even know why I'm telling you this. I don't know you."

"No, I'm sorry, Gracie. I didn't know," Dylan replied.

An awkward silence cast over them, as Gracie stood there watching the waves crash in the distance.

Gracie shook her head. "I'm fine." She wiped her eyes with the back of her hand. "So, where can a girl get some good ice cream around here?" A smile lit her face.

Dylan breathed a sigh of relief and laughed, "Oh, I know *just* the place."

*Portrait 2 :: Kathy Maloney*

# Brave Old World

Richard Nelson

## I

How it happened is uncertain. Where it happened was everywhere. When it happened was, well, it was sometime in the early twenty-first century. Why? Now that's the real question. Why did we wipe ourselves out? Why did hate become the new love? Why did we develop something whose only possible use was the elimination of the human race? And then why did we unleash it?

All good questions. Too bad there's no one left to debate them.

## II

In the Before, I was a Web page designer for a machine parts business in Omaha, Nebraska. The World-Wide Web? Now it's the "world-wide nothing."

I had a wife and a four-year old daughter. My wife was pregnant with our second child. We had just found out that it was going to be a boy.

But now all of that was gone as well. My wife and daughter both died in the plague that circled the earth, killing everyone. Well, almost everyone. For some reason, I survived. I watched my beautiful wife and daughter vomit out their entire insides and then die in their own filth. I buried them in our back yard. I didn't even get a cough.

The original estimates were that no one would survive. Not even the animals. Birds and insects, yes. Probably the fish. But no mammals. And then, just at the last dying scientist stated on the last television broadcast, maybe a few would survive. By some genetic anomaly. Less than a millionth of a percent. Six billion people reduced to a few thousand. Spread over the entire planet.

So that was what I was. A genetic anomaly.

Every morning since that day, when I first open my eyes, I wish I wasn't.

### III

After I buried my family, I sat in what we had called our family room. Not exactly an appropriate name any longer. I watched the television as the world died, the channels one by one going to snow. Some stayed on longer. An unattended camera in a studio or up on a rooftop, until the power went out in that particular city. And then the power went out in our house.

I must have sat there the rest of the day. I remember the room being light and then it was dark and I must have fallen asleep as I was still on the couch when I opened my eyes in the pitch black. My entire body revolted. I jerked forward off the couch and retched, but nothing came up as I hadn't eaten anything for a couple of days. I hoped that I was dying, but it was just the pain of loss. Of everything I held dear. Of everything that I had ever known.

And then I cried, for the first time since it happened. Horrible, wrenching sobs on my hands and knees – like my body was trying to get something out of it that was too painful to hold in any longer. After several minutes, I finally collapsed on the floor, my body jerking, slower and then finally still. I prayed for God to take me, but no such luck. I suppose cataloging billions of new souls into heaven must be time consuming.

And then the sun came up again. At least it still worked.

I used the toilet and flushed by instinct. It was a whole minute later that I realized that it had functioned properly. Why would that work when nothing else did? "Of course," I said aloud to the empty room. Water access was based on pressure and gravity. As I was probably the only person in town using any, the water pressure would last for a long time. A really long time.

I ate a meal out of canned goods. I had gone to the stove to turn it on and was even reaching for a pan, but then I caught myself with a dead laugh. We always were well stocked so I had enough canned goods to last for several days. But I would eventually need more. Many more.

I stood outside on our front porch, the city deadly quiet. Where I once could hear the hum of traffic on L Street even from two blocks away, now there was nothing. But the smell was there. The smell was everywhere. I could see bodies in yards, bodies in cars as they had tried to escape, the cars up over curbs, some having rolled into the sides of houses.

I realized that I couldn't stay here. I had survived the world's deadliest plague, and now if I didn't move, I'd probably die from the toxic smell of death. Where to go? Where to go?

# IV

It came to me in a flash. My grandparent's home town, Griswold, Iowa. I'd go there for now. The population had been only a few hundred. The smell couldn't be that bad. And if it was, I could always find a farm nearby. But I needed a few things first.

Luckily I had recently gassed up our SUV. More than enough gas for my trips around town and then the drive east. And even if I had been short of gas, it wasn't like I didn't have my pick of vehicles. I drove over to the Hy-Vee grocery store near our home, parking out back and entering through the freight entrance, which was standing wide open. There were a handful of bodies laying around the store, the insects having a field day. The smell was overpowering in the enclosed space, so I found some Vaseline and put a dab under my nose like in the movies. It helped a little bit.

Taking my time, not having any reason to be in a hurry other than daylight, I loaded our SUV with cases of canned goods from the back storage area. I also grabbed some fresh fruit and vegetables. Probably be the last time for those in a while, if ever.

I went into the manager's office and looked through their files. I was looking for the location of the closest distribution centers, where they would have enough canned goods to last me for years. Altogether, it took me a couple of hours to gather what I needed, the biggest problem being working in the dark. Power was off everywhere and I had to use flashlights and batteries. I added those to the SUV.

I also went through the pharmacy and loaded up on toiletries – soap (bath, laundry, dish), shampoo, toothpaste, toothbrushes, floss, even deodorant. I grabbed every roll of toilet paper they had. Analgesics and antibiotics as well. Not that I'd probably ever need them. After all, I had just survived a plague that had wiped out the human race. But no sense letting a cold get the best of me now.

Next I drove to Sol's pawnshop, looking for weapons. Considering I had no idea who else may have survived besides me, it seemed prudent to have some sort of protection. I grabbed rifles, shotguns, handguns and the appropriate bullets and shells.

By now the smell in the city was becoming unbearable. I tried to imagine what a city like New York smelled like. Even though the buzzing was driving me crazy, I thanked God for the insects. Hopefully, they'd clean up this mess soon.

It was April, the beginning of the season of rebirth. Grass turning green, trees budding out. Everything coming back to life after the cold winter. But not the human race. They had chosen to kill each other, in the name of religious hatred. I'd have a lot of time to lament that. But no one to share it with.

As it was spring. I gathered all the vegetable seeds that I could find. Griswold has an apple orchard to the west of town. Maybe I would be able to have fresh fruits and vegetables after all.

## V

I spent one last night in Omaha. Lying in bed, trying to sleep, I was bone tired, but my eyes wouldn't close. I stared at the ceiling, even though I couldn't see it in the dark. I rolled onto my side and stared at the wall which I couldn't see either. I reached across the covers, but nothing was there. I was alone. Not just out of town on a business trip alone. Not just taking a walk in the woods alone. Completely alone. Soul-crushing alone.

My body felt empty, like someone had scooped out my insides. I pictured some doctor performing an autopsy on my remains, turning to an assistant, saying, "Damn, this guy was empty. How did he stay alive?"

Maybe a better question would have been, why? Why did he stay alive?

\*\*\*

"Daddy. Daddy, wake up."

I heard her voice. My daughter's voice, clear and sweet. Like the purest crystal, tapped by the purest finger nail. I knew it was a dream. I knew she was gone. But I forced myself to remain in that world between sleep and reality. Between beauty and death. Between just out of reach and gone forever.

"Daddy, come play with me. Read me a story. Tickle my belly. Make me laugh."

They stood across the room. I reached for them. My daughter held out her hands to me, but my wife gently held her back, my daughter curling her body around my wife's leg.

My wife said to our daughter, "Not yet, honey. He's not ready."

My daughter smiled, knowingly. Wise in the ways of the dead and the living. Wiser than me. Far wiser than me.

The sun woke me up, filling the room with light. Free light. A gift from God each day. No need for electricity or nuclear power or coal or anything. Just open the shades and let it in.

I realized what else I needed. Books. Real books. The kind you still hold in your hand and read. I made a library run, grabbing everything that would fit in the car.

I went back home for the last time. Filling the tub with water, I took a

135

bath. No warm water, bracing to say the least. The water had turned brown when I first got in, but after several rinses, I felt clean. I put on fresh clothes.

I stood in our house for what I assumed would be the last time. The photographs, the mementos, the toys were all still there. But all they were now were sad reminders of all that was gone. Our latest family photo stood silently on the mantle. I blew it a kiss and stepped outside and got in my car.

## VI

I weaved my way through the maze of silent cars, down "L" Street to the new South Omaha Bridge. I stopped in the middle and walked to the railing, the lazy Missouri rolling away to the south, to the ocean.

I pulled out my cell phone and turned it on. Amazingly, it still had power, three out of five bars. All powered up and no one to call. I reached back and threw it as far as I could. It arced through the air, flashing in the sun for a few seconds, and then it fell out of sight.

I didn't even hear it splash.

Next, I pulled out my brand new e-reader. My wife had just bought it for me a month before, thinking as I was an avid reader, that would make it easier for me to do so. The battery was already dead. Black on black. I dropped it over the railing.

I got back in my car and looked at my cache – books, food, clothes, toiletries. Everything a single man would need, and I was definitely a single man now.

I started the car and drove east, back to the Stone Age.

# An Anchored Bond

Allyson Olson

I had never seen so many trees in my life. Seated in the back seat of the rental car, I gazed out the window upon never-ending amounts of Minnesota green. Red, orange, and yellow crept from tree to tree, bringing fall with them. Interest did not let my mother's neck cease from moving side to side to front in the passenger seat. My father supervised the wheel like an enthusiastic captain at the helm. A massive sign appeared. "Turtle Lake 5 miles" flashed by.

The car pulled over to a log cabin, where I assumed my father picked up the keys to our territory in the wilderness. Anticipation held onto me as we followed the dirt road. Finally, we reached where we would be spending the next week. Our cabin was everything you might imagine it to be: cozy, rustic, and reeking of the smell of pine. I looked around the front room. Being a fourteen year old, the principal and most imperative thing I noticed shocked me.

"Where is the TV? What am I supposed to do without a TV for a week?" I said frantically.

"You'll make do. Find other things to occupy your time," my mother nonchalantly informed me.

TV bonded my father and me. Since the divorce, trying to conjure up a conversation became difficult. Sports, movies, fishing, and TV became the set list of topics. Neither of us dared to roam away from it. Eagerness pushed me through the side door. I walked out onto our wooden, lightly stained deck. It overlooked a giant lake, Turtle Lake. August turned the trees into a fiery inferno surrounding peaceful off-blue waters. The deck led to a long, wooden stairway carved into the hill. As I wandered down the steep pile of mismatched timber, I did not notice my feet sink into the sand when I reached the bottom. A dock stood still in the water, while a boat laid next it. The two were companions secured together.

My father appeared behind me and said, "Tomorrow, we are going to go fishing, so be ready by 4:45."

I foolishly questioned, "At night?" His laughter echoed throughout the remote place as he strolled away.

A fourteen year old does not do well with mornings. At dawn, I do not believe many do. I lugged my body to the beach, where the fishing poles and tackle box had beaten me. The white motor boat sat still on the water, mocking me. My father packed the boat with the essentials: fishing gear and beer. The boat shook as I stepped in like an unbalanced seesaw. My father grasped the pull cord and looked at me with excitement. The boat slowly glided on top of the water, picking up speed as it reached the middle of the vast lake. I saw my dad searching for the spot. His eyes ignited as a fish breached the surface and gave up its coordinates.

The boat reduced speed and came to a halt. "Drop the anchor!" the commander ordered me. I looked around and found an old, rusty piece of metal. A doctor needed to mandate a Tetanus shot to everyone who encountered that piece of junk. In the exact seconds I threw it overboard, my dad instructed, "Make sure it is tied to the boat!" Panic rushed upon me. I peered over the side and saw no sign of a rope. I needed to handle the situation like a Band-Aid; tell him what happened and get the sting over and done. Disappointment flooded his face, which dwindled after the opening of the first Miller Light can.

No one can ever be sure of how long we baited and casted, but it felt like forever. Either way, the cooler for the fish we caught remained unoccupied. My father yanked the pull cord up. Nothing happened. Try after try, he only met failure. The engine flooded. My dad grabbed an oar and started to row. I watched as it pierced the water, making indents that rippled backward. The only sound heard was the swooshing melody of the irregular force pushing the water. I looked back at my father. He turned the color of the red leaves that floated by in the water, and sweat poured down his face. My eyes searched for a bucket in the boat just in case he flooded it. No, there stood only a cooler of beer; he would have declined that sacrifice.

I remember asking myself, "Is it that hard to row, or is he just getting old?" Finally, after a forty-five minute trek home, the boat docked. My father's originally light gray Oklahoma shirt turned dark. My mother stood on the beach looking at both of us curiously.

"What happened to you?" she laughed as she questioned him. As I stepped onto the dock, I looked at the side of the boat. A rope I had not noticed before caught my eye. It stretched straight down into the water. I tried to pull it up, but it stayed permanent. My father grabbed it and pulled with his tired muscles. Each hand forward played with my imagination. What waited on the end? A couple of hushed minutes passed by, he reached the end of the rope. The anchor rose from the water.

All three pair of eyes met instantaneously, and so did our laughter.

# Many Colors of the CTA

Bhavin Pardiwala

"This is Sox-35th. Doors open to the left at Sox-35th. This is the Red-Line train to Howard. Cermak-Chinatown is next. Doors closing."

"Nooo! Hold up! I'm coming, I'm coming." Whew, that was a close one. I hate how the CTA makes me run and look like a fool in front of everyone who had to wait for me, too. As I hop on the first cart, panting hard, I look for a seat and see a cloud of long, droopy faces staring me down like I came from another planet. But of course it's full as usual. That's ok though, riding the CTA after 4 years, I know how disgusting and sticky those seats are, probably from the drunk Chicagoans who pee in public, especially on the Red-Line. On this warm, Friday night, I see the glimmering lights from US Cellular Park brighten up this dark, ominous sky, and all I can think about is "Screw the Sox. Go Cubs!" I'd probably get shot if I yelled that out down here.

The train starts to move, although at this rate, I feel like I can walk home faster. Trying so hard to look at my phone because of the constant jerking from the train, I see the time. Great, its 8:00 p.m. Guess I'm not gonna make the purple line express to Howard, which means another 90 minute commute for me. Joy and excitement rushed throughout every inch in my body, if only that were true. Riding on the CTA can be fun at times, because of the interesting people I get to observe, but after 4 years, I just wish I didn't have to go through this long, tedious process of seeing my parents for the weekend. At least, I have my pencil and sketchbook.

As I look at the CTA Map that is normally located on each cart, although most people steal them either as souvenirs or for the shear excitement of almost getting caught in public, I see all the different trains that run in and out of Chicago. As a kid, whenever I would hear about the Red Line or Brown Line, I literally thought these trains were painted in their assigned colors. Much to my disappointment, they sadly were not.

"Yo, yo, yo.

What up, girl?

Why ain't you pickin' up your phone? You know I don't like to wait."

My curiosity and interest for this conversation grew dim, especially after characterizing in my mind how this person might look and noticing how he actually looks: a dark, African-American guy, 'bout 30-35 years old in a vibrant red button-up and a black striped fedora. Another interesting character I see on my weekly commute.

I never really realized how sheltered I was until after graduation, when I started taking the CTA. Living in Skokie, which is a suburb north of downtown Chicago, I thought I knew so much about the greatest city in the world, but boy was I wrong. Chicago, as a whole, praises the fact of how diverse it is compared to other major cities. Technically, it is diverse, but growing up in an incredibly diverse community and then moving into the city for college, I've noticed how segregated Chicago is.

Yes! Train going express to Jackson. Things like this always seem to work out for me whenever I run late on the CTA. As I enter downtown, I wonder if Chicago just seems to generate an infinite amount of citizens as the train becomes packed like head bangers in a concert. The constant shuffle of feet to squeeze in the confined space. The people in my cart quickly disperse as we reach Belmont, until it is left with a few people listening to their iPods, going home from work.

Finally, some entertaining people to accompany me on this endless route. "Thump!" A tall, rotund male slips and bangs his fist on the divider as his buddy, slightly taller and more jacked follows him in, tattoos and all. In an instant, you can tell these guys have already been drinking, even though its only 9:00 p.m, but their night isn't over yet, that's for sure. The cute, blonde nurse, mid-20s I'd say, stares upon them with her soft and angelic blue eyes, masked by her overshadowing glasses. She gives them a smirk, and me not knowing what she's thinking about; does she realize how drunk these guys are, or is she completely engulfed in this song playing on her iPod? I make my eyes toward the map again and gaze upon the L-system.

What a unique way to classify each train route. Usually, trains in cities have numbers or specific brand names to distinguish each train from each other. Why colors? Is Chicago trying to exemplify its diverse nature by portraying it on public transportation? Can each color be associated with the group of people who take it or live near it? Certainly in the loop, there is a vast mix of people from all different races interacting in a place where most eyes in the world see us as? But can the world see what happens when we venture out on our own CTA line? Do people know that the further south we go from Chicago, mainly using the Green and Red Line, the more dominant it gets with the African American community? Or traveling west with the Pink and Orange Lines resides the majority of the Mexican American community. Going north on the Red, Purple and Blue has more of a diverse mix, but it is still heavily populated with Caucasians.

One of my favorite moments I get to witness on my commute is the dramatic shifts in the types of people who leave and enter the train at certain stops on the Red Line. Getting on at 35th, going north, each cart mostly contains black people, who are dressed up going to work while others are in their usual attire, and the occasional white guy or Asian lady who is most definitely going to Chinatown, the next stop. At Chinatown, the cart is now half filled with Asians, and the other half African Americans. By the end of Jackson, most of the black people have gotten off, and the cart is mostly filled with white people.

It isn't until I get to the end of the Red Line, when the cart is taken over by mostly black people, and dead, exhausted souls suffering from that dreadful commute, like me. The worker ants complying with the dominant grasshopper's every command, rush through their days, not ever taking a moment to stop and think about the cultural change that occurs in their daily routine, as I sit in silence and become a witness to this amazing phenomena. To see the CTA do a complete cultural 360 as it rips through the city is something very few people get to witness. And as I hop onto the Skokie Swift, the cart is filled with my childhood, surrounded by an immensely diverse group of people and my sketchbook. I calmly look down at my black and white sketch in my black and white sketchbook, and see only one thing missing, color.

> *"Prose is architecture, not interior decoration."*
> - Ernest Hemingway

# The Schizotypical Insomniac
# Has Stopped Taking His Medication

Heather E. Pecoraro

When there are people living inside your head and you can't remember ever inviting them there and they are always talking and their music is too loud and they keep walking all over with muddy shoes, it gets a bit unfriendly and you're very mad and you're very mean and you post eviction notices on the doors, but they never leave. So late at night, if you get any sleep at all, you're perpetually waking up in a cold sweat because somebody up there keeps flicking the lights, making your eyeballs roll up and down inside of their sockets. Every room of the house smells like rotten lettuce, because one of your residents keeps putting out cigarette butts on the furniture. Someone is playing sad piano keys in the corner, a child screams and cries and crawls all over the floor. They are shoving Bible verses and peanut butter and jelly sandwiches down your throat, and you're saying "No, this isn't right, I asked for apple pie." But the words get stuck on the tip of your tongue and instead the whole world hears you begging "Please pull the wool over my eyes some more, please can't you spoon-feed me some more of those sweet n' salty lies?" And this happens all the time, every night at nine o'clock. You won't forget to take your medication this time, no, you've been reformed! You'll go to church and wait patiently in lines and grind your teeth and fold your shirts and lock up your windows. You've been reborn! No more strong drinks or green things, but at least your afterlife is safe and set, so long as you fold your hands, get on your knees, and sign the dotted lines. "You've lost yourself and become someone else," the residents will taunt and tease, "sold your spirit, your eternal soul, for one hot meal and a carton of cigarettes." God bless insomnia. Hallelujah, Amen.

# The Hero

Jennifer Peterson

We had crushed our way through three impacts by the time I got out a scream. I gripped the seat, the thin rubber window ledge, anything I could, as we careened over and over, flipping and rolling and falling. My teeth were clenched. I was still illogically clutching my bedraggled copy of *Jane Eyre* between my elbow and my side, trying to hold on to everything at once. It had taken us a moment to slide over the icy road, a second to break through the flimsy gray guardrail, and it was taking us a torturously charged eternity to fall.

I couldn't think. All I could do was hold on. One crunch over another, gravity pulling at my shoulders, then slamming me back down on the dingy Greyhound seat. I closed my eyes and tried to swallow. I felt the adrenaline pounding through my veins and the shock that pulsed through my body, as we slammed our way down the mountain. There were screams all around me in the darkness. Some of them were mine.

"Just a few more seconds," I chanted in my mind, trying to convince myself it'd all be okay. It was so dark I couldn't have seen out the windows even if I tried, but I could hear the trees crushing underneath the bus, hear the branches scraping the Plexiglas windows. Slowly... slowly... slowly the bus toppled and tumbled and rocked back to one side before crunching to a stop.

I knew we weren't moving anymore, but I couldn't open my eyes. I couldn't breathe. My shoulder was dully aching like a joint that needed cracking but wouldn't crack. I rolled it with a grimace, unable to remember which impact injured it.

I heard grunts around me, a cry. Then a man's shout. I opened my eyes.

"My name is Sergeant Greg Thuler. Is everyone okay?"

He shone a flashlight down the seats. The line of whitish glow caught the settling dust and lit up a battered interior of the bus, backpacks and suitcases, open and closed, strewn all down the aisle. Someone's portable cassette player lay cracked on the floor, its reel still spinning, its crunchy film spewing forth with a whisper. As the sergeant's beam passed over the rows of seats, it illuminated pale strained faces of different colors, genders,

143

and ages. But the look of fear each wore was the same.

"Come on folks! Let me hear ya. Is anyone injured?"

There was a pause as people examined themselves before looking around slowly, rightly scared of what they might find.

"Sir... officer?" a tentative voice called from a few rows back.

"What is it?" the sergeant responded, immediately moving towards her. My eyes followed him as he passed. He was tall, dressed in an army green shirt and cargo pants. His arms were muscular. The steady beam of light he held cast shadows around the bus, leaving his face in darkness.

"It's this woman," a girl who couldn't have been older than fifteen whispered. "I, I think she's, dead," her voice broke. "I don't even, Jesus, I don't even know her name," the girl cried, moving away from the elderly woman slumped onto her shoulder.

The sergeant stepped over the seats and put his hand to the woman's throat. He calmly bent down and put his ear to her mouth.

"Nothing," he said quietly. He stepped back and extended his hand to the girl who'd spoken. Freckles were splattered across her pale peaked face, and her shoulders were shaking. She took the soldier's hand and used it to fling herself out into the aisle where she sank to her knees and closed her eyes, burying her fingers in her thin brown hair.

"Anyone else?" the sergeant called out.

"Two up here," a man answered with a voice that almost, but not quite, achieved the level of calm it aimed to.

"All right," the sergeant answered. "What about the driver? You okay up there, pal?" he called up to the front. His voice practically echoed in the eerie quiet of hushed sobs and groans.

I saw a shadow get up and scurry to the wheel. He or she hunched and examined the man in the front. All I could remember was a pudgy balding man who'd opened the electric door with a look that made it clear he was on a minute by minute countdown to the end of his route.

The sergeant shined his flashlight to the front, illuminating a middle age woman who simply shook her head.

"All right people! Talk to me! How many of you are there? Who's injured?"

He started at the back of the bus and counted off people one by one.

"Two, three, four... fifteen, sixteen...."

I was seventeen.

"Thirty-four, five... anybody I missed?" he asked, coming to the front again

I tried to count it out in my mind. Thirty-five alive meant eight dead,

144

maybe nine.

There was a groan from the seat in front of me, and I stood up, trying to see more clearly. There was an old woman lying under a bulky black cloak. I was pretty sure he'd missed her.

"Here," I called softly, leaning over the seat and pulling the cloak off. She had a knitting needle stuck in her neck and another clenched in her veiny hands.

"Oh my god," I breathed as the sergeant's light shined onto her, and I saw the dark smear of blood trickling down her neck and across her floral peach shirt.

"What's your name, ma'am?" the sergeant asked, crouching down beside her in an instant, handing me the flashlight.

"Leah," she moaned so softly I could hardly hear.

"All right, Leah, stay with me. It's gonna be okay. Anybody got a scarf?" he yelled into the aisle. A woman a few seats up quickly unwrapped one from her neck and brought it over.

"You know first aid?" he asked her.

"No," she shook her head, backing away.

"You?" he asked me, urgently.

I blinked, and he asked again.

"I took it in high school, but God, I wouldn't remember,"

"Doesn't matter," he cut me off. "Give her the light," he jerked his head toward the scarf woman.

He turned back to the wheezing old woman.

"All right ma'am, stay with me now. You're our number thirty-six and thirty-six is my favorite number. You gotta stay with us. Can ya do that?"

She paused a moment and then closed her eyes and nodded.

"Good. We're gonna get that needle out of your neck, real gentle like. Then, we're gonna use this scarf to staunch the bleeding,"

"No," somebody in the seats said. "I seen shows like this before. You 'sposed to leave it in."

"Not this time," the sergeant said to them quietly. "We don't know how long we're gonna be here."

It was the first time I'd heard any trace of uncertainty in his voice.

"We need to get this out as quickly as possible and do our best to stop infection."

The sergeant took the lack of response as acquiescence.

"Okay, Leah, you're number thirty-six. And we're gonna get this done in thirty-six seconds. You ready?"

She grimaced and nodded again.

"All right then," he said, turning to me and starting to count. I took a deep breath, as he took my hands and placed one on each of her shoulders.

"Hold her steady," he whispered in the pause between six and seven.

He moved his hands to the puncture in her neck, gently placing his fingers around the thick silver knitting needle.

"Twelve... thirteen..."

He tugged on the needle, and the woman hissed. I kept my hands pressed against her shoulders, holding her in place.

"Fourteen," he grunted, nodding to me. "Fifteen, sixteen, seventeen,"

The needle slid out with a nauseating squelch. There was a ping as he dropped it on the floor and a metallic cadence as it rolled across the aisle.

"Twenty-two, twenty-three,"

The rolled scarf passed from my hands to his to mine. I pressed the layers of yarn to the woman's neck. She closed her eyes.

"Stay with me, Leah!" the sergeant called between numbers. "You got kids?" he asked. "Couple of grandkids? Think about them, stay with us now!"

The woman opened her eyes, and they were tight with a mix of pain and determination.

"Thirty-four, thirty -five, thirty-six," he finished, brushing the thin white hair out of her eyes gently. "There we go ma'am. You're gonna be fine now. We're all gonna be all right. Thirty six survivors," he said.

I repeated what he said without meaning to, and a few others did the same, "Thirty-six, thirty-six survivors."

"That's right people! That's all right! Let's be survivors!" he called out, keeping one hand on the elderly woman. "Now, let's all get near the back of the bus,"

"What do we do now?" a man asked. There was a woman crying into his chest.

"We try to get communications running, we stay warm, and we wait for morning,"

There was no argument, only a slow but steady migration to the seats in the rear.

"Help me with her?" the sergeant asked me.

"Sure," I whispered, moving out into the aisle and coming around the front of the seat. I bent down and got my shoulder under her arm, as the sergeant did the same. I bit my lip, as the weight crushed against my swollen joint. We carried the woman to the back of the bus and sat her down in one of the seats.

"All right? What's our count?" the sergeant asked. "Come on people!

Talk to me!" he called out when no one responded.

"Thirty-six, thirty-six," they murmured.

"Okay, now, who is injured? How many people hit their heads?"

Several nodded and raised their hands.

"Don't go to sleep. Sing, talk to each other. Do whatever you need to do to stay awake."

"What about you?" he asked, turning to me. "You all right? You look a little pale,"

"It's my shoulder," I grunted, my teeth still digging into my lip.

"Let me take a look," he said, stepping closer.

"No, it's nothing. Check the others,"

"What's your name girl?"

"Marnie," I smiled.

"Well, Marnie, now you're my number thirty-six. Let me have a look at that shoulder. I need you with us."

I cracked a smile, but I rolled up my sleeve like he asked.

"May I?" he asked with polite eyes and his light southern twang.

I nodded, and he placed his hands gently over my aching arm and neck.

"Does this hurt? he asked, tilting his head as he pressed down gently on my shoulder.

"No," I winced. It hurt, but no more than it did without the pressure.

"Now?" he asked, pressing back lightly on the joint.

I screamed. A rush of fire went through my back and arm.

"Marnie! Marnie! It's all right!" he reassured me, his hands gentle again. "It's your scapula - pretty sure it's broken. But you're gonna be okay, you got that?"

I blinked the tears out of my eyes.

"You're gonna be okay," he reassured me.

"Okay," I repeated.

"All right!" he said, turning to the group again. "Everybody huddle up and try to stay warm and awake! Holler for me if you have a problem, any problem. I'm going up front to see if the bus' radio is working."

"What if it isn't?" someone asked.

"I'm sure they realized something was wrong when we failed to arrive in Billings. My bet is they'll be here by morning,"

I looked around the darkened bus, hoping he was right.

"Marnie, grab that light," he directed. "You're with me,"

I did as he said, wondering why he wanted me. I had no experience with radio communication. I'd hardly even had experience with CPR. I was just a college student, trying to get home for the holidays.

We got to the front, and I tried to keep my eyes off the dead driver.

"Sergeant, what are we going to do if they aren't here in the morning?" I asked, trying to keep the hopeless tone of despair out of my voice. By the time they got mobilized, tracked their way to where we'd gone off the road, figured out a way to get down here, I knew it could be a long time.

"It's Greg," he said. "Don't worry about it. They'll be here. You'll be comfortably in Billings by this time tomorrow night"

He fiddled with the walkie talkie attached to the radio. There was nothing but fuzz.

"Hey, don't worry about it Marnie. They're coming for us. They'll be here."

His voice was so confident, so absolute that I believed him.

We walked back to the others and took a seat. I listened to Greg talking to them late into the night. I didn't say much, but I didn't let myself fall asleep either. I was still awake when the sky turned gray, then pink. I was still awake when gold morning sun started to shine through the needles of the pines surrounding the bus, and I was still awake as I heard the first rescuers' yells.

Greg said they'd be here, and they were. They climbed down the mountain and called in helicopters to lift us out. When they asked who was in charge, we all pointed to Greg. They examined the crushed exterior of the bus and the beaten interior. When Greg told them there were thirty-six survivors, their faces were amazed. It was a miracle, they said.

Greg was next to me as I took ahold of the rope ladder up to the helicopter. I shook his hand and thanked him. He told me to get my shoulder checked out. I told him I would and started to climb up the ladder.

I was ten feet off the ground before I turned around and called back down,

"Greg! Wait! You never told me. Why's thirty-six your favorite number anyway?"

He cracked a sideways smile and called up,

"Because that's how many of us there were," before turning and walking back to the others.

# A Strange Evolution
## Michael Pick

"We are going to go visit Grandma today," my parents said. It was the first time I remember going to visit my great Grandmother. I didn't really think twice about it because I was still riding the high from my recent birthday party. I had just received a plethora of teenage mutant ninja turtle action figures and miniature Lego sets as gifts. Naturally, my interest, attention, and focus was on Leonardo, Michelangelo, Raphael, and Donatello as opposed to the ensuing visiting experience that lay ahead.

"You really want to do this?" my friend Chris asked me. "You're positive? You're just going to hang it up, after spending so much time and putting so much effort into it?" I told him that I had thought it over repeatedly and had made my decision. I needed a change. Something different. Something worthwhile. Something meaningful. I wasn't sure what it was that I was going to do yet, but I knew that I could no longer work my desk job. I could not, and would not, work one more minute at that place. "Well I think you're nuts for leaving, but if it's what you want, go for it man," Chris lauded. Maybe I was nuts. Maybe it was a stupid move. Oh well, I knew I had to do it.

"Michael, put your toys away and get changed. We are going to visit Grandma today so I want you put on that nice blue collared shirt that you got for your birthday," my mom chimed. I knew what shirt she was talking about. It was definitely the most boring birthday present I had gotten that year. I could never figure out why all my presents couldn't be cool like the action figures. There was always that one gift that had underwear, socks, and some sort of humdrum piece of clothing that I was supposed to wear to events like church and Sunday brunch with my family. My mom would smile and tell me that she couldn't wait to see me wear it, and I would reluctantly smile and say, "Thank you." I carefully placed the turtles in a shoebox, slid them under my bed for after I got back, and put on that fancy new blue collared shirt.

I was nervous about putting in my two-week notice. I knew my boss wasn't going to see it coming. It was going to be a shock to my co-workers that I had gotten to know so well. I had been there for over 2 ½ years. It was a good job. It paid just fine, was stable, offered full benefits, a paid vacation, and sick leave. During this economic recession, it was a great job to have. I knew everyone was going to ask me why I was leaving, and that is what made me uneasy. I had no other job waiting, no other offers that I was going to jump right into. I surely wouldn't tell them that I mentally could no longer do the tedious, monotonous deskwork that they were doing. So, I lied and told them that I had another offer that I couldn't refuse. Everyone accepted that answer and bid me farewell.

On the drive to see Grandma, I realized that I had never met her or seen where she lived. "She lives in a home," my mom told me. Well, of course she lives in a home I thought, where else would she live? I didn't realize that the phrase "lives in a home" meant that she lived in a nursing home. As we pulled up, I was immediately terrified. I saw elderly people everywhere. Wheelchairs, walkers, and oxygen tanks were all new to me. Most of them looked angry or upset, like they had a permanent scowl on their faces. Some were shouting and screaming violently. I had never been so scared in my life. It smelled like mothballs, cabbage, and urine.

Walking out of the building, I immediately felt a weight lifted off my shoulders. I felt a freedom I hadn't felt in what seemed like forever. A mixture of excitement and fear engulfed me as I drove home from that building for the last time. What was I going to do now? I wanted to do something completely different from anything I had ever done before. I wanted to challenge myself. I wanted to see what I was made of. I needed to go in a completely different direction.

We finally made it to Grandma's room. The walk through the living room area to her room felt like an eternity. I was paralyzed with fear from all the commotion around me. It seemed as if all irritated eyes were on me. Upon entering her room, Grandma hugged me aggressively as I just stood there, my arms dangling lifelessly at my side. She told me "Happy Birthday," but I don't remember much else of what she and my parents talked about. I could not wait to leave. I had to get out of there. I never wanted to come back.

Three days after I walked out for the last time, my brother Pat ran an idea by me. "Have you ever considered being a nursing assistant like in a hospital or nursing home? I know a lot of people who do it and seem to like it." I immediately dismissed the idea. I didn't really like going to the doctor and hadn't been to a nursing home since the debacle with Grandmother, when I was 5. After thinking about it further, I decided to talk to some of his friends who were working as CNAs. They told me it wasn't a glamorous job, and it definitely wasn't for everyone, but they truly enjoyed the satisfaction they got from the work.

I have been working as a nurse's aide in a long-term care facility here in Omaha for over a year now. It is a tough job, and some days are better than others, but the fulfillment of helping people with their everyday lives is exactly what I was looking for. The void was finally filled. I never thought that I would return to the place that scared me the most as a kid, but I haven't regretted it for a second. I think back about my initial experience in that environment and just laugh at how things truly do come full circle.

> *"I try to create sympathy for my characters,*
> *then turn the monsters loose."*
>
> - Stephen King

# A Flash of Lightning

Montana Ringer

I woke in the early a.m. on the couch to a strobe light reflecting off the neighbor's fence. I had to teach the next day and decided I'd sleep better in my bed. As I clambered towards the west kitchen window, I saw the parade of lights illuminating from the low hanging, gray blur cloudy sky. A millisecond after one bolt, another would reveal an alternate low-hang of cloud above North Platte. I am enthused by storms and have been ever since I was a child.

Having been raised by frugal parents who lived off the land, I eventually absorbed their wariness of the approaching green walls of clouds. These clouds threw ice rocks from the sky. As the green wall continued to build, it would suddenly send a sweep of cold breeze to replace the hot day's swelter. Those breezes could be followed by a dangerous wind and lightning bolts which might spark a pasture problem in an instant.

We only had the public television stations and could only fully receive four of them; however, my family had plenty of true-life reality shows to watch. On those occasions, we would set the lawn chairs on top of the cellar mound where fireworks could be seen on the Fourth of July from five surrounding villages. We would "Oooh" and "Ahh" at all the sparkles of light, and in between, two little girls would giggle with the moonlight beaming on their rounded cheeks. We couldn't hear the boom and only see a few of the effects, but we were amazed.

The other reality show we dusted off the lawn chairs for was the evening storms. We would watch the evening storms as they approached our tiny, one bedroom house. After a long day of playing outside during the hot, dry summer days, it was nice to feel the cool breeze sweep out the lingering warm air. Current knowledge allows me to assess that my parents watched these storms in case we had to make a mad dash for the cellar, but as a child, I marveled at the sights and sounds of this reality show.

Of course, we drove ourselves back into the sticky, warm house and opened the windows to let the air flow when the storm came too close for my parents' comfort. To this day, I love the sights of flashes, the sounds of clashes, and the smell when the rain finally hits the earth.

With a flash of lightning, I was back to the present from my sentimental flashback. I lurched up the stairs from the kitchen and set my alarm just before climbing into bed. I opened a bedroom shade to draw a bit of the light show in. I slinked into bed and closed my eyes to the flashing through my eyelids. I was hummed to sleep with the *booms* and *bangs* as the vibrations rattled my windows.

*Old Market, Omaha :: Jason Bottlinger*

# Grandmother's House

Megan Schiermeyer

I can feel the rumbling of the gravel under the tires of my vehicle as I draw closer to the place where my mind is allowed to wonder and explore, where I can forget the concerns I have in my life and run free like a young child. I can feel the warmth of the sun shining through the windshield. As I turn down the familiar lane, I am reminded of the peace of mind this place fills me with. I put the car in park and step out. Molly, the overexcited, tail wagging, yellow lab, instantly greets me. The warm, fresh air fills my lungs and I let out a deep sigh of contentment. I enter the coolly kept garage and step up the wooden stairs. When I open the door to enter the house that provides the home-sweet-home feeling, my nose fills with the aroma of freshly baked chocolate chip cookies, making my stomach growl. Taking a bite of one, the chocolate instantly melts in my mouth. The rich sweetness satisfies my taste buds. Seeing my grandma's bright and cheery smile, I can't help but naturally fold into her welcoming hug. She continues to go about her busy way in the kitchen to prepare a delicious meal to be enjoyed in a few hours. I look out the window and find the glassed over pond, rimmed with cattails, that has provided countless memories. The memories of paddle boating, ice-skating, and fishing with my family and friends come flooding back to me, causing a smile to appear on my face. I am reminded of how much I love the peacefulness and the calmness of being outside and I decide to spend some time fishing at the pond.

I return outside with the fishing pole I have used for many years and a Styrofoam container of worms. I stop to take a look at what surrounds me. The clear blue sky allows the sun to cast its heat on my skin. The slight breeze throws my bangs in front of my eyes. The chickens are browsing through the bright green grass in search of bugs. The cows happily swish their tails back and forth as they enjoy their corn in the feed bunk. As I begin my walk down to the pond, I notice the bright red cherries just waiting to be picked from the tree. When I reach the edge of the pond, I sit down on the soft, grassy bank. Molly joins me, sitting by my side. I cast my worm and sit patiently waiting. As I quietly wait, I can hear the splashing of the bullfrogs frightfully jumping into the water. I can hear the chirping of the nearby crickets. I can smell the musk of the water and the moss lining the bank. Suddenly, I feel a jerk of my pole as a fish takes hold of my worm. I begin to reel in my catch and I can tell by the fight the fish is putting up that it will be a big one. I land the fish on the bank and remove the hook from the large mouth of the bass, and release it back into the water. I cast my worm for a second time and wait for another bite. My patience runs out when another bite never comes and I return to the house, hoping the delicious meal my grandma was preparing is about ready to be served.

As we sit around the dinner table enjoying the delicious meal, I take in the rich laughter, the wide smiles, the unforgettable memories, and the sweet love that is experienced at this place, Grandmother's house.

> *"I know that if I have been working on one paragraph and I have written it three times, it goes in the bin. Unless it comes straight out, it is wrong, it is awkward, it does not fit."*
>
> - Robert Rankin

# The Farm Laborer

Charles Scudder

When my twin and I were born in 1931, Mother and Father lived in a small Nebraska village, Juniata. That was my urban world until 1936 when we moved to Hastings. After 1939, we moved back to Juniata. We never lived on a farm, and yet, I did a great deal of farm work over a period of seven years between 1941 -1949. I'm so often asked: "Were you raised on a farm?" Of course the answer is "No, but . . . ." So, when my daughter asked me recently: "Did you work when you were a child?" I recalled the following events.

Our family was poor without seeing ourselves as poverty stricken. My father kept a large garden to raise vegetables to supplement our table. At the age of nine, my twin and I were required to work in the garden during the growing season when we weren't in school. Many times, we were given an assignment and left unsupervised to carry out Dad's designated chore. At the beginning of our performance in the garden, we were given but scanty instruction on the difference between vegetable plants and weeds. If we pulled out the little vegetable plants thinking they were weeds, we were criticized for our errors. And so, we learned the difference between weeds and vegetable plants.

My sister and I were given other assignments having to do with the care of chickens, a cow, goats and turkeys.  One of our garden assignments was to take a gallon can half full of kerosene and go down the rows of potatoes with a stick, examine each plant, and when we saw a potato bug, we were to shove the insect into the gallon can where it died as it came into contact with the kerosene.

We were children and, when we weren't in school, we were at home. The depression made jobs for people my father's age impossible. There really wasn't any place to go for entertainment, recreation, play, or visiting. All of those activities could be found in Hastings, but we had no money to spend even if we could get there. At home, all of our family from Father and Mother on down to the youngest child worked around the house. This style of living went on from 1940 through 1942, and, then a change took place in my circumstances.

The War effort had taken many young men away from Juniata and Hastings leaving employers without mature male workers to work the fields. Unknown to me, my mother arranged with John Hueske, a local farmer, for me to work on his farm. I was put to work harvesting potatoes. I was 12 years old. It was day labor, and I would go to the job early in the morning and after working all day, come home in the evening. The owners had me picked up at my house in Juniata, driven to the worksite and at days' end dropped me off at home. Paid $2.00 per day, the task I performed at that job was to pick up potatoes that had been unearthed by a plow built specially for that purpose. There were, perhaps, eight other field hands. I believe they were migrant workers. I was supposed to keep up with the group.

When I arrived at the field, the potatoes grown there lay exposed in long rows. Large canvas sacks were given to us. They were fastened on a belt around our waists. These canvas sacks extended down between our legs to the ground, and as we walked forward, they dragged behind us with the mouth of the sack open. Then, stooped over, we would walk forward picking up the newly dug potatoes and toss them in a backwards motion into the mouth of the bag attached to our waist. When the bag was full (or, so heavy it couldn't be dragged forward) we would carry the sack to a wagon at the end of the row and dump the potatoes into that wagon. We would then return to the field and renew our potato picking, filling up the bag, carrying it when full to the wagon, and then return to the field. This job lasted until the entire potato crop had been harvested. I was tired but upon completing that job I had to resume work in the family garden. That was my first job as a farm laborer.

I was the only boy in our family. My father finally found employment, leaving me to do outside work at our Juniata home, while my sisters stayed inside cooking, sewing, doing laundry, and other household chores. Gardening at that time, involved spading after the ground thawed out. Then came raking and smoothing the soil. Thus prepared, planting of the seeds, cultivating the young plants, picking weeds and harvesting fell to me. At the end of the day and on the weekends, my Father exercised control over our garden. Keeping up with the weeds was always a daily charge so, during the spring, summer and fall, I was in the garden every day when it wasn't raining.

Farmers surrounding Juniata were affected by the War. Their older sons were inducted into a branch of the armed forces leaving their parents without a work force. When they could, farmers employed their own children, but that work force had to be supplemented by laborers to do farm work. In this way, these local farmers were the nearest employers around.

Going to a larger community to find work in stores or factories involved travel. Even had I wished to work in Hastings located just seven miles to the east of Juniata, I had no means to get to work even if the employer would have hired a 12-year-old boy. We had but one car and Father drove it to his work and back. So, I had no choice but to stay at home and work in the garden and care for domestic animals.

But, once again, my circumstances changed. One day in the summer of 1943, my father, having just returned from the Juniata grain elevator with chicken feed, surprised me by commanding me to get my clothes together. I was told to go to the grain elevator in Juniata and meet a farmer who was waiting there for me. He farmed just a few miles North of Juniata. I was to live with his family that summer helping him farm his land. The farmer would pay me $2.00 per day, room and board. In the fall, I would return to my home and go to school. Sadly, I said "goodbye" to Mother and my sisters and did as I was told. Now being 13 years old, I wasn't ready to live away from home, but I couldn't oppose my father, so I took up residence with the farm family.

It should not have surprised me to be forced to go to work for a local farmer at such a young age. Father and his brother had been farm laborers during their teen years. Doing farm work involved every kind of farming task involving plants and animals. The level of farm technology in 1943 enabled farmers to do many different functions with a tractor. Still there were jobs machines were unable to do. Corn picking, for example, was done by hand as was milking. Cleaning the chicken house and the stalls in the barns involved only manual labor. Tractors drew wagons, plows, mowers, binders, cultivators, combine thrashers, and harrows, but there were still many tasks, which had to be done by hand. Upon entering my employment, I already knew how to do many of the ordinary farming tasks. My employer- farmer taught me how to use the tractor and the various implements of farming. He warned me about safety issues, particularly the possibility of overturning the tractor while working on slopes. Soon, I was assigned to do ordinary field operations using the appropriate appliances.

The farmer had electric lines to his house and barn. So, we had light and power to use shop tools. This farmer had no cows to milk so labor on that farm was done mainly in the fields. Arising at 5:30 am, I would dress for work, go to the kitchen for breakfast and go outside to begin carrying out the days' assignment. The farmer might direct me to "plow the South 40" for example, and then would tell me how to get to that parcel. I learned to tell time by the position of the sun, and when I thought it was noon, I would head back to the farmhouse for dinner. An additional signal that noon arrived was the "Town Whistle". It was blown at noon from the Juniata Volunteer Firehouse and again at 5:00 p.m. If I was outside, from my position in the field, I could hear the whistle faintly, but still, the sun was my principle timepiece.

The noon meal was described as "dinner" while the evening meal was "supper". Our meals would ordinarily be taken at the house, but occasionally at midday, if the farmer and I were working together, the farmer's wife would bring water and sandwiches to the field. Refueling the tractor had to be done before returning to the field. I would finish work in the field to which I had been assigned and, then, return to the house. If it was still light, I would be assigned to another task. One evening the farmer gave me a 22 rifle and a box of bullets. He told me to go to a certain field and scout for rabbits who were eating his corn. I was to shoot these rabbits. I did as I was told. Creeping up a hill to a position overlooking a swale at the bottom, I saw an incredible number of jack-rabbits situated in a circle eating the vegetation there. It made me feel bad to kill these animals. After shooting a few rabbits, the rest of them hurried away from the spot where they had been eating. I didn't pursue any of them and left the bodies of those I'd killed where they had fallen.

But, ordinarily, at sundown, work stopped. Supper followed, and afterward, casual conversation took place. Whenever another farmer would drop by for a visit, there would be talk of weather, corn prices, and other agricultural topics. We retired very early and arose very early.

It was not uncommon for one farmer to "loan" his worker to another farmer for undertakings at that other farm. I was loaned to a brother of my principle employer during haying season. I was to mow alfalfa hay and rake it into windrows. After being allowed to dry in the field for several days, the alfalfa would be baled using a hay baler. Then the bales would be collected from the field and stored in the haymow of the barn. This was very hard work for the rectangular shaped bales had to be lifted onto a trailer and then a load was taken to the barn, where the bales had to be lifted off again and, using a block and tackle, they were hoisted up into a haymow door. From there the baled hay had to be stacked bale on top of bale. I was glad when haying season was over.

I lived with the borrowing farmer while carrying out the particular task for which I'd been loaned. Here again, housing was provided. The farmer and his wife arose at dawn. I would be awakened and take my place, at the breakfast table. This farmer had cows to milk twice each day: morning and evening. Having learned to milk cows at my family home, I needed no instruction. There was a difference between the two farms insofar as entertainment was concerned. The second farmer had a small radio in the milk barn. As we milked the cows, the radio would be playing in the background. The farmer liked a music station featuring Texas Mary. She was a live performer and sang such songs as: "I Had a Rooster," "Starving to Death on My Government Claim," and "The Little Old Sod Shanty on my Claim." These songs were unfamiliar to me. Later in my life, I was to learn them and sing them to my children.

The milk from the farmer's cows had to be run through a separator. This device divided the cream from the whole milk. The cream was stored in one container and the milk in another. Cylindrical cans having a five gallon capacity were filled, and when full, they were set out by the roadside: one can for milk and the other for cream. Following a regular schedule, a dairy truck would pick them up for delivery to the dairy. There, the milk would be pasteurized and bottled and the cream churned into butter. After milking, I would be assigned to other farming tasks. Shocking wheat, oats, and barley were July activities. Cultivating fields of corn was another.

The wheat field combine crews came through Nebraska with and harvested wheat for those farmers not owning combines. My second employer's wheat fields were combined by a traveling crew, and for the first time, I drove a truck filled with wheat into town and to the Farmer's Co-Op grain elevator in Juniata.    .

There were dangers on both farms. One of them involved storing alfalfa in the haymow before it was dry. While living with the second farmer and doing the haying, he failed to allow the necessary length of time to allow the alfalfa to cure. We stored the baled hay in the haymow. Within a few days, I noticed smoke coming from the barn. Investigation revealed the hay in the haymow was burning. "Spontaneous combustion" was the source of the fire. There were no firemen in the sense of standing firefighters ready to rush to a fire. Neighbors tried to put out the fire until the volunteer firemen from Juniata came with their pumping equipment. The fire damaged the barn and its contents to a great extent. My job became one of cleaning up the burned hay. The days flew by, and the agricultural season drew to a close. I looked forward to going home and returning to school.

I was away from my family from June until the end of August. Returning home from my job as a farm laborer, I renewed my place in the family. For the entire summer, I had been out of touch with my sisters and parents. No one asked about what my experience had been like. No one called or wrote, and my experience went unnoticed. Neither had I written any letters to my family or asked my sisters what they had been doing over the summer. Very uncomfortable emotions attended my return to home, school and village life. Was I wanted? I didn't know. My peers had not worked on a farm that summer. They had been idle or worked in their homes. It was good to be back among them nonetheless.

In 1944, the war was still on, and during that summer, I once again found myself employed for a different farmer living near Holstein, Nebraska. All of the kinds of work I performed the previous summer were repeated here. I was put to work milking a larger number of cows, cleaning barns, caring for livestock, and doing fieldwork. This farmer had no children of his own. He didn't know how to work a laborer, and I was assigned to work under intolerable conditions. He did not work alongside me. I was savagely criticized when the job didn't get done in the fashion imagined by this farmer. I despaired about what I felt amounted to abuse. I called my mother and asked her to come and take me away from an unpleasant situation. I was not to escape farm-work however. Friends of our family living on a farm near Red Cloud, Nebraska, needed a laborer. This farm was located about 30 miles away near the Republican River. Again, my parents directed me to that farm and work.

This farm had but one small tractor and a team of workhorses. I had to learn how to harness them, hitch them to an implement, and work in the fields. Working farm implements with horses was a new experience for me, but I learned and performed my assigned tasks to the satisfaction of the bachelor farmer. Once again, however, I was loaned out to another farmer, a brother to my initial employer. He, his wife, and daughter lived on a farm several miles away in Burr Oak, Kansas. Milking cows in the morning and evening, caring for the horses, and working in a large garden was the nature of my work at that farm.

From 1945 to 1949, I worked at other kinds of employment than farming. Brief construction work involved different employers on different projects. Many of these jobs were away from home, and I resided in the town nearest the project. All of these jobs were outside, labor intensive, and had poor working conditions. I continued to do farm work in between these local construction projects. Becoming ill or suffering broken bones would have interrupted my employment. Only after a full recovery would I have been allowed on the premises. There was no health insurance and no such thing as working hours, weekends, or holidays. There were rainy days, and then I had time to read. There was only the radio, newspaper, mail, and the telephone to provide contact with the outside world.

Today, the farm laborer has contact with the world through telephones and other applications using cyberspace. A mobile phone erases space and time. This is only a recent development. Farm laborers of the 1940s

161

through the next 20 years were "out of touch" with the social and economic world. A farm laborer was, for the most part, isolated. Living at any of the farm homes was for me a spectator experience. I was always an outsider. "Going to town" was not favored except for supplies and hauling grain to the elevator. The farmer's wife canned and preserved food. For those activities, she needed supplies, but none of her work involved the farm laborer. Religion was part of the farmer's daily life. Prayers over food were something in which I could participate, but I was not invited to attend church on Sunday nor the Wednesday night prayer meetings. "Not one of us" would be the most appropriate denomination of my social status.

"Going on vacation" never happened in the farmer's life. Chores had to be done day and night and absence from the farm for any extended time was not practical. While working on the farm, I lived and worked within the framework of the family's rhythms, customs, weather conditions, and crop maintenance requirements. I always looked forward to a resumption of school because that meant time not working. None of the farmers for whom I worked, smoked or drank alcohol. They didn't go to dances and "going out for dinner" was unheard of.

My time of being a farm laborer ended in 1949 when I graduated from high school. Looking back on my life as a farm laborer, I'm aware that times have changed for farmers. The War imposed restrictions on the farmer, which do not exist today. Hiring a boy from town to do a man's work is no longer likely. The understanding of how to raise a child has changed from that which existed in the '40s. Developmental criteria for different age groups became common knowledge in the 1950s, but prior to those new understandings, children were treated as if they were adults. The admonition to "act your age" directed towards children was society's way of coordinating age with adult behavior. Times were changing in farm families, however. One farmer, for whom I worked, complained that he had to send his son to camp. He berated the fact that "children these days were being spoiled!" "Going to camp" seemed attractive to me, but that wasn't going to ever happen. Being isolated on the farm and in a small village, I had no idea of manners, etiquette, or customs found in larger communities. Later, at college and in a larger urban setting, I was frequently found wanting in skills associated with urban life, dress, and fashion. Social proprieties were a huge area of improvisation for me.

Children's games, parties, recreation, and family travel to have new experiences were all absent from my childhood. I had no prior experience with this lifestyle. Museums, libraries, art studios, symphony halls, an operatic performances were unknown territories for me.

In response to the question: "Did you grow up on a farm?" the answer is: "Just about!" In response to the question, "Did you work when you were a child?" The answer is, "Yes, I worked hard and long." If you were to ask, "How did your childhood experience affect your life as an adult?" Well, the answer would have to be: "Profoundly!" But, that is another story.

*Rose :: Kim Justus*

# An Almost Tragedy

Ciera Simbro

There I sat, believing my day was going to end pretty well. It was about 2:40 in the afternoon, I only had one class that day, and my homework for it was long done. Still, something squirmed at the back of my mind, trying to remind me of something long lost among the heaps of Cadence's concert reminders, story ideas,  and daily to-do lists. The itching at my brain became too much for me to just sit and ponder any longer, I had to get up and do something. I walked to my small vanity, really it was just a corner of my work desk where I kept a mirror, hair accessories, and makeup, and began straightening my hair. It was then, while looking at my emerald green eyes and my long, chocolate brown hair that I remembered. My paper was due at 4:00! I looked up at the small round clock on the wall, 3:05. *Plenty of time* I thought to myself, moseying across the room to my small stack of important files. I began searching, only once reaching the bottom realizing it wasn't there. I searched again, still no sign of it. Then it came to me, I had left it at Cadence's dorm yesterday when I went over there before class. *Better go get it,* I thought, heading toward the door.

I locked the knob behind me without a second thought, and started walking toward Cadence's dorm, five floors down and all the way across the building. I got there quickly, my long legs carrying me steadily through the halls without a moment's hesitation. I grasped the knob and began to push even before turning. Locked. *No!* I thought sternly to myself. *This cannot be happening right now.* I checked my watch, the vibrant turquoise seeming even bolder against my pale skin. 3:20. At this point, I began to panic. It would take me at least 15 minutes to get to my professors office which only left me twenty minutes to get back to my dorm and print off a new paper.

I started running, nearly tripping over another student several times.

It didn't take long until I was back at my own dorm. I twisted the knob, only then remembering I had locked it. After checking my pockets and the ground around me several times, I remembered one devastating fact, I had left my keys on the hook right inside the door where I always put them after arriving home. I checked my watch again, 3:30. It was fifteen minutes until I absolutely had to leave. I began sprinting toward the RA's office with no time to waste.

I pounded on the door, grasping the shiny brass knob and throwing it open without a seconds hesitation.

"Ineedthekeytomydorm," I said, out of breath and panicked.

"What's that Amory?" the RA replied, a look of complete confusion crossing her face.

"I. Need. The. Key to. My dorm." I tried again, this time saying each word between breaths instead of trying to fit them all into one. She handed me the key. I made it to my dorm in record time, barely even at a complete stop before the key turned and the door was swinging open.

I ran to my computer, thank goodness I had left it running, the old thing took forever to turn on. My paper was easy enough to find, saved directly to my desktop. I quickly opened it and hit the print button.

"Come on, come on," I muttered to myself squirming around. "I don't have time for this, hurry up!" The printer had barely let my paper out of its firm grasp when I at once had it in my hand. I hastily put on my navy blue coat and grabbed my keys, and there I was sprinting through the mint green hallways once again.

I checked my watch, 3:50. Its small hands informed me, it was simply mocking me now. Fifteen minutes away from my destination and ten minutes to get there. I was still sprinting, my legs burning as an unseen fire licked at them from behind, my lungs struggling to keep up with the oxygen the rest of my body demanded. I couldn't slow down, this paper had to be turned in. A quick glance at my watch told me, I had been running for five minutes. *Faster* I thought to myself, pushing my long legs to their breaking point, three minutes left. Two. One. 4:00. I missed my deadline, but still I pushed on, hoping maybe if I made it there before he left, my professor would appreciate my effort enough not to drop my grade. It was 4:05 when I got to my professor's office. Noting that all the lights were down, I walked glumly to the door and noticed that, on it, there was a small note. *"Home sick today. Papers due 4:00 tomorrow. No exceptions."* I was saved.

# Meeting Ryan

Emily Smith

As I walked into the building full of strange kids I'd never met, I was immediately wary and judging. I figure it was going to be like everywhere else, and nobody got to know anybody, and newcomers weren't accepted. So what would be the difference here? I looked around, and there were kids playing basketball, piano, and others mingling in groups. I could pick out the nerds, jocks, and the normal, or so I thought.

He had been playing basketball when he almost killed me trying to get the ball, and no apology was offered of course. The game was Tips, which is highly unpredictable, I have almost caused WWIII playing that game. Anyway, he handled himself like he was walking on water and was Jesus himself. I was trash talking some of his friends, and he was annoyed already.

While I was standing there looking like the biggest white elephant ever, I was invited to play the extreme sport. Needless to say I blew it. But, that night this kid decides to grace me with his presence and not only that but he spoke to me.

"Where are you from?" He asked.

"Omaha," I said, hoping he wouldn't ask for my address and try and kill me. I'd have had to put a restraining order on him, and that whole business is messy. Well, we stood there awkwardly for a second when I got the brilliant Idea to ask him a unique question.

"Where are YOU from?" Genius, I know.

"Wausa... Is this your first year here?" Well, have you ever seen me here before? Seriously, where are your critical thinking skills?

"Yep," I said stupidly.

"What's your name?" He asked attempting to save this Titanically sinking conversation.

"Emily, what's yours?" I'm really good at repeating questions.

"Ryan," he said holding his hand out. I stupidly took his hand hoping he wouldn't try and put me in a headlock or anything. He took it as a gentleman would help a lady out of a carriage. Then, he took his other hand into a fist. "Oh no," I thought, except his middle and index fingers and placed his hand on top of mine. I wasn't sure if this was a normal greeting or not, so I stared at him unimpressed.

"It's a beetle on a rock," he said, a little sheepishly.

"Wow, you know I could have come up with a more creative first greeting than this."

"Well, you don't play nice do you?"

"Nope."

*What'dyousay? :: Kim Justus*

# It All Fell to Pieces

Gabby Sullivan

The day my life changed forever started very early, as Jack shook me awake.

"Come on, Milo!" he said, "We've got to get moving, if we want to see everything in three days."

I groggily rolled over to look at the alarm clock beside my motel room bed. I groaned when I saw the time.

"Seriously, Jack? Seven o'clock? I thought this was supposed to be a vacation!"

Jack shrugged and casually tossed me my duffle bag. "Bree's always a slow walker. I want to get to the Trade Center before 8:30. The school tours start at 9:00, and it'll be busy at the viewing area then."

As Jack woke up Bree, his eleven-year-old sister, I went into the cramped bathroom and changed into jeans and a t-shirt. I accidentally bumped my wallet off the tiny countertop and everything spilled out onto the floor.

"Dang it," I muttered as I picked up the money and pictures. When I shoved them back in, my eye caught a picture of Jack and me. My mind wandered.

The picture had been taken just last May when we graduated from high school. We were all decked out in our caps and gowns, and Bree was photo-bombing with a creepy stalker face in the background. Jack and I had always been best friends. He was like my brother. As a graduation present, our parents let us go to New York City for a couple of days, as long as we'd take Jack's sister along. This was our second day in NYC.

It was September 11, 2001.

The three of us got to the Trade Center at around 8:30. Jack was right. Bree was a slow walker. My dad was friends with a corporate official who worked in the North Tower, so we got special, un-guided access, although my dad's friend wasn't going to be there. He took the day off work to take his daughter to kindergarten.

"This place is amazing!" Bree shrieked. "It's so huge!" She was right; it was enormous! The towers loomed over us, bright sun glinting off the plate-glass windows. They were so tall; we had to crane our necks to see the top.

The lobby alone was bigger than my entire house back home, and it was filled with more people, it seemed, than our entire hometown. People in business suits shoved past us to get to the already crowded elevators.

"Maybe, we should take the stairs," Jack noted. Bree and I agreed, and we started climbing the metal stairs. We climbed for about half-an-hour before we really started to rethink our decision.

"How... many... floors... are there... again?" I panted.

"110," Jack replied breathlessly. He leaned heavily against the wall. Bree glanced at the plaque beside him. She groaned.

"We're only on the thirty-fourth floor! What time is it, Milo, anyway?" she asked.

Looking at my watch, I started to say "8:49," but then there was an explosion high above us. Fire and rubble rained past the window like confetti. We were silent for a moment.

"What just happened?" Bree exclaimed, panicking. We heard screams from high above us. Jack and I looked at each other, alarmed.

"I've got no idea," Jack said, "but we'd better get out of here." Then, the lights went out. I pulled out my penlight on my keychain and shone it on the others. "Fast," Jack added.

As we stumbled down the stairs, my mind was whirling. What the heck just happened up there? Was it a bomb? No, they had to have security for that. It couldn't have been a fire. Too much explo-

"Watch out!" Bree screamed, snapping me out of my thoughts. I screeched to a halt. Good thing, too, or else I would have been a flattened Milo-cake on the ground. A steel beam had fallen, blocking our immediate descent. The dust made my eyes water horribly. Through the blur, I saw a plaque by the door. It read "10."

"Let's go in there!" I coughed, pointing at the door. "There might be another stairwell on the other side." If there wasn't, I knew we were toast.

The tenth floor was worse than I expected. People ran about, talking into cell phones and trying to get out. Office cubicles were pushed out of the panicky people's way, sometimes onto other people. Screams and yells were everywhere. Through the dust and confusion, I could barely make out the outline of a door. Another stairwell!

"Over there!" I choked out. Bree coughed her approval. Jack wasn't looking at Bree, the stairwell, or me. I followed his gaze.

A woman was trapped under a pile of office cubicles. She wouldn't be able to get out by herself; that much I could see. The rubble landed right on her legs, pinning her to the ground. She screamed for help. I knew exactly what Jack was going to do. He always was the braver one.

"Jack," I grabbed his arm. "We don't have time. The tower isn't doing well." I could hear the steel structure creaking ominously.

My best friend looked at me, his face set. I knew then that nothing Bree or I could say would make him change his mind. "Milo, take Bree outside, and keep her safe. I'll try to meet you across the street at that café. People always want to leave their mark on the world. This is my chance. Now go!" He hugged Bree and me tightly; all of us knew this could be the last time we would see the other alive. Then, he shoved us towards the stairs and ran to the woman.

"Jack!" Bree cried. "No!" She tried to run over to him, to drag him back here, but I grabbed around her waist and hoisted her on my back. I almost let her go, but I knew Jack wouldn't come. The last image I had of my best friend was of him throwing rubble to the side to get to the trapped woman.

Bree sobbed the entire way down the steps. I tried to hold it together for her, but inside I was breaking down, too. Then, I saw the best thing I saw all day, the lobby.

Firefighters milled about in the lobby. Some of the floor to ceiling windows were shattered, and dust covered the floor. I ran outside, keeping my head down. I just wanted to get out of the tower.

Somehow, the outside was worse. Some people were running and yelling as they tried to leave the terrifying scene. Others just stood there, dumbfounded, trying to decide if it was a dream or reality. I could hear crashes, one after another, from people in the towers who decided it would be better to jump than to be burned alive in that inferno. Dust covered cars were abandoned on the side of the streets.

The towers were the worst of all. I could barely see the top of the towers, because of all the smoke. It was as if they weren't even there. I could hear awful screaming, and Bree jumped off my back.

"Thanks, Milo," she said so softly I wasn't sure if I heard her, "for saving me." She hugged me tightly. Suddenly, my phone started ringing.

I answered it, "Mom?"

"Milo!" her voice said frantically. "Are you all right? What about Jack and Bree? Their mom called me. She said Jack wasn't answering his phone."

"Bree and I are fine, but Jack stayed inside to help. I couldn't stop him," I shook my head to clear the recent memory. "What even happened up there?"

"We don't know exactly," she replied, "only that someone crashed a plane into each of the Twin Towers."

After that blow, I told Mom I loved her and hung up. I handed Bree the phone to call her parents, and we went into the café Jack said he'd meet us in and sat down in a booth. If he didn't answer his phone, who knew what happened up there?

I shook that dark thought out of my head. No, Jack was still alive. He had to be.

I suddenly heard a horrible creaking sound. The South Tower was collapsing!

"Everybody take cover!" I heard someone yell. We hid under the table in the cafe. Dust and debris flew past the windows in a dirty brown cloud. The South Tower was history in less than half a minute, along with all the souls inside.

The two of us climbed out from hiding and sat in shock on the floor. Then my feelings turned to anger. What was going on in the minds of the sickos who crashed the planes?

Bree lay her head on my shoulder and fell asleep within ten minutes of the collapse. Who could blame her? She just wanted to get out of the world. The kid had seen horrible things in the past hour. I called the rest of my family and my friends to let them know I was all right.

I still couldn't believe what happened. I kept thinking it was just a dream that I would wake up, Jack would sit here laughing with me, and the South Tower would be standing up over NYC. However, this couldn't be, because I hurt all over from getting jostled around in the stairs.

Out of nowhere, the large building fell to pieces. With a loud roar, the North Tower, the last place I would ever see my best friend, collapsed into a cloud of dust.

Bree sobbed, "Jack!" My throat closed up. I could hardly breathe. What if he didn't make it out?

When the dust settled, Bree and I went outside to see if we could find him. When I saw the rubble, I knew it would be a lost cause. The pile of concrete and steel lay everywhere, nearly 10 stories in places. I picked up something small and shiny at my feet. It was a dented gold ring that said 'Class of 2001.' Then I looked at the identical ring on my left hand.

"Jack's ring," I whispered. That was when I knew my best friend was gone.

*** 

They found Jack's crushed body a month after 9/11. When we held his funeral, everyone in our small hometown plus a few special people attended. All *five* of the survivors Jack saved came to pay their respects and to meet the family of the man who saved their lives. They told us their stories. One woman with a broken leg, the first person Jack rescued, told us how once Jack gotten the rubble off her legs, he carried her down ten flights, gently set her down beside a nurse, and ran back inside the tower. One man recalled how Jack coaxed him down from the ledge from which he was going to jump. A girl about Bree's age remembered that Jack pushed her out of the way of a falling chunk of concrete when she was in shock from seeing her own father's dead body on the ground. He was only stopped by the falling of the tower; when it all fell to pieces.

So, it turns out that my best friend is now a hero. There is a small memorial to Jack in our high school's garden, so all will remember him. I know I will.

# Pre-electrical Sky

Douglas Taylor

During "dubya-dubya two," my mother told me that because of the threat of enemy bombing, they had to use blackout curtains to prevent aircraft from seeing houses and communities from the air at night. Citizens were urged to not smoke outside at night because a lit match or cigarette could be seen from high above. Even the car headlights used deflective hoods that limited the light beams. I wonder how bright the stars were with the lack of atmospheric light from the towns and cities?

Imagine virtually no light pollution! What a glorious night sky it must have been. I wonder how many people took advantage of the situation and went outside at night during the war? It must have been like the pre-electricity sky. I imagine it must be like the sky experienced by the frontiersmen, the natives, the founding fathers, and the early sailors under that magic blanket, that heavenly navigational chart.

When I am camping in the mountains, far from the electrical glow of civilization, I look into the deep wonder and marvel at those ancient universal thoughts that humans have been sharing and surely inheriting through thousands of years. Witnessing that amazing spectacle, that humbling forever dream, that unimaginable space must be the foundation of our spirit.

Now that we know more than we did before the telescope and space travel, now that we know more about physics, space, time and light; it is even more unimaginable. It continues to be a living mystery and bewildering wonder. Perhaps, wonder is one of the qualities that distinguish human beings for other critters, the ability to wonder and dream, to question, to transpose ideas into abstractions such as poetry, writing and visual art, to express the inexpressible, to see into the dark.

# I Hated My Dad

Tom Tomasek

The Spanish Flu pandemic of 1918 killed an estimated 50 million to 100 million people world-wide. Over 500,000 died in the United States. It spread quickly around the world in three waves.

Most flu varieties target the very young and the very old. This variety was more menacing. It targeted the young and the healthy. Ages 20 to 35 were particularly susceptible. It struck quickly and fiercely. Death could occur within two to three days of the first symptom.

The Spanish Flu devastated my father's family. In 1920, he was the oldest of seven children. There were five girls and two boys, ages one through seven. There was one set of twin girls. My grandfather, a recent immigrant from Croatia, was a poor tenant farmer in southern Minnesota. His 27-year-old wife cared for the seven children, while he worked 80 hours per week to put food on the table. The Spanish flu came, and it was cruel to the young family. It took 4 of the 9 family members. The mother, the twins, and another daughter became victims of the invisible killer.

With no one to care for the surviving children, my grandfather had to make some difficult decisions. He learned of work opportunities in the meat packing industry. He packed up their scanty belongings and set out for Omaha, Nebraska.

He placed his children in Saint James orphanage in Omaha, where they lived for several years. My grandfather stayed in boarding houses, while he worked and saved to buy a home. The shock of losing a mother, 3 sisters, and being thrust into an orphanage at such an early age had a life-long effect on the children.

For most of my life, I hated my father. He had 7 kids, just as he had been 1 of 7. He was an alcoholic and a gambler, which made my mother a saint. My father worked hard, but he drank and gambled harder. My mother could not depend on a weekly income, as the neighborhood barkeeper and local bookie took their cut off the top each week. The family lived on what was left, and it wasn't much. There were times when nothing was left. I didn't know how poor we were until I was older. Medical and dental checkups were far and few between. I hated him even more as I grew up.

Divorce was not an option for my mother, both financially and morally. Most Catholic couples just stayed together whatever the circumstances. I had two older siblings and four younger ones. My mother's time was taken up by the small children. I was raised partly by school nuns and my friend's mothers. My hatred for my father grew.

In my late teens, I met my future wife's father. He was the exact opposite of my father. I have never met anyone more unselfish. He put his family, his spouse, and his church first. On a list of 10, he put himself number 11. He showed me how to be a father, but I continued to hate my own.

As I grew older and had children of my own, I began to consider my father's childhood or lack of it. Although he made conscious choices, circumstances had not smiled upon him. He did not have a father figure as God had given me in my teens.

My father died at age 72. One night his heart just stopped beating, after he had gone to sleep. A few years before his death, I began to visit my father regularly. He told me things about his childhood I had not known. Finally, I let the past go. Someday, I will see him again, and now I can say, "I love you, Dad."

> *"Like everyone else, I am going to die.*
> *But the words--the words live on for as long*
> *as there are readers to see them, audiences to hear*
> *them. It is immortality by proxy. It is not really*
> *a bad deal, all things considered."*
>
> - J. Michael Straczynski

# Of Squirrels and a Nut

David Waller

Back in 2004, my family moved up to Omaha from Missouri, and Mom was *not* very happy about it. In addition to leaving her friends and family behind, she also had to deal with the fact that Nebraska gets 5 times the average snowfall of a Missouri winter. In one week. Fortunately, Nebraska does have one thing going for it: it is prime squirrel-feeding country. Prior to the move, Mom never really got to interact with our furry round neighbors. Not for lack of trying, mind you. Mom wanted to give handouts to the bushy-tailed critters since the time she visited a friend's house and saw them do the same, stuffing their squirrels until they were practically circular.

Unfortunately, our house happened to be right behind a small forest. Perfect for nature watching, bad for feeding squirrels. The little fuzzballs were either too readily able to find food on their own to need a handout, or they weren't even aware there was food at our place. I assume that squirrels see the suburbs as we would see that downtown area with the broken down windows, graffiti-covered walls, and an overall seedy atmosphere that tells that you're just as likely to find valuables as get mugged at gunpoint (or get cornered by an angry/overly cheerful dog, as I suppose must be the equivalent situation for a squirrel). Either way, they weren't coming to *Mom*, so she had to let them be.

I guess I had the impression that very few people wanted to feed squirrels anyway. I remember seeing bird feeders at the local Lowe's while growing up, and the box always advertised how squirrel-proof the feeder was. That's a lie, by the way. According to Heritage Farms' website about 80 percent of bird feeders – the people, not the apparatuses – have problems with squirrels, who will not only steal the bird food but destroy the feeder in the process. And by feeder this time I meant the box with the bird seed, though if you saw the box-art you might be tempted to think otherwise. They always had a yellow circle with a dash over this squirrel that looked like it was ready to beat the tar out of your birds, and then come over and hand you a "whupping," too. Apparently they can jump 3 to 4 feet high and 10 to 12 feet away, so good luck getting away from those little monstrosities.

Despite their negative press from the bird folk, the squirrels of Omaha, like the people, are actually quite friendly. The squirrels here are the kind that are used to living in the danger zone and love to spend their Friday nights eating, leaping, running in front of cars, and I'm pretty sure drinking. Considering those first three items there must be some sort of squirrel frat out there.

Well, for one reason or another, these little guys were more than happy to take the food Mom offered them. She began to get regulars, and started handing out names along with the corn. There was Pudge – named so because the more we saw him the fatter he got – and then there was Pashmina, an irritable black squirrel named after our cat of the same temperament. Then came Twitchy, Pudge's eventual replacement Chub-Chub, and various unnamed squirrels of Theta Tau Epsilon. At first, feeding them was a bit difficult. For one, apparently the bird's got wind that, despite their negative ad campaigns, someone was trying to ruin the neighborhood by giving handouts to the riff-raff squirrels. Well, they couldn't have that, so the birds tried to eat the squirrel's food, to the point that Dad and Grandpa tried to reverse the usual situation and build bird-proof squirrel feeders. In addition to this, the squirrels were a bit wary of Mom. Whenever they suspected that someone was coming, they'd flatten themselves against the ground as camouflage. I suppose they figured this was brilliant, but the conversations tended to go something like this:

Squirrel: Oh drat! Someone's coming! I'd better hide.

Mom: Oh, hey squirrel.

Squirrel: What's that? I don't know who you're talking to. There's no squirrel here.

Mom: Yes there is, I can see you right there.

Squirrel: No you can't! I'm flattening myself out so my brown fur blends right in with this bright yellow corn.

Mom: It'd probably help if you'd stop talking.

Well, at this point the squirrel would get embarrassed and slink on home in true spy fashion. But time and the occasional treats won them over, and the squirrels would not only stop running when Mom came to feed them, they'd actually come up to the door and wait for her to arrive. Mom was so proud that she had actually tamed these little fellows, and I had to admit I was impressed. This is assuming Mom had trained the squirrels and not the other way around, though both of us had to wonder.

Anyway, Mom was a very good caretaker to her furry friends. One winter in particular she really showed her dedication. Pudge, the most trusting, most friendly, and most well-fed of our squirrels was coming down with a bad case of mange. According to Purdue, this is often caused by mites and leads to hair loss and dry, darkened, thick skin (hair loss can be caused by fungal infections too, by the way). Mom called some wildlife experts and was given some medication she had to apply to walnuts and feed to Pudge (this course of treatment matched descriptions I would later find on SquirrelNutrition.com). Though Purdue insists that one shouldn't bother treating adult squirrels as their nests are probably infected and will lead to relapses, my mother's general animal mojo and literal ability to get a wild animal to eat out of her hand seemed to win the day, and Pudge was back with a full, luxurious coat in no time.

There are times I have to wonder about Mom though. Until recently one of the houses in our neighborhood had lodged a walnut tree, and Mom would sneak over and nab nuts from the yard. The neighbors didn't mind, thankfully, and said she could take *all* the nuts if she wanted. In fact they practically begged her to do it. Thank goodness for that. I read a story online a while back (on gawker.com if you're interested – try a Google search) where a woman was arrested on two accounts of trespassing for sneaking into her neighbors' yard to feed the squirrels. I had to laugh and wonder if Mom was the kind of person who'd get caught pulling a stunt like that. Then the evidence presented itself.

Eventually Mom found that not *everyone* was so accommodating of her habit. As she picked more and more nuts, one whizzed by her head, accompanied by an angry chattering sound. She looked up and the following scene ensued:

Squirrel: Hey you @#$% human! Get the @#$% off my lawn! (cocks a nut like a shotgun)

Mom: (staring in terror at the squirrel)

Squirrel: You heard me, get! Don't make me grab a stick and chase you outta here, 'cause I will!

Mom: (makes a run for it)

Squirrel: And stay out!

Well, Mother Nature apparently did not appreciate the squirrel's rudeness, as a storm hit Omaha hard and knocked over the walnut tree, leaving Mom without her supply of free treats. Shortly after that, we found that the miffed-off squirrel had taken up residence in our yard. We named him White-Tail.

I'm sure the squirrels appreciated Mom's efforts. After all, winter can really suck out here. VisitOmaha.com gives us temperatures in the 12 to 38 degree range on average in the winter months, though I have to wonder if their estimates aren't a little high. Either way, it sucks not to have a real house, so any method of keeping that body fat up has to help. Then again, it sucks even if you do have a house. Mom tends to have a harder time in winter, being an avid lover of plant and animal life alike. One particularly bad season she scribbled "I hate winter!" in marker all over our refrigerator. I have to wonder if this doesn't have something to do with the desire to feed squirrels – some need to have someone out there, a companion who understands the way she feels, and who will always be there when she looks out the window. Or maybe she's just nuts.

*Karleen Gebhardt :: Ed Vogel*

179

# Ha! Me Stay Quiet?

### Elaine Frain Wells

It's not easy to organize a book that is supposed to summarize one's life, especially a life as rich and full as mine has already been. My memory bank is like Fibber McGee's closet, stuffed so full of experiences that I can barely close the door, much less figure out how to create order from the chaos.

Should I simply begin at the beginning and proceed chronologically from my birth in a charity hospital, through school days and mundane jobs, to my beautiful life with the man of my dreams and his tragic death, finally leaving the reader hanging on the cliff of anticipation about what will happen in the last third of the story? Or should I divide the unruly mess into neat sections, such as "My Love-Love Relationship with School," "Summer Jobs All over the Place," "Real Jobs I Loved and Hated," "The Men in My Life," "Travel: Where in the World is Elaine Frain Wells?" "Transportation: From Boeing 747 to Camel Cart, and Life as a Rollercoaster?" Lots of people probably admit how hard it is to organize their own closet, how they keep putting it off until the space is so cluttered that they can't find anything. Well, I've been thinking of writing this book for years, and several strangers and friends encouraged me to put my pen to paper, but I was stymied by the overwhelming task of rereading all my journals and deciding what to put in and what to leave out.

Then in 2011, *"The Year of Paring Down,"* it occurred to me that I could finally write this book if I would list only the memories that stuck out in my mind, and instead of researching the details for accuracy, just write what I recall. "Eureka, I found it." So, I made the list, but then misplaced it before I had even begun to write. How appropriate in Fibber McGee's closet, don't you agree?

Recently, almost by coincidence, I met Imran Ahmad, whose autobiography, *The Perfect Gentleman: A Muslim Boy Meets the West* made Oprah's list of "must-read books." He explained how he followed the same procedure that I had in mind; he started with his earliest recollections and wrote about whatever he recalled up to the present. He testified that his life story poured out onto the pages easily and quickly, and he now travels the world, meeting fascinating people who love his book and him. He affirmed my process and got exactly the results I wanted!

The final push I needed came from 2012 *Fine Lines* Summer Camp for Creative Writers. Early in the spring, I signed up and waited eagerly for the first day of camp, knowing that what I needed most was feedback on my writing but feared that other writers (real writers, individuals with degrees in literature and creative writing, published authors) would not like my ideas or my style. My plan to avoid criticism and outright ridicule was to stay quiet and listen to the suggestions other writers received from the group. Ha! Me stay quiet? What was I thinking? After the first day at camp, I read a poem that practically popped out of me fully clad in metaphors, and the group liked it. The next day, I read them the first page of the book, and they made complimentary comments. That's all I needed to start writing in earnest.

***

(In the popular radio show, *Fibber McGee and Mollie*, which aired from 1935 to 1959, Fibber's closet was crammed with so much stuff that some of it would fall out whenever he opened the door.)

# Conquering My Biggest Fear
## Kaitlyn White

It was the first week of June, and for being so early in the summer, it was hot and humid. Life had been tough the past week, and my family had endured a life altering experience. It felt as if my world had done a complete 180, and I was not sure how I would ever cope with it. At the church garage sale that Saturday, everyone was trying to be comforting, nice, and gentle. My favorite saying for that week was, "Everything will be okay. It will all work out." How was everything going to be okay? How could God do this to my family and to me? What did I do to deserve this? Everyone around me was holding up so well, and I felt that at any second the dam was going to break loose and I would lose it. This is when an old family friend brought up the aspect of summer camp. The thought had never even come across my mind, and the second he said it, I shot it down. I am not the girl who "hates" her parents and can't wait to leave for college. I love spending time with my parents, and I fear the time when I don't get to see them every day. This is my biggest fear.

So here I am, this girl who is broken and devastated, and yet, they want me to leave my family for a week. After I let the thought sink in, I considered it. I didn't want to go home for the time being, and I knew I needed to heal, but how could I leave my parents? After a lot of thinking and debating, I realized I had to go. I had to go to conquer my fear and heal. So I signed up for what would be the most amazing experience of my life.

That Sunday at four o'clock, I headed to Calvin Crest, a church camp in Fremont, to spend a week without any outside connections. No phone, no computer, no car, no electricity, no air conditioning, and no family. I was lucky enough that Alice and Don Johnson ran the camp and I had my best friends Kaci, Kellon, Wayne, Taylor, and Carly to be there for me.

That Sunday after church, Don came up to me and asked, "You ready for the best week of your summer?"

I replied, "This will hardly be the best week of my summer." Little did I know how very wrong I was.

At home, we had a long list of things to pack, and we had to go to the store to buy some things we didn't have. I had to accomplish this in only three hours so I could make it to camp on time. After packing all the appropriate clothing and hygiene products, we ran to the store to pick up a lantern, sleeping bag, and lots of bug spray. Now that we were done packing and shopping, the time had come to leave. On the 45 minute drive over, I had a million thoughts racing through my head. What if something happens while I'm gone? How can I not see my parents every day? What if I hate camp? If you couldn't tell, I have horrible anxiety, and it was worse than ever on this short drive.

Once we were there, it only got worse. My pulse was well over the normal 100 bpm, and I was so frightened. Once there, we went in the main lodge, signed in, and took care of all the paperwork. Outside by the tractor that would take us to our campsite, I saw all of the kids for ranch camp. They were all there smiling and talking and getting to know one another, and I was attached to my mother.

Looking back on this moment, I was such a baby. I feel like I was so dramatic, yet I know, in that moment, this was my biggest fear.

As we packed my hundred bags onto the trailer, it was becoming so real. As the car was unpacked and the engine of the tractor started to rumble, we said our goodbyes. I hugged my mom as tears threatened both of our eyes. I told her how much I loved her.

She replied by saying, "You just have fun, and don't worry about us. We love you so much! Just enjoy every minute."

With that, she got in her car, and I got on the trailer. I watched, as her car drove down the road and out of sight. It was then that I realized there was no turning back. I sat with Kaci on my right side and Kellon on my left. At the camp, we got situated and unpacked. It was not what I expected it to be. When I walked in the door of the cabin, I could see our cabin was made up of three bunk beds: one on the left, one on the right, and one straight ahead. I got the bunk on the bottom to the right. The bath house had no lights or doors on the stalls, and the water that came out of the showers smelled like rotten eggs. Outside of all the buildings though, there was nothing but trees and fresh air! It was so calming, just what I needed.

At ranch camp, we spent the morning riding and grooming horses. That in itself was a therapy session for me, and I loved it. After we got done with the horses, we went back to camp and ate lunch and then had F.O.B, which stands for flat on back or better yet, naptime. After naptime, we would do a craft and then have a little Bible service. Next came game time. I was introduced to my all time favorite game, Gaga ball. It is like dodge-ball, but more fun. After games, we ate dinner and had a bonfire, which was a therapy session. Everyone who was there went through something different, and we were all there to support each other; we bonded. With these therapy sessions, I started to heal and mend my relationship with God! Within a short week, I overcame my biggest fear; I made new friends, and I started the healing process.

At the end of the week, my mom came and picked me up! I had an amazing week, but I was so happy to see her.

She asked, "Did you have a good time?"

I replied, "Yes," knowing that I couldn't possibly tell her about my whole week in that time. There is no way to describe the joy and peace you feel at ranch camp. Only those who have been there know how difficult it is to describe.

After a lot of goodbyes to new friends, I headed home. I knew it was not going to be easy to face reality and maybe all this week did was allow me to push my pain to the side, but somehow I felt more at ease and that I could do anything. I knew that with my family and friends, and more importantly God, I could overcome any obstacle.

> *"A great deal of talent is lost to the world for want of a little courage."*
>
> - Sidney Smith

# I Wish to Be Happy

Noni Williams

In the future, I wish to be happy. Every time I start to ask myself what is it that I want to do when I grow up, I get stuck. I started out wanting to be a marine biologist, but my mother reminded me that not only did I not seem to like large bodies of water, but that I also was not that fond of animals. My next goal was to be a lawyer, and the unavoidable fact of about a decade's worth of post-secondary education tainted that idea quite thoroughly. After that came a string of technology related professions until I finally settled on civil engineering.

After going to countless engineering presentation at the Peter Kiewit Institute, and attending many science and technology related summer camps, I realized I liked civil engineering. I would not say that it is my passion, but it certainly holds my interest. I have come up with numerous ideas and experiments that could potentially better our world and I would like to put them to use. Engineers Without Borders piques my interest the most. The ability to do for others that want the help, but do not have to means to better themselves on their own has always been a source of pride for me. Compared to the rest of the world, we are the minority. Those of us that eat every day and have had a chance to go to school, we are the minority, which means the majority is in need. I want to be able to provide that for others.

This past summer, I realized that I hated civil engineering. I just could not see myself being an engineer for the rest of my life. So I changed my major to Mathematics, and  I am almost finished with that. But I just cannot decide what it is that I can see myself doing for the rest of my life. I could be a teacher. I could be a housewife. I could be a journalist, analyst, even an actuary.

One of the few things that I see myself doing until the day I die is writing. I have been writing poetry (and winning contests with that poetry) since I was nine years old. Ten years later, I still write poetry and have expanded my interests into song writing and short essays. I have always seen myself as a writer. My vision, even while currently fixated on my goal of attaining a degree in math, will remain on writing. It is my life's passion

185

and I will pursue it.

Writing is my passion, but I just want to be happy.

*Painted Child :: Kim Justus*

# The Best Gift

Emily Woods

Her name was Ms. Rose. She is the reason I fell in love with English during high school. I had always been a straight-A student, and I always liked English. She made her class fun and exciting. My love for the subject grew as my respect for her increased. Ms. Rose did not mind my in class questions. She took her time to make sure that everyone understood the subject. The questions I asked challenged her, and she was grateful to have a student so engaged and driven to learn. Her specialty was English, and she knew it forward and backward. I thought of new ways to diagram sentences and challenge exceptions to English rules. Often she would say to me, "I do not know the answer to your question, but I will look it up tonight, and let you know tomorrow." She never forgot.

We had a close personal relationship as well. I worked for her in the library, and also on her other "baby," the school newspaper. She taught my drama class. Every Friday morning she would bring cinnamon rolls for her workers. We all appreciated that weekly treat, but few of the students wished, as I did, that they could give something back to show equal gratitude. I truly appreciated the knowledge she imparted to us on a daily basis. Her class was tough. All the seniors would lament and warn the underclassmen about the term paper, the memorization, the senior class play, which she directed, and a few other class assignments that were difficult. They were right, that term paper was difficult. She kindly demanded perfection during rehearsals for the play. I have locked into memory so many prepositions and tenses of words, I am surprised that anything else fits in.

Ms. Rose believed that she was doing her job well when she was being tough on us. She told us that she was preparing us for college. I regret that I did not test her theory the fall after graduation. I have found, however, the knowledge that found its was into my memory has not left. It may be dusty and rusty, but it is still there, and at my disposal. That is, by far, the best gift she could have ever given me.

## CAMPER FEEDBACK

"*Fine Lines* is not only something with which to cozy up in front of a roaring fire, but it is also a way to explore the world through the eyes of other authors and to discover one's own voice as a writer. I enjoy reading poems by writers of all ages, and it reminds me of who I am, who I was, and who I aspire to become. It is important to encourage writing at all ages and stages of life. It is especially important to encourage writing at a young age, when it is easy to become discouraged. *Fine Lines* is unique in the aspect that it publishes work by authors and artists of all ages and backgrounds and is an enjoyable way to delve into the literary world."

-Anne James, pursuing a PhD in biology at Creighton University

> *"The greatest good you can do for another is not just share your riches, but to reveal to him his own."*
>
> - Benjamin Disraeli

# The Superior Patience Man

Ali Mohammed

I am the superior patience man.
I am the bringer of burgers.
I will walk with you to and fro.
My days are for anyone to keep, but especially you.
Waiting outside the bathroom door is exhilarating.
Missing you after work crushes my soul,
But slowly,
For I am the superior patience man.

If you hold me, I will hold you back.
I will even hold you when you don't.
If you strike me down, I will come right back.
You can strike me down again.
If you hurt me, I will stand so still.
Only my tears shall move.

I am the superior patience man.
My skin cannot be closed.
I will paint your toenails regardless.
Massaging your back should not make me as happy as it does.
It's always nice to see you smile.
It's even nicer to hear you laugh.
Even if it takes all day, I'll get my chance to tickle you,
For I am the superior patience man.

# Dawning

Syndey Anderson


From the snow-covered blankets
To the hot summer nights
The changes just like that
Not knowing when it's right
The deer in the spring
And the leaves in the fall
It's a new day that's dawning
To care for it all
The flowers
To the crops
With the corn stalks
To plan on growing tall
The sunrise in the east
And the sunset in the west
The pink in the clouds
White fluffy pillows
Angelic beds
Horses in the hot summer sun
The cattle in the water
June bugs to call
Into the night to spread their song
Of joy and happiness
The stars in the sky
Flying into another galaxy
Into another world

# Affirmation

Gladys Naomi Arnold

The change in seasons is a time
that makes us pause

to search for meaning in our lives.
The natural laws

proclaim that spring can give the answer . . .
An affirmative right

to know all things show inclination
toward the light.

Response

The strong March winds
Swept broken branches
Into the fires of spring,
Clearing the way
For the April greenings
That gentle showers bring.

There comes a night when the velvet darkness
Knows a sudden need . . .
The warm wind answers
And comes to whisper
A call to the sprouting seed.

# My Daydream

Mary Bannister

Easy-going rays of sunshine peek through my window
And invite me out to play.
I try not to surrender to this seductive enticement,
But then an impulsive gesture latches on
As a quick glimpse suspends my thoughts.

Seeing the gentle breeze of the trees is too much for me to handle,
And I easily and naturally slide into my splendid daydream.
All semblance of my previous reality has vanished.
An afternoon passage has allowed me to enter once more,
And like Alice in Wonderland, I have crossed the threshold
into my secret place.
Everything is just as I left it.

My gardens greet me with their pungent fragrances of lavender and chives.
The song of birds welcomes me to my reverie.
The fresh air tingles my cheeks,
And the radiant sun, like cupid's arrow, aims for my heart.

But suddenly I sense a presence-something new.
The brilliance of this musing is heightened by a whisper,
And I see you there.
The certainty of this euphoria
Entirely replaces the reality of what was left behind.
And the daydream has become even better than before.

# A Student Speaks of Mountains

Makayla Bell

I've known mountains,
I've known mountains as steep as the heavens
and older then the first breath.

I have witnessed mountains so majestic,
tops covered with snow like a precious treasure
is hidden below.

My dreams have grown steep like the mountains!

I drank from the fountains of life's possibilities.
I have dreamt of drinking from the Nile
when you couldn't see life for miles.

My life is built in the midwestern plains,
and I am peaceful as I sleep.
Unlike uprooted soil my soul runs deep.
I have looked into and studied the Egyptian
pyramids and admired the multi-toned leadership there,

I have heard the singing of the choir where my grandmother lived,
in old Arkansas when the sun was bright,
and I've seen the notes rise from their
voices and caress the pain and hurt.

I've known mountains...
Wise and sturdy mountains,

My dreams have grown steep like the mountains!

*London Eye :: David Martin*

# Imagine

Larissa Boyd

Escape this world,
Escape the sorrow,
Escape my pain.

I have an Escape,
I have another world,
My world, My Escape.

My Escape is peaceful,
No Sorrow or Pain,
My imagination.

My world is not real,
My Escape is fake,
I can only Imagine.

# Early Mourning

Jackie Byers

oven clock blinks 6:05
distant trees showing breeze
I blink at sun pouring in patio door – screen ajar
on another screen, a head informs me: sixty-
three degrees
sipping hazelnut coffee, I think about sliding
open the door
to step into more of morning.

swift shadow catches my eye, vanishes quickly –
hawk hunting breakfast
startled dove intent on safety escapes hawk
but not glass door
feathers and hollow bones settle softly
on the deck
dove had no sense of imminent demise
did it seek door as exit?
stunned, I hope for dove heaven

screened head still talking:
"June 12, 2012 is the anniversary of . . .
so today is that day
an anniversary I no longer celebrate
I remember two doves on a cake to honor a union
dead as dove on deck

what cost, escape from predator?

# Cinco de Mayo

David Catalan

The Fifth of May is an all-American holiday
Borrowed from Mexican history
The defeat of a French army at Puebla in 1862
Crossing the border into California
During the American Civil War
Gaining cross-country popularity
Fueled by the 40s Chicano movement
Americans like to say *Cinco de Mayo*
Foreign, yet familiar imagery
Adding a touch of *gringo* sophistication
Americans want to be connected
Connected to their family
Connected to their neighborhood
Connected to church and community
Beyond this Hierarchy of Needs
Then to a global connection
Demonstrating worldly knowledge
In prideful celebrations of alien cultures

St. Patrick's Day parades
Oktoberfest beer tents
Chinese New Year fireworks displays
Santa Lucia saintly processions
Juneteenth's African roots
Cinco de Mayo today is a community festival
Smiling mayors and area politicians
Exhibiting their parade marching skills
Tiara-topped queens riding in convertibles
Fundraising activities by nonprofits
Another American-born economic driver
Tortilla tossing contests for kids
Taco and beer vendors
Adults of all ethnic ancestry
Savoring the most popular tequila drink in America
With a personal sense of exotic discovery
The *Margarita* in salt-rimmed glasses
Just another American concoction
Most likely a re-mixed Texas *Daisy*
*Cinco de Mayo* is a call to celebrate
Heritage, diversity, and culture for some
Tolerance and hesitant acceptance for others
While the Mexican backdrop fades to gray
Overpowered by a hunger for American Manifest Destiny

# Moving Rocks

Ardiss Cederholm

When I see a field of newly plowed black dirt
it reminds me of growing up on the farm
when in the spring of the year, our dad would
have us picking up rocks, throwing them on the
flat bed trailer, so many that it made me wonder
wonder where they came from,
why they kept coming
like weeds in our yard, if not controlled

not controlled like my thoughts
of the father who labored long hours
to provide for his family and
who taught me right from wrong
thoughts of the guilt I felt
of not being there with him
as often as I should
even near the end.

# Content

Neil Chaparro

no one calls my
phone anymore but
i'm not upset

moments of solitude were
hard to come by for
me in the past

it seems every breath i
take, the less depressed
i am

racing thoughts used to
define my brain, even in
sleep my brain wouldn't
slow down

vast amounts of sedatives
artificially eased my
nerves to the point of
addiction

content is a word i
rarely use

i am in love with the
current life i live

no longer frowning; this
makes my facial muscles
happy

looking forward to the future,
this is so foreign to me

socializing, no longer hiding
behind books, this is
something i now
embrace

i am a
walking
miracle

though i've destroyed millions
upon millions of brain cells,
my hard-drive is not yet
garbage

it's been over a year since
i've put my pen to paper
but this simple act
cleanses me,
pleases me,
makes me
smile

and today, as the rain
pours from the clouds,
a real smile and felt
emotions will
surely
suffice

# Not a Clown

Katie Davison


Why so much makeup?
Why so much hairspray?
Be yourself.
Everyone else is taken.
Be yourself.
Don't look like a clown!
Look like a girl.
A human!
Don't be a show!
Be yourself!
The perfect human you are.
Makeup and hairspray don't make you perfect.
You are perfect.
Just the way you are.
So be a girl,
the perfect human you are.
Not a clown!

# Highway 29

Randy DeVillez

Surrounded by dead flowers,
the dirty white teddy bear
affixed to the guard rail
appears crucified, horribly
out of place, more-deserving
the welcoming fingers of a child
beneath clean, warm comforters.

Like so many other monuments
along this road, it is a visual
reminder of life's uncertainty,
death's unpredictability, the
grief, emptiness, tragedy
for those left behind to wonder:
how did it happen,
why to him or her or them,
why now... here...
the eternal never-answered
questions. So we place bears,
flowers, wooden crosses roadside
where loved ones died, to say
you are missed, not forgotten.

As we drive by, if we dare see,
think, they are monuments, also,
to our mortality, a reminder we
are all driving on life's journey
toward our destinations, never
certain what lies beyond the curve.

# Empty Meadow

Lorraine Duggin

The empty lot next to Alice's house slopes toward the street,
wrapped in tall green grass where once red, ripe tomatoes grew.

Potatoes, cucumbers, green peppers, zucchini, beans, Brussels sprouts,
onions, beets, stalks of yellow corn—her garden flourished every
summer since I've known her, followed by flurries of canning activity.

"Keep dancing," she told me yesterday when I brought her home.
"Keep doing whatever you're doing. Don't get like me."
I lift her metal walker up the flight of three short
stairs to her front door, holding onto her arm with my other hand.

At 88 she's a miracle, a marvel, still hosting book club, chairing
a church committee, writing poetry, reading the latest biographies,
taking a short story class, playing the piano. All of us want
to be like Alice when we get old. What does she mean,
"Don't get like me."?

But this year, there is no garden. She doesn't mention it,
and neither do I, the huge lot beside the house
a wide meadow of ripe green grass wrapping the slope
where tomatoes always grew.

*Bench and Stream :: Mardra Sikora*

# Flying

Grace Erixon

I close my eyes
And spread out my wings
Desperate to be free
Of the dark, lonely sadness inside of me.

I break down my walls
Brick by brick
And no longer confined
Let go of everything and cry

I want to stay here
But must return
To take on everything I fake
To keep my deepest secret, so I awake

# My Friend

Tony Gebhardt


We united with immediate friendship,
in the town marked Mile High.
The tale I wish to wag and tell,
embarks a voyage until the day I die.

Both He and I so very young for sure,
both stuffed in baggage, feeling spirits low.
At this landing ground we were,
where big jets plane over, to and fro'.
With end's plane landing on truth,
most friends don't touch the sun either.

Returning from a parent's home I did,
whether grand or step it did not matter.
'Cause all was real.... the kitty held the riches.
I never knew one day I'd say one trip I took,
had bourne my heart so full of gold.

My buddy was also robbed of comfort,
since he too was a very young age.
So young in fact, it wasn't fair.
My hand held friend whom I did tend,
was apt to catch a deal of cards.
We didn't know how it would end.

I named him Victor, with eyes so trusting.
His keen eyes so full of hope and warmth,
piercing hope as I did, already knowing victory.
Our introduction likened a stricken match.

Homeward bound to one of many homes,
we left days' prior sorrow's past.
Knowing light was soon ahead,
another tunnel's track lay below,

six feet beating at a time.
The clickety increments paced our lives to last.

There we were at the place I lived.
I showed him around for quite a little while,
where I dined and the places I crashed.
We got used to this daily style.

A year now elapsed just moments ago,
we tossed the ol' ball around all through the day,
fending off this distant foe's laughing voice,
"you have to go, be on your way."

We bid farewell to the Rockies that day,
kissing every aspen and boulder goodbye.
We had a respect that could only have come,
from running and playing on mountains so high.

So packed up we did, locking this and that,
we destined new things, so we began to chat.
"What will it be like?" was the look he gave to me.
"I'm not sure" I said, "but soon we will see."

We bounced around on top of all our stuff,
feeling the dry Mojave' heat.
Looking back to the east we both agreed,
a mountain's cool is hard to beat.

We pulled up to the front of our new house,
in front of a big boulevard.
If that wasn't enough there was the 405,
right next to our home, next to our yard.

Without thinking much
about the light on the track,
I grabbed my friend's leg,
and we walked around back.

Regardless of the nice big pool,
we both agreed there was too much commotion.
That day was nice and now we lived close,
only three miles away, so went to the ocean.

For many days the ocean front ebbed,
at our always smiling faces.
For the water healed our wounds,
like the tall snowy pines in mile high places.

As we stood with the forest it quenched our thirst,
we tasted its icicles so purely sweet.
We finally agreed the sea was good,
and by the way, just down our street.

We swam and played,
for another year or so.
With such heart stopping notice,
where did he go?

We didn't get enough time together,
as we had so much to do.
He kept me warm on many nights' chill,
I kid you not, this friend was true.

There he lay, forever fast asleep,
on Artesia Boulevard.
Cars honked and swerved as they drove by,
when I carried him back inside our yard.

# How My Family Joined the Circus

Daphne Goetzinger


I'm going on a vacation
To Nashville, Tennessee
To see the representation
Of the circus with my family.

We're riding on a plane
On the way to the show
We started to play a game
That no one seemed to know.

We finally got to the hotel
I put away our bags.
Upon the bed I fell

When I woke up
Everyone was getting ready to go
I raised my head a bit, my brother said "sup"
My mother then said it was time for the show

We got to the festival
The man at the ticket booth said "$9.20"
I was excited because it would be fun, like a carnival
But then my father realized he forgot his money

A sign read "Here in Tennessee
The circus is always free
To the members of the circus."

To my surprise
My father said excitedly
"I'd like to join the circus
Me and my family"

We walked into the room
Where the acrobats got dressed
I heard a loud boom
A man said he hoped I wasn't stressed

I put on a clown costume
I jumped out of the doors and oh the fumes
(It smelled like sweat and popcorn)!

After the show we got into a car
At the end of the train.
It was next to the tiger's part
We had early fame

This is how my family joined the circus!

*2013 USA Flag Bench :: Ed Vogel*

# Silence of the Brain

Barb Greer

My thoughts have escaped to the bottomless abyss.
Perhaps they went over the fiscal cliff,
When I wasn't looking.

Finding the name of an old actor or actress,
or lyrics of an old song, but it
Surfaces, approximately twenty minutes after first trying.

It's as if it is buried within a knowledge bank,
And must travel through a search and retrieval process
To find it, on some brain disc or flash drive.

It is difficult to say or at least unpredictable,
The amount of trivia that has already been dumped, never to be revived,
or how much may somehow arrive at the most unusual time.

Over seventy years of experiences, over the cliff, into the abyss,
"Clinging" to the crags of memory by my fingertips,
"Struggling" with one toe in a crack trying to keep a foothold.

But Oh! The experiences I've had,
The fun, the friends, the faces I've seen, the places I've been.
The memories are there, fugitives in the silence,
Escaping to recollection and relish when they surface at
The most surprising time.

*First Presbyterian Church, Madison, NE :: Kristy Stark Knapp*

# Purple

Sarah Guyer

Irises, tall and proud
Reach up the fencepost
Safety out-voted
By curiosity,
Trying to see
How high they can go,
Flowers blooming,
Smells wafting,
Purple all around.
Bees buzzing,
Standing out
Against the color,
The outstanding color,
Butterfly fluttering,
Leaves green
Soaking sunlight
Making food,
To feed the plant,
To purify the color,
The color purple.

# Scaled Impressions of the Titanic

Debra L. Hall


"All aboard and in your places!"

Crystal clear propriety
Acquaintance through camaraderie

Words spoken…
precise and plush

A quick response in broken English
Pristine ballrooms and champagne

Memories linger full of pain
Romance set in diamond brooches

Arranged for marriage hope approaches
Charming etiquette thee elite

Borrowed shoes for little feet
Paltry promises quickly spoken
Vows uttered…
never broken

A gentle waltz about the floor
Foot stomping
hand clapping
give me more

Silks and satins
Homespun lace
Beauty
Radiance

A comely face
You may bow and kiss my hand

Heads held high
they take a stand

Elegance befits aristocracy
In life or death...
a place for me!

*2013 Claire's Bench :: Ed Vogel*

# Two Little Bunnies

Kathie Haskins

Two little bunnies chasing each other,
Through the garden, darting in and out.
One running through rows of Marigolds,
The other scampering behind the Irises.
Back and forth, weaving in and out of the
Lilies and tomato plants.
Their game of Hide and Seek complete,
The two tiny bunnies settle in for breakfast,
Nibbling on pepper plants and a bright
orange Marigold.

Meanwhile ...

Two large dogs with retrieval instincts,
Sitting on the gated deck,
Standing perfectly still, ears perked,
Heads bobbing in unison,
Watching the scene before them,
Wishing ... waiting ... exhibiting
incredible patience.

Meanwhile ...

One medium sized mom,
Sipping her coffee, taking it all in,
Smiling ... grinning ...
Her heart overflowing with joy.

# Advice from the Sun

Cayla Hawkins

Dear Darkness,
Begin everyday with a fresh start
Think big
Rise to a challenge
Let your light shine
Feel the fire within
Shine with beautiful colors
Be hot
Reflect your light in others
Don't let a cloudy day get you down
There is always tomorrow

> *"A story isn't about a moment in time, a story is about the moment in time."*
>
> - W. D. Wetherell

# My Crackling Flame Heels

Haley Heibel

Slinky gold embracing my
Heels, bolstering me on a
Pedestal, creating my exclusive runway
As I gaze down at the world.

Tip-tap, tip-tap
Each stride glides with
Confidence as a champion on
A victory lap.
I am golden
Radiating my energy
Through the spectacle of
The Crackling Flame Heels.

Complemented with an effortlessly
Elegant vestment
Whose intricate lace encompasses
My figure and flows out at the waist.

Balance is achieved, a perfectly
Noticeable yet modest appearance
Heel-toe, heel-toe
Poised with each movement

I take each step with caution,
For the dark has come
But I shouldn't fear
My heels still shine
Reflecting a path
That will guide me through the dark
And keep me flaming.

# Impermanence

Daisy Hickman

Searching for myself within the
confines of letters called a name
was futile, a string of letters void
of explanation, empty of feeling,
except for what was remembered
from mornings, even entire days,
hazy with repetition, but when the
afternoon light pierced the glass of
my studio window, I reached for my
paints and brushes to capture my
ephemeral nature in reds browns
soft yellows and a fleeting blue sky.

---

*"Originality does not consist in saying
what no one has ever said before, but in
saying exactly what you think yourself."*

\- James F. Stephan

---

# Green

Hannah Holl

Green is growing
Its vines
Its new leaves
And fresh blades
Of grass

Green is softness
It's a field of clover
Its lily pads
And seaweed
And moss

Green is strength
It's a lush mountain
It's a pine tree
And a cactus
And bamboo shoots

Green is life
It's the new beginning
Of another cycle
It's springtime
And most of all it's hope

# Opening Doors

Cecilia Huber

If you look carefully enough,
You might see opening doors.
These doors are opening for a reason,
For you to become courageous and do what's right.

These doors open for you to step into.
So don't be a waiter.
Be a doer,
Because for example, doers get published and famous.

Waiters don't get anything except shame and sorrow.
Doesn't that sound horrible?
But doers don't have to worry about that,
Because they're courageous enough to see.

Opening doors open to new sparks of imagination,
They also open wider to new inspiration.
So come on and step right in, don't be shy!
And don't ask why, because doers never do.

There, now don't you see?
There's a whole different world out there.
All it takes is a little courage
to step into opening doors!

# Mid-Town Tapestry

David Prinz Hufford

I am weaving stories off the windy streets
Back where I walked some fifty years ago.
Nothing has changed. Everything is different.
Some things are the same. Some things never
happened before.
Cars move like shuttles up and down the streets.

A billowing newspaper snags in the bushes
By a garage with broken windows. Here we will
read of hope.
Some threadbare child runs through
the whirling wind.
The war is winding down. We will pull out
In time to stop over-population. Aha!
Oil is the culprit.
Money is the culprit. Borders are the culprit.

Here are threads enough to make
a storied pattern
That we can weave like a picture book
of dusty memories.
Move away. Move away; I'm busy now.
You made me forget what I was saying.
What was I saying? What was I trying to say?

Nothing has changed. Everything is different.
No one is listening anyway. Some things
are the same.
There may be hope. See? Children still run
in the wind.
So what? I am busy now weaving some stories.

# "batting practice"
Tom Hyde


i watch a mother with her son,
face, form, and hair,
shows days of exuberance,
waning.
however, she knows his
days of good times,
are not quite beginning,
as she tosses the plastic ball,
so he can smack it,
with his orange plastic bat.
she laughs,
when his wild swing
whiffs widely by,
making his body
move in an arc
with the bat,
almost making him fall.

it takes time,
and a heaping amount
of little boy frustration,
before he cracks at
that little ball.
when he does,
mom laughs
and praises him.
his short pudgy arms,
try to encircle her
as she kneels.
tears fall.
he sees them,
asks what's wrong,
she answers nothing.
he crinkles his face,

looking up at her,
hugs her again,
she leans and grasps
his fat digits,
and helps him
into the house.
inside,
as she sees the bat and ball
lying in the grass,
and wonders,
if he'll ever play
in those big parks,
in front of masses,
hoping he'll remember;
not to swing wildly.
but then

*2013 Camp Writer :: David Martin*

# She Doesn't Care (The Unfairytale)

Anne James

If life was a fairytale,
he'd be my prince charming,
fighting dragons and evil queens,
rescuing me from the plots of all my foes,
wrapping up the tale with a kiss astride his steed.

But life's not a fairytale,
and he's no prince;
he has no royal blood,
but he magically comprehends me,
understanding all my whims.

We don't ride off on horseback,
he drives a black Dodge Stealth,
which takes us to places
where we create our own fairytales,
despite their everyday appeal.

We create our own adventures,
battle brigands in our homes,
reading stories of legendary quests,
and recreating them in our world,
where our imaginations never end.

We build castles from building blocks
and submarine-cars of Legos,
swimming in a pool we pretend is the ocean,
we're children at heart,
playing cowboys and aliens.

He sees the world as a playground,
the possibilities endless.
He the wanderer,

I his Sacajawea
on the adventure of a lifetime.

Life's not a fairytale,
there is no prewritten end.
It can be something better,
for within our hearts, minds, and souls
lies a unique, endless potential.

Life's not a fairytale
and he isn't my prince charming.
No dragons nor evil queens lurk in the shadows,
no rescues from evil plots,
but sometimes our days wrap up with a kiss.

> *"And as imagination bodies forth the forms*
> *of things unknown, the poet's pen turns them*
> *to shapes, and gives to airy nothings a local*
> *habitation and a name."*
>
> - William Shakespeare

# Best Friends

Ellen Jesina

Each best friend is unique

With their own special feature.

They are heart's food and won't go away.

They are with you always and never let go of the heart they hold.

They support you and are your shoulder to cry on,

Not watching you face it alone.

Be joyful to have a friend.

You are one, too.

# Annie Girl

Kim Justus

I knew the time was drawing near
as I watched the clock run down
I truly did not want to see her time had come to
move from me
It was hard to watch her struggle each day

Treats comforted the love I brought
Finally, I prayed for guidance, strength,
and to do the right thing
We cannot cheat destiny, but we can meet
it with grace
The answer that came was etched on her face

She looked in my eyes with focused intent
Raising her paw to rest on my shoulder
she let me know our life was great
She was brave so long

Trying to ease my heart, wanting me to channel
her looming new start
I called the doctor, saying, "The time has come."
Willing and quiet as I stroked her gently
I felt her soul lift, as her body went still

She was gone, transported to her final journey
I whispered, "I love you," though I knew
she was gone
Her spirit soared beyond the moon and the sun
Tears stinging my eyes in the piercing quiet

I lingered a moment, gathered her collar
in my hand
Rising to leave her, memories scattered like sand

# Individual

Tenley Kahl

I am a sister, a daughter, a niece, a cousin.
I am a best friend, an acquaintance, an unknown.
I am the shy one, the funny one, the smart one.
I am a lover of science, avid reader, French speaker.
I am an artist, an author, a creative creator.
I am a chef, counselor, peacekeeper.
I am a traveler, inventor, putter-off-for
later.
I am opinioned, watchful, and looking deeper.
I am quiet and loud, hopeful and negative.
I am a finder of new ways to live.
I am always changing.

> *"No tears in the writer,*
> *no tears in the reader."*
>
> - George Moore

# Symphony of the Plains

Katherine Kramer

The meadowlark's trebling melodies
compliment the syncopated calls
of the insects and the prairie dog's chirp.

The high whistling notes of the wind
weave in between all of these
during the gentle calm of the first movement.

I am caught up in this as I am transported to
a time past. I hear the grumbling bass notes of the oxen
as they plod down the rutted dirt road
pulling a creaking wooden wagon
holding the worldly possessions of those
who have decided to seek their fortunes west.

Tin washtubs and pots clang like cymbals during a vigorous Sousa march
but fade out and back into the meadowlark's solo.
The percussive sounds of hooves pounding on the hard, dry earth
a running buffalo herd signals the new movement.

The wind picks up and adds its own scream
as the clouds darken
thunder rumbles and crashes.
I am caught up in the bombastic climax
long after the last note has faded.
I am back in the here and now.
The symphony of the Plains remains with me.
It's earthier, natural song
a comfort from the cold, impersonal,
mechanical concerto of modern life

# Our Bei Da Huang – (Life on the Farm)

Kate Ku-Gregory

**I**

After three days and three nights by train, we –
a group of middle and high school students from cities, finally
arrived at Bei Da Huang – which is lying in the northernmost part
of the northeast part of China - Heilongjiang - the border province
between China and Russia.

No buildings, no roads, no electricity, no running water, only
the largest grassland I've ever seen in my life.
The tall green grass pasture stretched so far away.
I saw its end meeting the sky. I thought I could
touch the white clouds if I walked to its end.

**II**

We cut down the grass, dug the earth to make bricks to build our barracks.
How many times the bricks were turned black rather than red.
How many times the walls fell before it finally stood up.
The green grassland looked prettier after we decorated it with red brick
barracks.
The color stands out.
Joys, laughing, and screaming, just like any our sportsmen
celebrate their victories.
The breeze was sending our delight high into the sky.
We see the white clouds saluting to us -
as they passing in our sky.
They know this accomplishment is phenomenal for a group of teenagers -
who NEVER had any experience as pioneers.

**III**

We planted corn, rice, wheat, and millet.
We grew cabbages, squashes, tomatoes, beans, peppers,
cucumbers, potatoes, egg plants, and radishes in our vegetable garden.
The soil is so rich. Our cucumbers are about two feet long; our potatoes
are almost a half size basketball;
and our eggplants are as big as soccer balls.

Growing up in the city, we never knew that these vegetables
could grow so big!!!
We believed that we were the BEST farmers in the world!
We kept cabbages, potatoes, and radish in the cellar as our winter supplies.
We raised pigs. Like any other young people at our age, we were craving for
meat, after –
day after day's cabbage and potato stew; cabbage and bean curd stew;
and radish and potato stew during the long winters.

## IV

How could I forget these summer days on the farm?
We had to get up before the day break to work in the field.
We left our barrack before the stars' retreat for home, and
returned with the stars over our heads.
Our parents never knew how hard we worked on the farm, only
the stars knew.
The stars saw us marching to the field
with a sleepy head and a hoe on our shoulders.
The stars also saw us returning exhausted and dusty.
We enjoyed those rainy days on the farm.
We used (Kang), our big bed built by bricks, as a stage and our sheets as
curtains
to perform "The White Haired Girl" and "The Red Lantern" - the very few
plays
were allowed to perform during the Cultural Revolution.
Our barrack was filled with amateur performers' voices and
roommates' teasing and laughing.
We wished tomorrow would continue to rain.
So we could have fun again!

## V

Winter came after the harvest.
None of us liked the winter at Bei Da Huang - it could reach
below zero 50 degree centigrade, plus
the brutal wind from Siberia.
We built a stove connected with a brick wall in the middle of our room to
keep us warm.
The room became warm when we built fire to heat the water on the stove
to wash before went to bed.

But when we awoke the next morning,
the room temperature dropped to below zero.
The water in our basin is frozen, so is the wash towel.
There was frost on our eyelashes.
No one wanted to get out the warm bed to enter the cold world.
Those brave roommates who got out first and started to build fire to heat the room
were greatly appreciated. You could hear
a resounding shout "Xie Xie!!" ( Thank you!!) from everyone who was still
tightly wrapped in the quilt.

We were longing for the spring – it is not just the first season in a year, rather
its spirit. The spring shows us –
the beauty of our earthly Mother and her courage, regardless
a harsh and wearing winter she had just experienced.
She teaches us never to give up, no matter how hard and how unfair life is.

> *"Fundamentally, all writing is about the same thing; it's about dying, about the brief flicker of time we have here, and the frustration that it creates."*
>
> - Mordecai Richler

# The Reporter Reminisces

Robert Levine


I loved covering the beat—I learned
to pursue each new source or reference
from the last, to persist in probing,
asking interviewees to elaborate each fact
and explain each explanation. A story formed
in my mind like a germinating seed:
for its body to break above ground
its roots had to dig as deep
as they could, branching off and spreading
until they tapered into nothing.

I loved erecting the facts
into a pyramid that stood on its head
(a feat matched by no architect):
up top, the lead—the broadest and most basic;
beneath, the take—its background;
down to the narrowest piece
of news that could endure the structure's pressure.
I learned to judge whether a detail
could slip into this matrix
to fill out the story more perfectly,
or added dead weight that would cause its fall.

I loved casting the facts into words.
Journalism compelled my words to dwell
on human effort and fate—
scholarships won, leukemia suffered—
not just trees and my own soul or navel.
I learned to slice the mass of facts into simple,
pithy sentences, brief paragraphs.
I had to enable readers to know
before I could provoke them to ponder.

My electronic typewriter clacked onto
the robin's-egg blue or canary yellow
paper that distinguished the *News Review*'s copy
as smart black letters trailed the platen like a
train engine's smoke. I loved the sound
of the impact on who I was
of my name and work printed for the public,
never more resonant and crisper
than that day they first appeared.
I learned from the newspaper's check,
though modest, that my byline and writing
could mean as much as money in the bank.

# In Honor of Porphyria

Blaze Livingston


Oh, how Porphyria sang and danced,
How she loved the love or romance,
Strangled by her own hair,
She was so fine, so fair—
Oh how she's gone, withered—
And how her lover, slithered—
Away.

Oh dear Porphyria, you will be
Remembered, we
Shall never forget—
But your lover might regret
His actions of that night,
But now you will see
The light,
Shining down upon you.

In honor of Porphyria, we sing,
In honor of Porphyria, we dance,
In honor of Porphyria, we rise,
In honor of Porphyria, we chant,
And allow the rain
To fall, to bring
A cure for the pain.

A cure for the pain suffered,
For the marks on her throat,
But at least she died quickly,
The best the lover could do at most.
Her eyes, bloodshot, stare outwards,
Her mouth, gaping open, cannot draw breath,
As her lungs refuse to expand.
Ironically, her lover caused her death.

Dear Porphyria, in the skies,
Shed memories of the storm,
Forget the cottage, and the man,
For it is you that we mourn.
Your love was not true, Porphyria,
It was merely a mirage of hate,
Of confusion. Porphyria, true love
Is much better than what you've experienced.

A picture sits upon a podium,
Of Porphyria dressed in white,
Similar to her presence as of now,
Due to the occurrence of just one night.
She was brave, courageous,
And her soul was not one to follow,
But her soul has left the casket,
Leaving her body hollow.

Oh dearest Porphyria,
Your beauty, untouched,
Warms the hearts of others.
Simply, your beauty causes the grate to
Blaze up,
As the coffin is buried.

# In a Combat Zone

Wayne Lund

Serving in a combat zone
I sense a lot of fear,
But I keep telling myself,
it's only for one year.

Out on patrol I suddenly receive fire,
quickly hitting the ground,
I hear a lot of yelling up front,
And the enemy has been found.

A grenade explodes,
I am hit with shrapnel and lying in the rain,
I know pretty soon it will stop, yes
but not my pain.

Finally, after awhile I'm
flown out on a medi-vac flight,
At a forward aid station,
I'll spend at least a night.

Waking up, I find a Purple Heart medal
pinned on my chest,
A doctor stops by saying, "You're lucky son.
Now, it's time to rest."

After months in a hospital,
I can now walk with a cane,
Doctors say I'm fine,
but I'll always feel the pain.

# Tyler, Tyler
Wendy Lundeen

Tyler, Tyler…you naughty boy,
You can be so loving and such a joy.
Why must you be two little boys
One so sweet, one full of noise?

Often times, you are overlooked
We know that's when your schemes are cooked.
Dillon's needs come first sometimes
And we see you hatch your dastardly crimes.

Tonight your sleep study will reveal
Why your behavior is so unreal.
Is your airway blocked when you dream each
night?
Is this the reason you cry and fight?

Do you need more oxygen to your brain
To gain control over your domain?
We only want the best for you
A joy-filled life is overdue.

This October you will be seven
We want to forgive your transgression.
Don't let another year go by
Where we think of you as the "wise guy."

We love you so, we really do
But your loveable moments are all too few.
Please get a grip and help us know
Why you continue the status quo.

We're hoping tonight as you sleep and dream
The test will divulge a pattern or theme.
We pray for answers and knowledge for you
Before we send you to Lima, Peru!

Our darling, spunky, loving Tyler
You're as fierce as a roaring, growling tiger.
Please be the boy we know in there
The one who's the answer to our prayer.

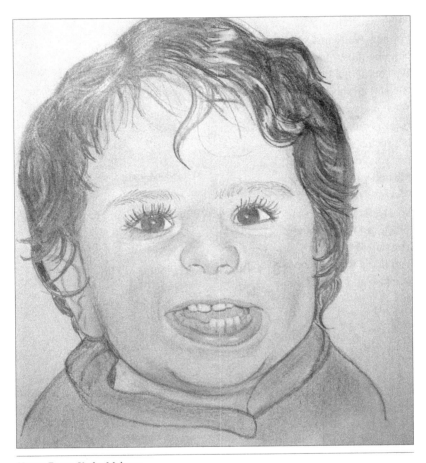

*Happy Face :: Kathy Maloney*

# Color to You

Nick Lynam

Living in this sea of red
I don't know, am I dead?
Forever blue because we're only two
In a perfect world, you would love me
And I would love you
For now we're just yellow
Nothing more than hello
We could light this cold gray world up
But still all this is is, "Sup"
What more can I do to spend a day with you?
Is it too much to ask?
It's such a simple task
For you and me
Me and you
I feel we're still two
What's that to you?
When can I get through
To you
You know we don't need to be two
Because all I need is you.

# In a Rain of Light

Fred MacVaugh

On ice-slick stairs,
She shivers:
"7 . . . 6 . . . ."
Her coat's inside, warm
Beside his.

*—Thump! Thump!—*

As New Year's rockets rise,
He trembles:
"5 . . . 4 . . . ."
Their breath buoyant
As balloons:
"3 . . . 2 . . . ."
She turns then.

*—Boom! Boom!—*

"Will you . . . ?"
Stars fall,
White as rice.

# Neville Nerves

Bridget McKeon


I am nervous
I have butterflies in my stomach
I try to calm down but it is too hot to concentrate
My makeup is sticky and the microphone tape is pinching my skin
My costume is so tight I can hardly breathe
I leave the hot make-up room and push my way through
the crowed green room
I think hard
I step out into the cold room
I try to remember my lines but I can't think straight
The only thing that comes to mind is the place I'm in
So I think of the old dressing rooms that are upstairs above the stage
I remember the old cracked mirrors and the rugged brown carpet
I think of the costumes, which hang on their hangers or pile on the floor
I think of the balcony at the back of the theater
I remember the seats that have had the serious and playful conversations
I think of the gargoyles and decorations you can see from the balcony seats
I think of the sound and light booth above those seats
in the back of the balcony
I remember the hole through the wall and the big spot lights
Then I think of the Patty Birge audition room
I remember the games we played and when we got too riled up Alison
would tell us old stories of the Neville
I also think of the old pictures of past plays on the walls of that room
I remember my mom being in "The Music Man"
I think of the kitchen where my friends and I stole sugar cubes and laughed
so hard when I fell down at lunch
Finally I think of the stage
The stage is so familiar I can almost smell the wood
I can remember the smooth cool touch of the dark wood on my bare feet
I also know the way the curtain flows when you run behind it
But this time it will be different
With the hot lights, the audience, and the microphones
Nothing will be the same

I'm so nervous but so excited at the same time
When I think of all these places, I calm down
I can breathe
They call me to the green room
"Let's do this," I say

*The Modern Teenage Reader :: Ana Turner*

## Life

Will Morrow

Life can be depressing
It also can be stressing.
Sometimes it is wonderful
Other times it is horrible.
Life is mostly funny
Also life is not too sunny.
Never let yourself rest
Until your better is the best!

# So, This Is Church?

Nicole Moulds

So, this is what eagles say church is,
A cult that is nothing more,
A cult that thinks better of itself,
A cult that rebukes the eagle's ignorance,
But adores its beauty.

Whatever the eagles say, church is more,
More than good deeds and light-filling smiles,
More than meaningful songs
and powerful messages.
It is more than a mere cult or religion.
It is a community, a city,
God's city.

A city that shines like the morning sun,
A city that has people on their knees,
A city with only one king,
A city that hopes the eagles will see
That church is much, much more.

So, this is what I say church is,
A city that is my home, my Safe Haven,
A city that loves with the love
That is above all that can compare,
A city that loves even the eagles
But prays that they will see
A city that is what church is to be.

*Rainbow :: Shari Morehead*

# Beautiful Things

Gina Nield

A spider web freshly made glistening with morning dew

A dragonfly landing on a fishing pole resting its wings glossy blue

A chorus of frogs croaking after rain

A rose blooming in early summer, a sight that never could be plain

A leaf falling blown on a fall breeze deep wrinkles from a year on the tree

A willow tree by a flowing stream curving branches reaching out for me

# A Good Day

Lisa O'Neal

I know the day will go well
When the sun begins to swell
In a bright pink hue between the trees

When golden leaves pave the way
And gentle breezes make branches sway
As a dance while the morning still awakes

These are the days I love
As I thank God in heaven above
And ask Him to send more days my way

# Moving Diana

Julie Soaring Eagle Paschold

It is time
for raking leaves, trimming dead foliage
and moving the rocks
to anticipate new landscaping.
The boys tote piles of stones via wagon
while my daughter finds them hidden in the dead weeds
on an atypically warm day in November.
Time has already changed
so darkness hastens its gradual tendons
all too soon.
One ornament that must be carried carefully
whose origin has a tale of its own
is my headless fountain statue.
I call her Diana
and she moves about the front yard;
once near my roses,
once at the foot of the stairs,
once propped by the railing to ascend.
Now Diana sits
white and pensive
almost leaning beneath the ash.
She is waiting;
patiently waiting and asking,
"When is winter?"

# My Outdoor Palace

Lucy Peterson

For others it is just a tree
But that is different for me
In my tree I can feel the textured bark
I see the leaves create a stunning arch
How I love the height of my tree
For the long distances I can see
In my tree, I am in a safe place
Even in tag, my tree is the base
In my grand tree I hear the birds call
Always I am careful not to fall
An undisturbed place is up in my tree
The feeling I get, the feeling of free
For alone in my tree, I am not
My tree is where animals are brought
For some animals my tree is their home
For other animals it is a place they roam
Welcome always, are animals in my tree


They are the ones who hold the key
The key can unlock me to a new space
So that I may see another face
Many faces the Earth can display
Everyone changing day to day
The furious storms that destroy many lands
The sun shining bright on the hot beach sands
My imagination
Is a great combination
When I can be up in my incredible tree
Knowing that everyone is special, including me

# Summer

Chasey Ridgley


Lying out in the sun
Thinking once again that I'll get a tan
But knowing that I'll once again get a sunburn
The thought doesn't exactly comfort me
My eyes miss the faces of my friends
Getting tired of staring at tiny screens
Yet hopeful at the thought of hanging with someone
Relief floods me in the embrace of my best friends
The only time to get peace and comfort is in the cool night
The stars shining so beautiful and bright
I feel the need to escape
The need to get out into the night
Too often the hot summer sun beats down
Making it exhausting to go outside
The freezing hose water doesn't even help
And once again I find myself stuck inside next to the fan
I find myself thinking about school
The thoughts are brought again when I pass it on the street
How much I enjoy sitting in the air-conditioned classrooms
I don't want to admit that I miss school
I would love to wake up at noon
When no one is in the house
But my darn puppy needs to get up at six
So he can go outside and pee
I love summer as it is
But unfortunately I need the structure
The school day provides
I love the summertime

# To Be or Not to Be

Devin Roberts

To be, or not to be, still I don't know my destiny.
In time I will see what is meant to be of me,
but I have lots of time to find myself in the midst of darkness in my life.
That has been brought to my attention.

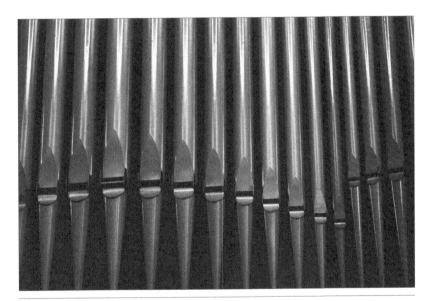

*Pipes :: Kris T. James*

# Blue

Esmeralda Rodriguez

Blue, the color of the beautiful waves running through the hot, rusty sand
Making it cold and wet.

Blue, the color of peace, tranquility, faith, and sincerity
Is as beautiful as watching the gorgeous night sky

I look through my window and feel that inner peace surrounding me
It's that same feeling when I look at the quiet, mysterious beach
During the sunset from a small distance

It's that amazing connection to the water I feel when tears run through my
eyes and
fall into the water.

# My Dearest Kim

Kay Scheinost and Mardra Sikora

Everyday I still love you
and feel the loss
Every day I wish
I could have you back
no matter the cost
Your smile was beautiful
your laughter was true
These are eternal
elements of you
You forgave me
for decisions made in haste
To forgive myself
that is a challenge
harder faced
Your death
was senseless, but
your life was not
There are many lessons
left to be taught
Although I feel alone
I look around to see
Although I feel defeated
you are fighting
these battles with me
We have much to say –
you and I
Protect Each Other!
Is the battle cry
The days have passed
and turned to years
When I see you in heaven
you will dry these tears

# Stories

Cecilia Seger

I like all kinds of stories.

Short stories,
Long stories,
Wrong stories,
All-right stories,
Happy stories,
Sad stories,
Good stories,
Not-bad stories,
Fact stories,
Just-draft stories,
Clipped stories,
Even ripped stories,
Plain stories,
Information stories,
School stories,
Cool stories,
Bright stories,
Flight stories.

But three kinds of stories that I like best,
Much better than all the rest:
Especially celebratory, epilogue stories,
And come-along stories.

# When I Perform

Mia Sherlock


The spotlight brightens
The music begins

I'm up on my toes
I twirl and spin

I jump and I leap
From one side to another

Feeling just the music
And not any other

I rise up on pointe
Then down in plié

I just do what I've practiced
So much every day

To dance is my dream
I can't let it die

For when I do dance
I feel I can fly

The world disappears
My troubles do cease

And just for a moment
I am finally at peace

# Advice for a Friend

Lisa Shulman


If I were a flower
And you the bee,
I would but die eventually
Despite each morning's shower.
For bee who does cower
From caring for his partner
Soon will find he is left without her
And his heart shall remain but sour.

So if, my friend, you care for me,
Then do your duties well,
As the wind doth whisper to the tree--
To me your secrets tell.
For if you neglect to these simple rules abide,
You'll find me no longer at your side.

# Climbing

D.N. Simmers

There is a second chance that loses all words.
There is a second thought that has no tongue.
All move into the afternoon when mists come in,
and bees are back inside and safe.
They rumble noises and protest
jesters that they will sting,
but only move their wings.
Against a sun that is setting
near the edge of all silence that has
fallen like an old wasp,
even he has no sting left.
He staggers like a shattered piece of cloth
away from the moment.
One last meal remains
a moist noise of falling into
night, splitting after impact.

# Born in 1974 -
# An Autobiography With Round Stone

Michael Simon

Everyone has an omphalos though often
We're surprised the first time we find it.

Thunder has found me living here, a thousand miles
From my rock, from the valley where a cloud is a bird
With a necklace. When the rumble walked over the hill
It was like glimpsing the bird.

Years ago I paused in Lodge Grass, following the trail of
The voice I heard. Hiking in the Wolf Mountains,
On a hillside full of grandmother's knuckles and dragons' spines
Exposed by the song that weathers the world,
I mistook the sound of thousands of grasshopper wings
For the rattles of snakes coming out in May.
I ran from the hillside, from rock to rock to rock, until a quiet
Like the floating center of the earth offered a round rock singing
"I am the center of the universe and the verse is the center of me."

The spin and circle of the world was too much to hear,
Too much to see. The soft concentric lap of rock
Drowned me. I ran, running as if bees are electrons
And electrons are bees. The hillside of spines and knuckles

Chased me to a valley of clouds where the day gave me
Two drawings, a walking bird with a strand of jewels,
And a tadpole swimming in the night sky.
I believed they could change weather.

Years ago I left Lodge Grass with two drawings.
I've tried to forget them. Scraps of prayer chip my teeth.
My finger tries to trace the outline. The jewels are missing,
But something is coming back, singing about it,
Erase the diagrams in the dirt quickly.

*Imagination :: Timothy Wright*

# an old crutch
Carey Glenn Smith

Writing beautiful words apparently isn't enough
anymore.
Beauty needs a story now.
And that's the scary part.
That beauty isn't enough in and of itself
for people today.

I know affluent enough people to whom
this doesn't apply.
They even have favorite words that
roll their tongue around magically.

Liz's is "insatiable,"
Ivy mentioned "synergy" off the cuff.
Maybe in defense of elegance
I can find a bit of debutant
in all of people's lazy words.

A bit of beauty in their arrogance.
A bit of waltz to their existence.
It just makes me nervous
because their story is mine as well.

And maybe that's where the
scary, beautiful narration
truly resides.
Not in their words.

# Time Kept through Nature

Chandler Solomon


I say goodbye to nature, my mom,
Glow of the lamb all gone.

Cigarettes burning through the tying webs of my life,
Wounds growing deeper each day cut by a different knife.

I say goodbye to time, my father,
Sinking into the darkness even further.

Sand castles gone with the wind just like my homes,
I'm another lost cause like each one of my poems.


> *"Poetry creates the myth, the prose writer draws its portrait."*
> - Jean-Paul Sartre

# Pink

Haidyn Sosalla-Bahr

Pink is a sunset, warming and calm
Like a blooming petal, as soft as deer's call
A kitten's fur, happy and purring
A transition from the sun's blurring

Lighter than lavender, darker than cream
A pale-colored cotton candy stream
The color of roses and taffy and lace
A playful color, a friendly chase

Starburst wrappers with candy
I think pink is quite dandy
A valentine's heart, as dark as a rose
The fresh scent of pink fills my nose

Ballet and ribbons, a twirling display
A cheerful, bright start to your day
Pink like a dress, graceful and slim
A magical fantasy with imagination and whim

The color of happiness blooms inside me
A flower being pollinated by a bee

# Mother's Day

Laura Streeter

Why did you go?
There was too much more to know
and nothing you could tell
You knew me very well

You're not here to tell me anymore
You're not here to make it all 'ok'
You're not around to ease the trouble
or to just sing a song with me for one more day

Thoughts transcended words
and though it seemed absurd,
You left, and I was right
The dark somehow seemed bright

You're not here to tell me anymore
You're not here to make it all 'ok'
You're not around to ease the trouble
a stolen moment seized the day

You used to validate my convictions, give me praise
And then my turn for you
But how was I suppose to make sense
of a mess that grew and grew?

You're not here to tell me anymore
You're not here to make it all 'ok'
You're not around to ease the trouble
All of that's been taken away

Time became the battle
An uphill climb for sure
We did everything that could be done
We knew there was no cure

You're not here to tell me anymore
You're not here to make it all 'ok'
You're not around to ease the trouble
or to just sing a song with me for one more day

*Romance :: Kris T. James*

# The Crash

Madison Taylor


One day Ally woke up
And went to the deck
The boards were creaky
And it started to wreck.

The boards trembled
Then started to creak
They started to shake
Then let out a squeak.

And with a thud
Ally went down
She hit the table
Then fell to the ground.

She didn't get hurt
As it would seem
But what she doesn't know,
It was just a dream.

# Progression

Edward Vogel

A granule of sand
not predestined but only subject:
the welcome of flow
a rejection
of ebb.
No sense in that dark abyss
But be mindful of direction.

The hawk struggles 'gainst
Aeolus' blow.
Seemingly gliding but
stationary in axis.
To progress it but only must crawl.

An apple, felled to the mantle,
subject to worms and no polish.
Stay as it were,
rotting.

My soul aided,
but unguided be it so.

# The Great Fire of Chicago

Nicole Vawser

Now that the fire is done,

Our burdens are laid down.

Our bodies are somewhat renewed,

And the people are wiser.

No longer shall we fiddle with wood,

But we shall chisel the city of stone.

This fire has imprinted on us,

And we shall do the same to the city.

# Poem for Dad

Hope Weber

Dad

You picked me up when I was down

You dressed me in my finest gown

You calmed me when I was feeling the tide

Never a dull moment with you by my side

Love you, Daddy!

> *"The best way to have a good idea is to have lots of ideas."*
>
> - Linus Pauling

# Biographical Notes

**Russ Alberts** lives in England.

**Syndey Anderson** is a first time writer with *Fine Lines*.

**Gladys Naomi Arnold** was born August 3, 1896, at Verdon, NE. She taught American literature at Clinton High School in Iowa from 1923-60 and made a regional name for herself as a published poet.

**Brad Ashford** is a Nebraska State Legislator and ran for Mayor of Omaha in the 2013 election.

**Dani Bachmann** is a student at the University of Nebraska at Omaha.

**Matthew Ball** is a student at Metropolitan Community College in Omaha, NE.

**Haley Banks** is a first time writer with *Fine Lines*.

**Mary Bannister** teaches writing at the middle school in Albion, NY. Poetry has always been her favorite genre. Even as a child, she composed little songs that fluttered away with her vivid imagination.

**Makayla Bell** is a student at Omaha Northwest High School.

**Jeanie Boll** is a student at the University of Nebraska at Omaha.

**Jason Bottlinger** is an attornye in Omaha, NE.

**Larissa Boyd** is a first time writer with *Fine Lines*.

**Jackie Byers** is a published poet and taught English at Brownell-Talbot School in Omaha, NE, for forty years. When she is not with her grandsons or on the tennis courts, she may be writing, walking a trail, attending one of several book clubs, or watching a movie.

**Jessica Franke Carr** is a student at the University of Nebraska at Omaha.

**David Catalan** is the founder of Catalan Consulting. Prior to establishing his consulting practice in April of 2008, he was the executive director of the Nonprofit Association of the Midlands from August 2002 to February 2008. David is the President of the South Omaha Business Association and the author of *Rule of Thumb: A Guide to Small Business Marketing*. He is currently working on an autobiographical collection of poems drawing from relatives, friends, and locations. The working title is *vagabundo*, Spanish for *Vagabond*.

**Ardiss Cederholm** writes for a variety of reasons: to leave a legacy for family and friends and to tell stories in her narrative poems. She has been published in *Nebraska Life*, *Plain Songs Review*, and *Times of Sorrow Times of Grace*.

**Neil Chaparro** is a philosophy student at the University of Nebraska at Omaha.

**Sophie Morrissey Clark** is a sophomore at Westside High School in Omaha, NE. She loves writing. She is a triplet, and her brothers play in a band with her.

**Spencer Cox** is a student at the University of Nebraska at Omaha.

**Shelley David** is a nursing student at Metropolitan Community College, Omaha, NE.

**Katie Davison** is in the eighth grade at Dawes Middle School in Lincoln, NE.

**Randy DeVillez** died unexpectedly on February 19, 2013, at his home. He will be missed. He was the beloved "Papa" to seven grandchildren. He taught at the University of Evansville, Miami University in Ohio, and Moraine Valley Community College in Illinois. A tenured college professor of writing and literature, he was often nominated for regional and national Master Teacher and/or Professor of the Year awards. He wrote nonfiction articles, poems, and essays on various topics. Recently, he was published in *Art Times*, *The Writer*, and *Fine Lines*.

**Deborah Duffy** "I was encouraged by John Robinson to submit my story for your consideration in *Fine Lines*. I live in the Bitterroot Valley in western Montana where he leads a writing group. My story is of loss and of the healing power that nature can provide, especially for those of us who are lucky enough to call Montana home."

**Lorraine Duggin** followed the metamorphoses of *Fine Lines* since its inception, and her poetry has been published in several editions. Having written for her own pleasure and self-expression for most of her life, her love of reading led to a desire to write and publish. She is a Master Artist with the Iowa and Nebraska Arts Councils, a speaker for the Nebraska Humanities Council, and enjoys teaching writing to international students, immigrants, and refugees.

**Trinity Eden** is a student at Metropolitan Community College in Omaha, NE.

**Grace Erixon** is an eighth grade student at Millard (NE) North Middle School.

**Hayley Faber** was born and raised in Omaha, NE. Currently, she is a medical student with an interest in international health and preventive medicine. In her free time, she enjoys creative pursuits of writing and painting. Hayley has had the fortune to travel to England, France, and India and is planning further adventures, as her medical training allows.

**Marcia Calhoun Forecki** lives in Council Bluffs, Iowa. Her academic background is in the Spanish language and literature. She earned a Master of Arts degree from the University of Wisconsin-Milwaukee. Her first book, *Speak to Me*, about her son's deafness, was published by Gallaudet University Press and earned a national book award. She has published articles, short fiction, and once wrote a screenplay for hire. Her story "The Gift of the Spanish Lady" was published in the Bellevue Literary Journal and nominated for a Pushcart Prize.

**Tony Gebhardt** lives in Fort Calhoun, NE, and is a project superintendent for an Omaha based construction and property development company. He has been waiting patiently for years to start writing about the lessons of the heart, the places he has seen, and the people he has met.

**Cindy Goeller** is an amateur photographer living in Nebraska.

**Daphne Goetzinger** is in the sixth grade at Western Hills Elementary in the Omaha Public Schools.

**Adriana Gradea** was born in Cluj-Napoca, a large and important city in the Transylvania region of Romania, where she studied English and experienced the 1989 Anti-Communist Revolution. Then, she studied Advanced International Studies at the Johns Hopkins University in Bologna,

Italy. She came to the U.S. in 1997, worked in banking, and went back to school for her MA in English (2010) at Bradley University in Peoria, IL. She is now in a PhD program at Illinois State University in Normal, IL.

**Susan Graham-Ulsher** is a first time writer with *Fine Lines*.

**Barb Greer** is Kentucky-born, a high-school graduate, retired, and has experiences covering a broad spectrum of joy and heartache. She loves to "try to figure life out" by writing and can see by her musings that some periods of life were particularly "muse-able." She worked at many jobs over the years: working at a cemetery, a women's prison, a metropolitan police department, a natural beef company, a fast food chain franchisee, an alcoholic/drug treatment center, and a large mental health community treatment center.

**Maria Gutierrez** moved from Querétaro, México, to Omaha, NE, to live close to her children and grandchildren. She is a translator in English, Spanish, and French, and studies at Metropolitan Community College.

**Sarah Guyer** is in the seventh grade at Morton Middle School in the Omaha Public School District.

**Debra L. Hall** is a published novelist and resides in Omaha, NE.

**Shawna Hanson** is a student at the University of Nebraska at Omaha.

**Kathie Haskins** grew up in Papillion, NE, and currently lives in Millard with her husband and two children. She enjoys writing poems, reflections about nature, and hopes to one day publish a book of her poetry. Writing and gardening are her creative outlets, and she also enjoys reading in her spare time.

**Cayla Hawkins** is a first time writer with *Fine Lines*.

**Haley Heibel** was born in San Antonio, TX. At the age of two, her family moved to Lincoln, NE, for her father to start his dermatology practice. She received a Catholic education and excelled in academics, as well, as volleyball and tennis. She enjoys traveling, her two pugs, fashion, and spending time at the lake with her family. Next year, she plans to attend Southern Methodist University.

**DiEtte Henderson** loves photography and lives in Sioux Falls, SD.

**Daisy Hickman** was the editor of the *Lincoln Journal* Editorial Page in Lincoln, NE, is a graduate of Stephens College and Iowa State University, and writes poetry in Brookings, SD.

**Abby Hills** is a student at the University of Nebraska at Omaha.

**Hannah Holl** is a freshman at Millard (NE) West High School.

**R. C. Hoover** is an English professor at Metropolitan Community College in Omaha, NE.

**Cecilia Huber** is a seventh grader at St. Margaret Mary's Middle School in Omaha.

**David Prinz Hufford** has spent his life teaching and writing, 38 years in the US, the last 30 of which were at Iowa Western Community College in Council Bluffs, IA, and he taught in Slovakia and China. Since then, he has traveled to many countries, often on missions for his church. He has published over 250 poems in 20 publications, including three self-published chapbooks and one full-length poetry book.

**Tom Hyde** is a first time writer with *Fine Lines*.

**Anne James** is pursuing a PhD in the department of biomedical sciences at Creighton University. She completed her BS in biology and French at Creighton. In her free time, she enjoys writing poetry, playing the trombone, knitting, and scuba diving.

**Kris T. James** is a contributor to *Fine Lines*.

**Ellen Jesina** is a fourth grade student at Reagan Elementary School in the Millard (NE) School District.

**Shelby Jones** is a first time writer with *Fine Lines*.

**Kim Justus** was in professional sales for thirty years, and then she decided to direct her attention to her creative side, expanding a life-long interest in photography, writing, and producing her own radio show.

**Tenley Kahl** is a sophomore at Omaha Burke High School.

**Parth Kapadia** is a senior majoring in Civil Engineering at the Illinois Institute of Technology in Chicago. He started his own online international business, GlobalPetals.com, in May of 2009. Upon graduation, he plans on continuing his entrepreneurial adventures.

**Dr. Jody Keisner** is an English professor at the University of Nebraska at Omaha.

**Kristy Stark Knapp** is a full-time artist living in Madison, NE.

**Katherine Kramer** is a freelance writer and blogger from Sioux Falls, South Dakota.

**Kate Ku-Gregory** grew up during the Cultural Revolution in China. Encouraged by family and friends to write her recollection of this stressful time in China, she took the first steps and started putting things down on paper. She earned a BA in Western Language and Literature from Peking University, then came to the United States and earned an MA in Gerontology from Hood College and a PhD in Anthropology from Case Western Reserve University.

**Wendell Kuhlman** is a retired English teacher.

**Robert Levine** grew up in Greenbelt, Maryland. He earned a B.A. in English from the University of Maryland, where he received the Henrietta Spiegel Creative Writing Award. He earned an M.F.A. in Creative Writing from Emerson College, where he received the Emerging Writer Award. His poetry and book reviews have appeared in several magazines—including *The Baltimore Review*, *The Alembic*, *The Lyric*, *The Isle Review*, *SAGGIO*, and *Poet Lore*. He has self-published two collections of poetry, *The Account* and *Mystical Symphony*. When not writing or reading, Robert's interests include Judaism, nature, and just about anything in the arts and humanities. Robert lives in Brookline, MA, and works as a supervisor at a market research company, a private tutor, a freelance editor, and a proofreader.

**Blaze Livingston** is a student at Omaha Northwest High School.

**Dr. Loren Logsdon** "I believe in the mission of *Fine Lines*, especially in its intention to reach a wide audience of readers and to include a wide variety of writers. I like the emphasis on clarity of writing which is central to the purpose of the journal. So much writing today defies clarity and seems to delight in obfuscation. Write on."

**Norm Lund** was in corporate work for most of his adult life, first the software business, then general business consulting. Prior to that, he was a college student, followed by time spent as a U.S. Army officer. He is currently retired and contemplating another career. His life experiences and age have given him a perspective that can apply to the written word. It is a challenging and interesting exercise to write creatively, so that someone else can enjoy reading the work.

**Wayne Lund** joined the Army in 1960 at the age of eighteen and retired after twenty-one years, serving on multiple posts throughout the world. He completed three tours of duty in Germany and happened to be in Berlin during the building of the Berlin Wall. He served two tours in Vietnam, 1965-67 and 1970-71. During the second tour, he was wounded. He retired in 1980 but was recalled to active duty during Desert Storm, 1990-91. He received many awards during his military career.

**Wendy Lundeen** is a retired Spanish teacher for the Omaha Public School District.

**Nick Lynam** is a first time writer with *Fine Lines*.

**Fred MacVaugh** is a first time writer with *Fine Lines*.

**Kathy Maloney** is a retired English Teacher and a "new" portrait artist in Omaha, NE.

**David Martin** is the managing editor of *Fine Lines*.

**Garrett May** is a first time writer with *Fine Lines*.

**Magie McCombs** is a high school student in Papillion, NE.

**Bridget McKeon** is a first time writer with *Fine Lines*.

**Ali Mohammed** is a first time writer with *Fine Lines*.

**Sharie Morehead** lives in Salem, NE.

**Will Morrow** is 10 years old, a 6th grader at Loveland Elementary School in the Omaha Westside School District, and has attended the *Fine Lines* Creative Writing Summer Camp for three years. "I have a lot of journals that are filled with short stories, comic strips, and poems. I like to listen to Dad read out loud, and I draw pictures to create stories. In addition to writing, I love sports and play hockey year round."

**Nicole Moulds** "My age isn't important because it is only a number. One can assume that I am a female because of my name. It's true that I am a female, a student in high school, a senior to be exact. I love to write. I've always been asked why I love to write, and I have always given the same answer, 'I love it because it's an art.' My mind is complicated, so I'm used to the fact that I need to write. I write because, to me, it's the easiest way to communicate with people. I was born mute, and so I grew up with the love for the art of writing and poetry."

**Sosuke Nakao** is a native of Japan and a student at Metropolitan Community College in Omaha, NE.

**Lauren Narducci** is student at Metropolitan Community College in Omaha, NE.

**Richard Nelson** wanted to be an author all of his life, but things got in his way: military service, college, work, marriage, and children. After his full-time work ended, he began reading voraciously. Now, he has written six novels, two novellas, four short-stories, and a play. He is a living example of what happens when a writer never gives up.

**Gina Nield** is a freshman at Logan-Magnolia High School (IA).

**Allyson Olson** is a *Fine Lines* summer intern and a student at the University of Nebraska at Omaha.

**Lisa O'Neal** is an Honors student at Des Moines Area Community College in Iowa.

**Bhavin Pardiwala** is a student at the Illinois Institute of Technology in Chicago, IL. He likes to write creative non-fiction.

**Julie Soaring Eagle Paschold** has tried her hand at being a pizza maker, telephone operator, soil science research technician, overnight supervisor for a homeless shelter, research assistant for ruminants, advocate for water quality, coordinator for statewide art project, assistant to a town development organization, encourager of composting, and 911 operator. The titles that have sustained her are mother, wife, poet, and pencil sketch artist.

**Heather Pecoraro** is in the depths of a Graphic Communications (Art & Design) major at Metropolitan Community College.

**Jennifer Peterson** is a junior at Duchesne Academy of the Sacred Heart in Omaha, NE. She loves writing short stories and poetry and is working on a novel. She won first place in the 2011 Durham Museum regional essay contest and placed second internationally in the 2011 Jewish Partisan Educational Foundation essay contest. She was a Round 2 qualifier in the 2012 Anti-Defamation League of Holocaust Education's "Tribute to the Rescuers" essay contest, the state winner for Nebraska in the 2013 Colonial Dames National Congressional Essay Contest, and will attend the winners' Washington Workshops Congressional Seminar in Washington, DC, in June 2013.

**Lucy Peterson** is in the eighth grade at St. Vincent de Paul Middle School in Omaha.

**Michael Pick** is a student at the University of Nebraska at Omaha.

**Chasey Ridgley** is a student at Omaha Burke High School.

**Montana Ringer** teaches English at Hershey (NE) Middle School.

**Devin Roberts** "I go to middle school in Falls City, NE. I am thirteen years old. I write because it is the easiest way for me to express myself. I learned about *Fine Lines* through my teacher Karen Flynn."

**Esmeralda Rodriguez** is in the seventh grade at Norris Middle School in the Omaha Public Schools.

**Kay Scheinost** is a first time writer with *Fine Lines*.

**Megan Schiermeyer** is a first time writer with *Fine Lines*.

**Charles Scudder** is a retired attorney and lives in Omaha, NE.

**Cecilia Seger** is a fourth grade student at Harrison Elementary School in Omaha, NE.

**Mia Sherlock** is in the eighth grade at Omaha Beveridge Magnet Middle School.

**Lisa Shulman** died in 1990 at the age of 19 from a rare childhood cancer, Ewing's Sarcoma. She wrote poetry and stories all of her short life. A member of the yearbook staff during her junior and senior years at Millard North High School, she was awarded entry into The Quill and Scroll International Honorary Society for High School Journalists.

**Mardra Sikora** - In 2011, she retired from the position of president for Omaha's Wright Printing Company in order to pursue completion and publication of her first novel, *The Innocent Prince.* This new adventure led to many hours in the public libraries where she discovered and enjoyed reading *Fine Lines.* This discovery further inspired her to share her work with like-minded souls and hope for inclusion prevailed.

**Ciera Simbro** attendsThomas Jefferson High School in Council Bluffs, IA.

**D. N. Simmers** writes poetry and lives in British Columbia, Canada.

**Michael Simon** is a retired teacher and lives on a forested hillside near Eugene, Oregon.

**Carey Glenn Smith** received a Masters' in Art Education from Lander University and a BFA in Studio Art along with a minor in philosophy from the College of Charleston in South Carolina. The creation of visual art and the act of writing are intimately linked on fundamental levels. Currently, he is an Associate Professor of Art History at Piedmont Technical College in Greenwood, S.C.

**Emily Smith** is a first time writer with *Fine Lines.*

**Chandler Solomon** is a frequent writer with *Fine Lines.*

**Haidyn Sosalla-Bahr** is a seventh grade student at Millard (NE) North Middle School.

**Laura Streeter** is a photographer, artist, singer, and graphic designer. She is a graduate of both Metropolitan Community College and the University of Nebraska at Omaha and hopes to pursue a graduate degree in Gerontology.

**Gabby Sullivan** is 13 years old and lives in Fairview Heights, IL.

**Douglas Taylor** lives and writes in the Bitter Root Valley, Montana.

**Madison Taylor** is a fifth grade student at Skyline Elementary School in Elkhorn, NE.

**Tom Tomasek** is a tax accountant, lives in Blair, NE, and is a first time author in *Fine Lines*.

**Ana Turner** is a first time contributor with *Fine Lines*.

**Nicole Vawser** is a freshman at Millard (NE) West High School.

**Edward Vogel** is a creative writing teacher at Omaha Northwest High School.

**David Waller** is a first time writer with *Fine Lines*.

**Hope Weber** is an eighth grade student in Lincoln, NE.

**Elaine Frain Wells** is a musician and counselor and lives in Omaha.

**Kaitlyn White** is a first time writer with *Fine Lines*.

**Noni Williams** is a graduate of Duchesne High School and a current student at the University of Nebraska at Omaha.

**Emily Woods** is a student at Metropolitan Community College in Omaha, NE.

**Timothy Wright** is a photographer in Omaha, NE.

## *Fine Lines* Membership

Membership with *Fine Lines* includes four perfect bound journals delivered to your front door. Frequently, we send an e-letter with *Fine Lines* news, upcoming events, and the inside scoop on special issues.

In addition, we provide hundreds of copies to students who have no means to buy subscriptions. Your membership will help provide copies for young writers who cannot purchase *Fine Lines* for themselves.

We offer two methods of payment for your *Fine Lines* donations.

- U.S. residents should make checks payable to *Fine Lines* for $50. Schools and libraries in the U.S. should send $40. Those living outside the U.S. must send their checks for U.S. $60. Please include your name, address, and e-mail with your payment and send to:

  *Fine Lines* Journal
  PO Box 241713
  Omaha, NE 68124

- We also accept credit card payments via PayPal on the *Fine Lines* website: www.finelines.org

## Submissions

We accept e-mail, file attachments, CDs formatted in MS Word for PCs, and laser-printed hard copies.

No overt abuse, sexuality, profanity, alcohol, drugs, or violent articles are reviewed. Editors reply when writing is accepted for publication, if a stamped, self-addressed envelope or e-mail address is provided.

Address changes and correspondences should be sent to *Fine Lines*, PO Box 241713, Omaha, NE 68124

Do not send "whole class projects." Teachers may copy *Fine Lines* content for classes and submit student work for publication when they act as sponsors for their students.

Please contact *Fine Lines* for assistance.

# Kathleen K. Maloney
## designs

The Deem Corporation
P.O. Box 451117 • Omaha, NE 68145 • USA
Tel: (402) 895-5748 • Fax: (402) 895-2306

kathmalo@cox.net

---

**Dan Botos, AAMS®**
Financial Advisor

**Edward Jones**
MAKING SENSE OF INVESTING

8424 West Center Road
Suite 200
Omaha, NE 68124
Bus. 402-391-2100  Fax 888-224-8764
TF. 888-391-2112
dan.botos@edwardjones.com
www.edwardjones.com

---

**Epilepsy Affiliate of Nebraska**
Epilepsy Foundation of North Central Illinois, Iowa, Nebraska
**Laura Neece-Baltaro**
Volunteer

9315 Pauline Street
Omaha, NE 68124-3836

(402) 827-7080
(402) 319-4744
QKRLaura@aol.com
www.epilepsyheartland.org

*Adult Education Transformation*

*Empower Your Learning*

SJON F. ASHBY, PHD
SJON.ASHBY@AETRANSFORMATION.COM
WWW.AETRANSFORMATION.COM
PO Box 642237
OMAHA, NE 68164
402.403.9774

---

## System Integrators

**Sebastian Arul**
Communication Systems Engineer
14513 South 25 Avenue Circle
Bellevue, NE 68123

402-614-6996        sebastian.arul@cox.net

---

## TAX AND BUSINESS CONSULTANTS
"Your Tax Specialists"

### Tom Tomasek
Tax Consultant

229 So. 17th St.
P.O. Box 390
Blair, NE 68008
(402) 426-4144
Fax: (402) 426-4156

2816 North Main, Ste A
P.O. Box 815
Elkhorn, NE 68022
(402) 289-5756

E-mail: tomt@rvrco.net

Julio's Restaurant
is proud to
support *Fine Lines* and the
hard working people who
produce these wonderful
works of the human spirit.
Thanks to all who make this
publication another great
"Omaha Original!"

---

# WRITE ABOUT LIFE

---

www.WriteLife.com

Whether you want to write
a novel, a biography, or even
a "how to" book, our web
site has been developed
with you in mind, and we
offer numerous advantages
to those interested in
collaborative publishing.

# NELAC
*Nebraska Language Arts Council*

Nebraska Language Arts Council (NELAC) is a statewide professional volunteer association of language arts educators who join together to network through conferences, meetings, journals and conversation. NELAC is Nebraska's official state affiliate with Nebraska's Council of Teachers of English, and membership is open to all educators of language arts, kindergarten through college level.

## NELAC Promotes:
- Excellence in Student Magazines
- Young Writers' Programs
- Achievement in Writing Awards
- Promising Young Teacher Award
- The Nebraska English Journal
- The Nebraska Student Journal
- Nebraska Literary map
- Guide to Nebraska Authors
- Annual Nebraska Poetry Month
- Annual High School Quiz Bowl
- Plum Creek Children's Festival
- SLATE (Support for the Learning and Teaching of English)
- AFCON (Academic Freedom Colation of Nebraska)
- Nebraska Center for the Book

## JOIN NELAC this year!

Send $10 to:
NELAC
PO Box 83944
Lincoln, NE 68501-3944

Contact:
Clark Kolterman
Ckolte00@connectseward.org

# AFCON
## Academic Freedom Coalition of Nebraska

Academic Freedom Coalition of Nebraska promotes academic freedom in education and research contexts. This includes freedoms of belief and expression and access to information and ideas.

## As a Member, you can help us:

- Support applications of the First Amendment in academic contexts, including elementary and secondary schools, colleges, universities, and libraries.

- Educate Nebraskans about the meaning and value of intellectual freedom, intellectual diversity, mutual respect, open communication, and uninhibited pursuit of knowledge, including the role of these ideas in academic contexts and in democratic self-government.

- Assist students, teachers, librarians, and researchers confronted with censorship, indoctrination, or suppression of ideas.

- Act as a liason among groups in Nebraska that support academic freedom issues.

## To become a member:

Send dues, organization or individual name, address and phone number to:
Cathi McCurtry
15 N. Thomas Avenue
Oakland, Nebraska 68045

## AFCONebr.org

# Facing the Blank Page
## by David Martin

"In his collection of personal essays, Martin gives us no less than a series of prescriptions for how to conduct an examined life."
Dr. J.J. McKenna

"These essays are an interesting journey from introspective curiosity about what makes Martin's soul tick to excellent narratives about motivating one to write."
Richard Koelling

"I am delighted to see the essays I have read through the years in one book where I can turn the pages, taste the ideas, and savor!"
Colleen Aagesen

"Martin is devoted to his calling and is an inspiration to fledgling writers and diehards in the field."
Mary Bannister

### Facing the Blank Page

A Collection of Essays and Poems
from the First Ten Years of *Fine Lines*,
a Literary Journal, 1992-2001

David Martin

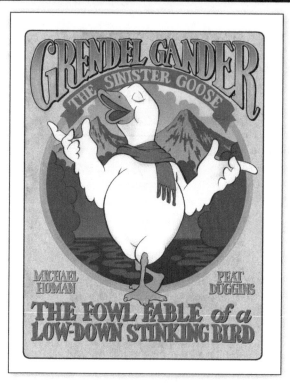

# BOXES

## The Secret Life of Howard Hughes

Eva McLelland was good at keeping secrets, and she had a big one. Sworn to secrecy for thirty-one years until the death of her husband, Eva was at last able to come forward and share a story that turns twentieth century history on its head and fills in puzzling blanks in the mysterious life of the tycoon Howard Hughes.

How could Hughes appear to witnesses as an emaciated, long finger-nailed, mental incompetent, yet fly a jet aircraft four months later? How could a doctor describe him as looking like a "prisoner of war," when at the same time investment bankers, politicians, and diplomats who met him said he was articulate and well-groomed? The answer is a perfect example of the brilliance of the elusive billionaire. He simply found a mentally incompetent man to impersonate him, drawing the attention of the Internal Revenue Service and an army of lawyers who pursued him, while he conducted his business in peace from Panama with his new wife, Eva McLelland. Sound fantastic? It is. However, after seven years of research and verification, Eva's story produces the final pieces in the mysterious puzzle that was Howard Hughes.

ISBN: 978-1-60808-017-5

## BOXES

### The Secret Life of Howard Hughes

#### DOUGLAS WELLMAN

# Now Available:

In the title story, *Hurricane Blues*, you will meet a Louisiana blues piano player who protects her home-alone son by averting hurricanes with a whiskey shot glass and a mother's love. In *The Reader*, a dreamy bookworm stumbles into manhood. In *Soul Most In Need*, the friendship of two southern widows is the one truth at a tent revival. *Nahualli* presents a sharp-tongued Mexican recluse and her shape-shifting lover. Meet a good-hearted deacon doing reconnaissance on a philandering preacher from a classic car in *T-Bird Recon*. A cruel medieval father, a frontier lawyer's silent child scrivener, and an aspiring teacher caught in the 1918 influenza epidemic also populate this eclectic collection of previously published and new short fiction.

ISBN: 978-1608080434

**www.WriteLife.com**
**www.Amazon.com**
**www.Amazon.co.uk**
**www.BooksAMillion.com**
**www.AbeBooks.com**
**www.Alibris.com**
**www.BarnesAndNoble.com**

CPSIA information can be obtained at www.ICGtesting.com
Printed in the USA
LVOW01s2004141013

356832LV00003B/30/P